T0229813

Current Applications of Deep Learning in Cancer Diagnostics

This book examines deep learning-based approaches in the field of cancer diagnostics, as well as pre-processing techniques, which are essential to cancer diagnostics. Topics include introduction to current applications of deep learning in cancer diagnostics, pre-processing of cancer data using deep learning, review of deep learning techniques in oncology, overview of advanced deep learning techniques in cancer diagnostics, prediction of cancer susceptibility using deep learning techniques, prediction of cancer reoccurrence using deep learning techniques, deep learning techniques to predict the grading of human cancer, different human cancer detection using deep learning techniques, prediction of cancer survival using deep learning techniques, complexity in the use of deep learning in cancer diagnostics, and challenges and future scopes of deep learning techniques in oncology.

Jyotismita Chaki, PhD, is an Associate Professor at School of Computer Science and Engineering, Vellore Institute of Technology, Vellore, India.

Aysegul Ucar, PhD, is a Professor in Department of Mechatronics Engineering, Firat University, Turkey.

Current Applications of Deep Learning in Cancer Diagnostics

Edited by
Jyotismita Chaki
Vellore Institute of Technology, India
Aysegul Ucar
Department of Mechatronics Engineering, Turkey

CRC Press is an imprint of the
Taylor & Francis Group, an **informa** business

First edition published 2023
by CRC Press
6000 Broken Sound Parkway NW, Suite 300, Boca Raton, FL 33487-2742

and by CRC Press
4 Park Square, Milton Park, Abingdon, Oxon, OX14 4RN

CRC Press is an imprint of Taylor & Francis Group, LLC

Library of Congress Cataloging-in-Publication Data
Names: Chaki, Jyotismita, editor. | Uçar, Ayşegül, editor.
Title: Current applications of deep learning in cancer diagnostics /
[edited by] Jyotismita Chaki, Aysegul Ucar.
Description: First edition. | Boca Raton : CRC Press, 2023. |
Includes bibliographical references and index.
Identifiers: LCCN 2022039588 (print) | LCCN 2022039589 (ebook) |
ISBN 9781032233857 (hardback) | ISBN 9781032223193 (paperback) |
ISBN 9781003277002 (ebook)
Subjects: MESH: Neoplasms—diagnosis | Deep Learning | Early Detection of Cancer |
Image Interpretation, Computer-Assisted Classification: LCC RC270 (print) | LCC RC270
(ebook) | NLM QZ 241 | DDC 616.99/4075—dc23/eng/20220822
LC record available at https://lccn.loc.gov/2022039588
LC ebook record available at https://lccn.loc.gov/2022039589

ISBN: 978-1-032-23385-7 (hbk)
ISBN: 978-1-032-22319-3 (pbk)
ISBN: 978-1-003-27700-2 (ebk)

DOI: 10.1201/9781003277002

Typeset in Times
by codeMantra

Contents

List of Figures

List of Tables

Introduction

Cancer diagnostics is a term used to describe a group of medical tests that are used to diagnose infections, disorders, and diseases related to human cancer. To obtain results, biological samples like blood or tissue are extracted from the human body.

Several approaches have been developed in recent times to automatically diagnose different cancer conditions. These approaches can essentially be split into two types: hand-crafted features and classifier approaches based on standard instruction. The second solution is focused on completely automatic approaches based on deep learning. The first type uses manually segregated characteristics and is given to classifiers as data. In training, the classifiers do not change the functions. However, in the second category of attributes, parameters may be modified to execute unique training data activities. Deep learning does not use hand-crafted features and has successfully been adapted to solve the cancer diagnostic problems. As a result, deep learning is now playing an important role in the advancement of cancer diagnostics.

Deep learning is being used by researchers to train algorithms to spot malignant tissue at a level equivalent to that of trained doctors. Compared to numerous domain experts, deep learning has demonstrated the ability to achieve greater diagnostic accuracy results. While this may be a point of disagreement among physicians, many potential victims can't wait for the technology to arrive. This book demonstrates the core concepts of deep learning algorithms that, using diagrams, data tables, and examples, are especially useful for deep learning-based human cancer diagnostics. After introducing the basic concepts of deep learning-based cancer diagnostics, this book will examine deep learning techniques for modeling the diagnosis and the properties and merits of the deep learning network models. A particular focus is placed on the application of different types of deep neural networks, which are useful for detecting different types of human cancers. The theory behind each deep learning architecture will be supported by practical examples in this book. Also, the pre-processing techniques needed to enhance the digital cancer data for proper identification of human diseases will be included in this book. Lastly, highlights will be on how the use of deep neural networks can address new questions and protocols, as well as improve upon existing challenges in cancer diagnosis.

This book is organized in the following way. Chapter 1 delivers the contemporary trends in the early detection and diagnosis of human cancers using deep learning techniques. This chapter analyzes the usage of deep learning architectures for early detection and diagnosis of human cancer. The recent progress involving the use of different deep learning techniques for the early diagnosis of various cancers is discussed; the current limitations and challenges for the implementation of deep learning techniques are assessed, and solutions to some of the common challenges faced by researchers are presented. Finally, directions for future research are outlined.

Chapter 2 deals with cancer data pre-processing techniques. This chapter discusses various cancer data pre-processing techniques that are necessary for data enhancement by reducing reluctant falsifications or improving some data features that are important for additional cancer data processing and automation in retrieval, classification, detection, and diagnosis.

Chapter 3 is devoted to a survey on deep learning techniques for breast, leukemia, and cervical cancer prediction. In this chapter, different ML and DL techniques are discussed to diagnose breast, leukemia, and cervical cancer; also, a comparison of different techniques is discussed with both advantages and drawbacks of the model. To reduce the time complexity and to increase performance, deep learning is used. Outcomes from the existing model proved that deep learning performs better for the prediction of cancerous cells.

Chapter 4 is devoted to a case study on an optimized deep learning technique for detecting lung cancer from CT images. In this chapter, a novel optimized CNN-based classifier is presented to alleviate the practical hindrances in the existing techniques such as overfitting, pre-processing, and data augmentation, and detection of lung cancer from CT images using CNN is performed on the LIDC-IDRI dataset. The tested results show that the presented CNN-based classifier results are good compared to the results from the machine learning techniques in terms of quantitative metrics.

Chapter 5 introduces the reader to a case study of brain tumor segmentation utilizing MRI multimodal images with deep learning. In this chapter, a pre-processing strategy for the operation of just on a limited section of the data instead of the entire image is suggested for the production of a versatile yet robust brain tumor segmentation method. This strategy helps in reduction in processing duration and fixes the concern of overfitting in a cascade deep learning network. In the subsequent stage, an effortless and coherent cascade convolutional neural network (CCNN) is suggested considering the employment of typically coping with a reduced portion of brain data in every layer. The CCNN model harvests all regional and universal characteristics in dual independent ways. In addition, unique extensive evaluations are carried out on the BRATS 2018 dataset, demonstrating that the suggested model gains fair performance.

Chapter 6 deals with an ensemble approach towards detection and classification of brain tumors using lightweight convolutional neural network (CNN). The entire flow of this chapter has two distinct sections, namely, brain tumor detection and classification. A lightweight CNN based on MobileNetV1 is designed for detecting the presence of brain tumor. Another similar CNN with more layers and filters is used for brain tumor classification among meningioma, glioma, and pituitary tumors. The lightweight CNN-based proposed approach of detection and classification of brain tumors is found to be efficient in terms of computational cost and efficiency.

Chapter 7 presents and analyzes the main researches about parallel dense skip-connected CNN approach for brain tumor classification. In this chapter, the parallel dense skip-connected CNN architecture is proposed to classify the brain tumors. The proposed architecture consists of 43 layers with parallel convolution and skip connections. The proposed architecture is tested with Kaggle dataset brain tumor small 2C and large 2C datasets. The brain tumor classification accuracy results achieved are superior as compared to conventional machine learning and the start-of-the-art deep learning networks. Since the skip connections are used in architecture, the redundant features and gradient vanishing problems are reduced. Also, the parallel convolution operation helps to reduce the number of parameters used and to find the best and optimum features to increase the tumor classification accuracies.

The focus of Chapter 8 is on how to perform the liver tumor segmentation using deep learning neural networks. The proposed research uses CT imaging to segment liver cancers. The liver lesions in abdominal CT images are segmented using automatic segmentation techniques. The hybrid U-Net model is employed with using the Deep ResNet34 model architecture. Hyperparameters and epoch scores are utilized to determine the model's accuracy. Finally, the CT scans are employed to train the proposed model to segment multiple liver tumors, and the performance is analyzed with the average losses and Dice score. This will serve as the foundation for developing an automated liver tumor diagnosis system for clinicians with increased accuracy, reducing the risk of manual mistakes during diagnosis.

Chapter 9 deals with deep learning algorithms for the classification and prediction of acute lymphoblastic leukemia. The automation of the classification of acute lymphoblastic leukemia is demonstrated by using Kaggle datasets in this chapter. To achieve this purpose, the variants of CNN along with different activation functions are experimented and achieved the highest accuracy with ResNet50, which are better in diagnosis compared to the efficiency of manual diagnosis, reducing the risk of cancer in mankind.

The focus of Chapter 10 is on cervical pap smear screening and cancer detection using deep neural network. In this work, an integrated convolutional neural network (CNN)-based approach is being proposed to detect and classify cervical cell abnormalities as per Bethesda system. The CNN-based YOLOv5(L) architecture is used for cell classification in multicell pap smear images. The proposed model is fine-tuned and tested on an exhaustive pap smear dataset SIPaKMED with five different classes of cells (parabasal, metaplastic, dyskeratotic, koilocytotic, and superficial intermediate). It can accurately predict the respective class of different types of cells present in the multicell test sample.

Chapter 11 deals with an ensemble approach towards cancer detection using deep neural network: differentiation of squamous carcinoma cells in oral pathology. This chapter presents the data engineering tasks involved in the diagnosis of anomalous tissues. The advent of modern tools and techniques used for feature selection and extraction using microscopic images of the tissues will be explained. Deep learning workflow for the well differentiation of squamous carcinoma cells using histopathologic images is illustrated with implementation using deep learning modules and technologies. Towards the end, summary on research challenges in digital pathology is presented. Finally, this chapter concludes with future research directions.

Chapter 12 provides an overview of challenges and future scopes in current applications of deep learning in human cancer diagnostics. This chapter brings out how AI-based assistance could help oncologists to give an accurate therapy by combining biology and artificial intelligence. Deep learning uses an artificial neural network (ANN) to process data, including medical images, to mimic human neural architecture. In order to decode the molecular start of cancer, clinical oncology research is now more focused on understanding the intricate biological architecture of cancer cell proliferation. Generalize AI, Super AI, and Tight AI are the three types of AI. With the evolution of AI technology, attempts have been made to construct robots that can perceive biological changes by pulling real-time data and comparing it to data from a population pool for the accurate clinical interpretation of cancer test results.

Jyotismita Chaki
School of Computer Science and Engineering
Vellore Institute of Technology
Vellore, India

Aysegul Ucar
Department of Mechatronics Engineering
Firat University
Elazig, Turkey

Contributors

I. Amrita
Department of Computer Science and
  Engineering
Global Academy of Technology
Bangalore, India

M. Angulakshmi
School of Information Technology and
  Engineering
Vellore Institute of Technology
Vellore, India

Nirmala Vasan Balasenthilkumaran
Department of Sensors and Biomedical
  Technology
Vellore Institute of Technology
Vellore, India

Karthik Balasubramanian
Department of Electronics and
  Communication Engineering
National Institute of Technology
Tiruchirappalli, India

Oishila Bandyopadhyay
Department of Computer Science and
  Engineering
Indian Institute of Information
  Technology
Kalyani, India

Soumi Bardhan
Department of Computer Science and
  Engineering
Indian Institute of Information
  Technology
Kalyani, India

Arindam Biswas
Indian Institute of Engineering Science
  and Technology
Shibpur, India

Jyotismita Chaki
School of Computer Science and
  Engineering
Vellore Institute of Technology
Vellore, India

C. Chellaswamy
Department of Electronics and
  Communication Engineering
SRM TRP Engineering College
Tiruchirappalli, India

M. Deepa
School of Information Technology and
  Engineering
Vellore Institute of Technology
Vellore, India

Jayanthi Ganapathy
Faculty of Engineering and Technology
Sri Ramachandra Institute of Higher
  Education and Research
Chennai, India

T. S. Geetha
Department of Electronics and
  Communication Engineering
Sriram Engineering College
and
Department of Electronics and
  Communication Engineering
Vellore Institute of Technology
Chennai, India

Jaydev Jangiti
Department of Computer Science and
    Engineering
School of Electronics Engineering
Vellore Institute of Technology
Vellore, India

Sumit Kumar Jindal
Department of Embedded Technology
School of Electronics Engineering
Vellore Institute of Technology
Vellore, India

N Jothiaruna
School of Information Technology and
    Engineering
Vellore Institute of Technology
Vellore, India

Anny Leema A
School of Computer Science and
    Engineering
Vellore Institute of Technology
Vellore, India

M. Loganathan
Department of Academics and Human
    Resource Development
National Institute of Food Technology
Entrepreneurship and Management –
    Thanjavur (NIFTEM-T)
Thanjavur, India

Munakala Lohith
Department of Computer Science and
    Engineering
Indian Institute of Information
    Technology
Kalyani, India

R. Malmathanraj
Department of Electronics and
    Communication Engineering
National Institute of Technology
Tiruchirappalli, India

R. Mangayarkarasi
School of Information Technology and
    Engineering
Vellore Institute of Technology
Vellore, India

S. Markkandan
Department of Electronics and
    Communication Engineering
SRM TRP Engineering College
Tiruchirappalli, India

R. Meenatchi
Department of Primary Processing
    Storage and Handling
National Institute of Food Technology
Entrepreneurship and Management –
    Thanjavur (NIFTEM-T)
Thanjavur, India

Sabyasachi Mukherjee
Department of Information Technology
Indian Institute of Engineering Science
    and Technology
Shibpur, India

V. Naresh
Department of Electronics and
    Communication Engineering
National Institute of Technology
Tiruchirappalli, India

P. Palanisamy
Department of Electronics and
    Communication Engineering
National Institute of Technology
Tiruchirappalli, India

Charit Gupta Paluri
Department of Computer Science and
    Engineering
School of Electronics Engineering
Vellore Institute of Technology
Vellore, India

P. Thiruvalar Selvan
Department of Electronics and
  Communication Engineering
SRM TRP Engineering College
Tiruchirappalli, India

Snigdha Sen
Department of Computer Science and
  Engineering
Global Academy of Technology
Bangalore, India

Sumedha Vadlamani
Department of Computer Science and
  Engineering
School of Electronics Engineering
Vellore Institute of Technology
Vellore, India

M. Vanitha
School of Information Technology and
  Engineering
Vellore Institute of Technology
Vellore, India

C.S. Vidhya
Department of Primary Processing
  Storage and Handling
National Institute of Food Technology,
  Entrepreneurship and Management –
  Thanjavur, Affiliated to
  Bharathidasan University
Tiruchirappalli, India

G. Yogeswararao
Department of Electronics and
  Communication Engineering
National Institute of Technology
Tiruchirappalli, India

1 Contemporary Trends in the Early Detection and Diagnosis of Human Cancers Using Deep Learning Techniques

Nirmala Vasan Balasenthilkumaran
and Sumit Kumar Jindal
Vellore Institute of Technology

CONTENTS

1.1 INTRODUCTION

Cancer refers to cellular changes that lead to an uncontrollable growth of cells in the body (Hassanpour & Dehghani, 2017). Cancers are a form of malignant tumors. Cancerous cells belonging to malignant tumors can grow uncontrollably and spread to different sites via the bloodstream. Metastasis is the spread of cancer from the point of origin to other parts of the body. The first step in cancer formation is the transformation of healthy cells to malignant or cancerous cells. They can arise due to physical agents that include ionizing and non-ionizing radiations such as X-rays, magnetic-electron field particles (Pambuk & Muhammad, 2018), natural and synthetic mineral fibers (such as asbestos, erionite, wollastonite, attapulgite, asbesti-form, and particulate matter found in air) (Soffritti et al., 2003), biological agents that include exposure to microorganisms (such as certain viruses, bacteria, or parasitic organisms), or chemical agents (including acrylonitrile products, aflatoxins, beryllium, nickel, cobalt, cadmium, silica-based compounds, chlorination products, DDT-based products, gasoline, formaldehyde, ethylene oxide, etc) (Huff, 1993). Exposure to different carcinogens leads to different cancers, whereas some cancers are also due to specific reactions and genetic changes. The five most common types of cancers include carcinoma, sarcoma, leukemia, lymphoma, myeloma, and central nervous system (CNS) cancers (Mitra et al., 2018). Cancers arising in different parts of our body tend to elicit different symptoms, and each cancer is diagnosed by specific screening tools. These tools include imaging tests (such as magnetic resonance imaging (MRI), X-ray scans, computed tomography (CT) scans, and positron emission tomography (PET) scans), blood tests detecting the presence of biomarkers, images from biopsies, etc (Hamilton, 2010). There are currently more than 100 reported cancers (Cooper, 2000). Some of the most common ones are as follows.

Brain and CNS cancers represent abnormal cell growth originating in the brain or the spinal cord. They are mostly genetically inherited or sometimes caused when the head is exposed to radiations (Buckner et al., 2007). Major symptoms include severe headaches, vomiting, nausea, seizures, or focal neurologic defects, and these cancers are mostly diagnosed using imaging modalities such as CT scans, T1-weighted MRI scans, T2-weighted MRI scans, and PET scans (Wilson, 1979). Breast cancer is a term used to define abnormal cell growth in breasts and is the most common cancer found in women (Prusty et al., 2020). It is mostly genetically inherited and is due to gene mutations and is not very dependent on one's lifestyle (Shah et al., 2014). Commonly observed symptoms include nipple abnormalities, breast pain, axillar lump formation, and breast ulceration (Koo et al., 2017). Mammography, ultrasound, MRI scans, and tissue biopsies aid diagnosis (Shah et al., 2014). Lung cancer represents the most common forms of tumors originating in our lungs and is the leading cause of cancer mortality throughout the world (Lemjabbar-Alaoui et al., 2015). Major risk factors include tobacco smoking, exposure to particulate matter, air pollution, family history, and older age. The most common symptoms include cough, chest pain, shortness of breath, and fatigue. Lung cancers are diagnosed using chest X-ray scans, chest CT scans, and tissue biopsies (Bradley et al., 2018). Colorectal cancers begin in the colon or the rectum; the risk factors include environmental factors such as smoking, alcohol intake, increased body weight, and familial factors; they are usually diagnosed using colonoscopy where a tube is inserted to take images of one's colon; the tissue samples collected through this procedure are also used for diagnosis. Early symptoms include rectal bleeding, abdominal pain, and change in bowel habits (Smith et al., 2006). Leukemia describes an abnormal proliferation of the hematopoietic stem cells present in one's bone marrow. It might be due to exposure to ionizing radiations, benzene, or several genetic abnormalities including Down's syndrome and neurofibromatosis. Common symptoms may include lymphadenopathy, bruising, nose bleeds, weight loss, fever, and bleeding gums; these symptoms can be diagnosed using a combination of complete blood count (CBC) tests, bone marrow biopsy, flow cytometry, cytogenic tests, and CT scans (Davis et al., 2014; Shephard et al., 2016).

Skin cancer refers to the abnormal growth of skin cells and includes squamous cell, basal cell carcinoma, and melanoma; it mostly occurs upon exposure to ultra-violet (UV) radiations from the sun, skin creams, tanning beds, and lamps, or it is also due to excessive smoking, exposure to environmental pollutants, or genetic disorders (Saladi et al., 2005). Major symptoms include appearance of pigmented or keratinized, non-healing skin lesions, white cystic papules or nodules, ulceration of the skin, bleeding of skin lesions for sustained periods of time, and these symptoms are diagnosed using total body examination, optical coherence tomography (OCT), dermatoscopy, and photodynamic visualization (Jones et al., 2020; Apalla et al., 2017). Prostate cancer refers to the increase in number of gland cells of the prostate and is the second most common cancer observed in men. Its risk is known to increase with age and prior familial occurrences. The most common symptoms include visible hematuria, lower urinary tract infections (LUTIs), nocturia, and erectile dysfunction (Merriel et al., 2018). They are commonly diagnosed using digital rectal examination (DRE), prostate specific antigen (PSA) blood tests, 3D MRIs, and ultrasound-guided biopsies (Borley & Feneley, 2009). Ovarian cancer denotes the abnormal multiplication of cells in the ovary and is the most lethal cancer diagnosed in females. The reported risk factors include prior familial history of ovarian or breast cancer, BRCA1/BRCA2 gene mutations, increasing age, hormonal therapies, smoking, perineal talc usage, use of oral contraceptives and anti-inflammatory drugs, and weight gain (Doubeni et al., 2016). Abdominal and pelvic discomfort, increased abdominal size, change in bowel habit, weight loss, and loss of appetite are the most commonly observed symptoms (Dilley et al., 2020). Rectovaginal examinations, transvaginal ultrasonography, liver function tests, CBC tests, and CA125 biomarker test are the commonly used diagnostic tools (Doubeni et al., 2016). Lymphoma is a term used to represent cancers associated with the lymphatic system and is of two types, namely, Hodgkin and non-Hodgkin lymphoma. Patients who have congenital immunodeficiency disorders or have acquired immunodeficiency are at an increased risk of developing lymphoma. Other risk factors include family history, or exposure to certain radiations or chemicals. The most commonly observed symptoms include recurrent fever with chills, swelling of lymph nodes, weight loss, and fatigue; these symptoms are mainly diagnosed using a combination of imaging tests such as CT scans, MRIs, X-rays, PET scans, single photon emission computed tomography (SPECT), serum lactate dehydrogenase (LDH) tests, and tissue biopsies (Zinzani, 2005; Jaffe, 2019). Multiple myeloma represents cancer associated with plasma cells in the bone marrow. Initial symptoms include anemia, fatigue, bone pain, renal impairment, and unexplained weight loss; these symptoms are diagnosed using a combination of serum and urine protein electrophoresis, calcium tests, CBC tests, bone marrow examination, bone marrow biopsies, whole-body fluorodeoxyglucose (FDG) PET-CT, and MRI scans (Gerecke et al., 2016; Rajkumar & Kumar, 2016). Risk factors include old age; race (African-Americans are more prone); familial history; sex (men are at a greater risk); and exposure to asbestos, benzene, and other chemicals (Padala et al., 2021). General information regarding the cancers discussed in this chapter is summarized in Table 1.1.

TABLE 1.1

Symptoms Observed for Various Cancers and Various Diagnostic Tools Used

Cancer Type	Symptoms	Diagnostic Tool
Brain and CNS cancer	Headaches, vomiting, nausea, seizures, focal neurologic defects	CT scans, T1- and T2-weighted MRI scans, PET scans
Breast cancer	Nipple abnormalities, breast pain, and ulceration	Mammography, tissue biopsy, ultrasonography
Lung cancer	Cough, chest pain, fatigue, shortness of breath	CT scans and X-ray scans
Colorectal cancer	Rectal bleeding, change in bowel habit, abdominal pain	Tissue biopsy, CT scans, colonoscopy
Leukemia	Nose bleeds, weight loss, fever, bruising, bleeding gums.	CBC tests, CT scans, bone marrow biopsy, cytogenic tests
Skin cancer	Appearance of pigmented or non-healing skin lesions, nodules, papules, ulceration	OCTs, total body skin examination, dermatoscopy, photodynamic visualization
Prostate cancer	LUTS, hematuria, nocturia, and erectile dysfunction	DRE, PSA tests, 3D MRIs, and ultrasound-guided biopsies
Ovarian cancer	Abdominal, pelvic pain, increased abdominal size, change in bowel habit	Rectovaginal examination, liver function tests, CBC, CA 125 blood tests, ultrasound
Lymphoma	Fever with chills, fatigue, weight loss, swelling of lymph nodes.	CT scans, X-ray, MRI, SPECT, PET, LDH blood tests, tissue biopsy
Myeloma	Anemia, fatigue, bone pain, renal impairment, unexplained weight loss	FDG PET-CT, MRI, serum and urine electrophoresis, CBC tests, bone marrow biopsies

Artificial intelligence (AI) is defined as the ability of computer-based systems to perform human activities (Chanal et al., 2021), in this case diagnose cancer using patient data and test results. Machine learning (ML) is a subset of AI, and it denotes a collection of algorithms trained to find patterns, make predictions, and perform classification problems (Belyadi & Haghighat, 2021). Deep learning (DL) is in turn a subset of ML and utilizes multilayered neural networks (NNs) to make predictions (Belyadi & Haghighat, 2021). NNs are computational systems designed to mimic the flow of information in an animal brain. AI, ML, and DL have gained renewed interest in medical image analysis and in computer-aided diagnosis (CAD). DL models can extract complex and high-level features from a dataset directly, are scalable and cost-effective, can work with unstructured data, and have amazing self-learning capabilities (Frank et al., 2020; Mohan & Subashini, 2019). CAD systems are constructed using ML, DL, and image processing algorithms to aid doctors in making diagnostic decisions using data from medical images, blood tests, and other diagnostic information (Alhinai, 2020). CAD can potentially reduce a radiologist's workload, enhance prediction accuracy, and perform faster and remote diagnosis (Alhinai, 2020). With the advent of Picture Archiving and Communication Systems (PACS), CAD systems are increasingly used for diagnosis in the United States and have been used to reduce the number of false negatives (Doi, 2007; Castellino, 2005). This chapter summarizes the current trends in the usage of deep learning architectures (DLAs) in CAD systems for cancer diagnosis.

1.2 DEEP LEARNING ARCHITECTURES COMMONLY USED FOR CANCER DIAGNOSIS

Two common DLAs are mostly used for the cancer diagnostic process. They include artificial neural networks (ANNs) and convolutional neural networks (CNNs). They are an integral part of CAD systems and are generally used to analyze data, find patterns in data, and perform classification. However, sometimes NNs are also used for segmentation, data acquisition, and to predict missing data. DLAs are mostly used in CAD systems utilizing medical images.

1.2.1 ARTIFICIAL NEURAL NETWORKS (ANNs)

ANNs are computing systems modeled using biological NNs. Their multilayered architecture closely resembles the arrangement of neurons in the brain; ANN consists of various interconnected neurons or nodes arranged in many layers. The feedforward neural network is the most popular ANN architecture; here, acyclic arcs connect neurons from different layers (Sairamya et al., 2019). The first layer is the input layer, and it consists of input from medical images or other diagnostic aids. The last layer is known as the output layer, which consists of the predictions made by the model. The layers in between the input and output layers are known as the hidden layers; these layers are responsible for recognizing patterns and establishing relationships from the given information.

Each node is assigned with a weight and a bias. The output of each node is the sum of the bias and the product of the weight and the input. These weighted sums are also passed through activation functions. Commonly used activation functions include binary function, real-valued function, sigmoid, hyperbolic tangent, etc. These weights are assigned during training, and a major chunk of the dataset is utilized for training. Backpropagation is mostly used to update weights during the training process. An error (or loss) function is initialized and minimized during training. Examples of loss functions include mean square error, binary cross entropy, categorical cross entropy, and sparse categorical cross entropy.

1.2.2 CONVOLUTIONAL NEURAL NETWORKS (CNNs)

CNNs are a class of DL networks used to analyze images and have learnable weights and biases. Like ANNs, CNNs are also arranged in layers; the layers can be convolutional, fully connected, pooling, dropout, normalizing, softmax, activation functions, or many more. The first layer is usually the input image, followed by feature extraction layers. Every architecture consists of its own combination and order of arrangement of layers and neurons; some of the most common pre-made architectures used by researchers for image classification include Inceptionv3, DenseNet201, GoogleNet, Nasnetlarge VGGNet, Xception, ShuffleNet, AlexNet, MobileNetv2,

NasNetmobile SqueezeNet, ResNet, and InceptionResNetv2. The weights in these architectures are modified when trained with input images from a dataset. The training and weight modification process is similar to the training process of ANNs.

1.3   USE OF DEEP LEARNING IN CANCER DIAGNOSIS

DL has been effectively used for cancer diagnosis, and several researchers have illustrated the same with the help of CNN-based classifiers. A comprehensive study was conducted, and DLAs for the ten cancers discussed in the previous sections are delineated in this section. DL-based cancer diagnostic systems for the ten cancers listed were searched in IEEEXplore, Springerlink, and ScienceDirect databases (Keywords used: "Cancer name" cancer diagnosis deep learning), and suitable research papers were considered for our study. Research papers with similar classifier evaluation metrics and papers from Scopus-indexed scientific journals were prioritized.

T1-weighted, T2-weighted, and fluid-attenuated inversion recovery (FLAIR) MRIs are widely considered as the gold standard for brain cancer diagnosis. Ismael et al. (2020) utilized a pre-trained GoogLeNet CNN model for feature extraction and ResNet-50-based CNN models to differentiate and diagnose pituitary tumors, meningiomas, and gliomas. Gonbadi et al. (2019) trained a CNN from scratch to diagnose gliomas using MRI slices; they used batch-normalization layers, optimization loss functions, and a dropout layer. Aboelenein et al. (2020) proposed a segmentation mechanism using Hybrid Two-Track U-Net DL architecture. This CNN mostly utilizes Leaky-ReLU activation and batch normalization layers. Sultan et al. (2019) classified brain tumors from MRIs using a 16-layered CNN with an accuracy of 98.7%. The CNN consisted of three convolutional layers, three ReLUs, a normalization function, three max-pooling layers, two dropout layers, a fully connected layer (FCN), and a softmax layer. Finally, Ge et al. (2020) explored the use of generative adversarial networks (GAN) to learn the features and classify brain tumors from T1-weighted, T2-weighted, and FLAIR MRIs.

DL techniques exist for the diagnosis of breast cancer using a variety of diagnostic tools. Prakash and Visakha (2020) developed a 99% accurate five-layered ANN model for the diagnosis of breast cancer using a combination of features extracted from CT and MRI scans. Haq et al. (2020) proposed a three-layered CNN (max pooling, convolution, batch normalization, and dropout layers) to diagnose invasive ductal carcinoma using histological images. Chen et al. (2021) used contrast-enhanced ultrasound (CEUS) videos to design a 3D-CNN-based breast cancer diagnostic aid. Modules in the proposed CNN extracted temporal and spatial information from the videos. Feng et al. (2020) utilized deep manifold preserving autoencoders to diagnose breast cancer using histopathological images of different resolutions. Saha et al. (2018) proposed the addition of a trapezoidal long short-term memory (TLSTM) layer to a conventional CNN architecture and obtained a 98.33% accurate DL model for breast cancer diagnosis using HER2-stained pathological images as input.

Leukemia is traditionally diagnosed by analyzing microscopic blood cell images, and therefore, DL architectures mostly used blood smear images or blood cell images as input. Anilkumar et al. (2021) proposed a custom-made CNN using a few layers from the AlexNet framework to diagnose leukemia using smear images. Nazari et al.

(2020) used DNA microarray data (which mostly consists of gene expression data) as input and designed an ANN with three hidden layers. Increasing the number of hidden layers from one to three increased the accuracy by nearly 30%. Kumar et al. (2020) exploited blood histopathological images as input and univariate feature selection to design a dense CNN consisting of convolutional, pooling, and fully connected layers. Boldú et al. (2021) built a CNN model with modules for recognizing abnormal promyelocytes, distinguishing the lineage of blasts (myeloid or lymphoid), and diagnosing acute leukemia using blood smear images. Lastly, Das et al. (2021) deployed a depthwise separable CNN MobileNetV2 along with a ResNet18 framework to create a hybrid model, preserving benefits of both approaches.

Lung cancer is diagnosed using CT scans and X-rays in hospitals; however, in certain suspect cases, patients are asked to undergo bronchoscopy resulting in bronchoscopical images, histopathological images, and whole-slide images (WSIs). Wang et al. (2020) combined the OTSU pre-processing algorithm with a fast fully CNN and feature aggregation for lung cancer diagnosis. Ozdemir et al. (2020) and Wang et al. (2021) utilized low-dose CT scans as input. Ozdemir et al. (2020) detected and classified lung nodules using a 3D CNN consisting of encoder-decoder pairs, ReLU layers, convolution, and instance normalization. Wang et al. (2021) detected lung cancer using a DLA consisting of a fusion of two 3D ResNet architectures, long short-term memory (LSTM) network, and fully connected network layers. Tan et al. (2018) modified a pre-trained, transfer learning-based model – DenseNet CNN – to diagnose lung cancer and tuberculosis from bronchoscopical images. Ibrahim et al. (2021) tested the combination of various pre-trained CNN models with gated recurrent units to diagnose lung cancer, COVID-19, and pneumonia from lung CT images and X-rays, and found the VGG19 model to be most accurate.

Histopathological images obtained by analyzing tissue samples (obtained from biopsies) have been most effective in detecting and diagnosing lymphoma. Steinbuss et al. (2021) used a pre-made CNN "EfficientNet" to diagnose lymphoma from histopathological images with 95.56% accuracy. Achi et al. (2019) combined image processing operations such as smoothening, sharpening, intensification, and enhancement with a CNN classifier to diagnose lymphoma using eosin-stained WSIs. The model achieved 100% set by set prediction accuracy. Li et al. (2020) used pathological images to propose a deep CNN transfer learning network, which consists of features from a combination nearly ten pre-trained CNNs. Syrykh et al. (2020) designed Bayesian neural networks – an altered CNN consisting of the Bayesian function to diagnose lymphoma using WSIs. Alternatively, Lippi et al. (2020) diagnosed lymphoma using PET-CT images. They utilized the principle of multiple-instance learning where support vector machine (SVM) and Random Forest (RF) ML classifiers were used as final classifiers.

Diagnosis of myeloma usually occurs using microscopic blood cell images or WSIs. Tehsin et al. (2019) utilized AlexNet for feature extraction and SVM for classification and were able to achieve 100% accuracy for sample-wise detection. Sanju and Kumar (2021) tested out various pre-trained CNN models for myeloma diagnosis and were able to demonstrate a classification accuracy of 99% using the MobileNetV1 model. Gehlot et al. (2021) built a CNN model using a combination of 2D convolution filters, batch normalization, parametric ReLu, and loss projection loss layers to diagnose myelomas using microscopic blood cell images. Vyshnav et al. (2020) modified the ResNet architecture and proposed the use of a mask RCNN for the segmentation of microscopic blood cell images and myeloma classification. Lastly, Wang et al. (2022) adopted cascade RCNN as the base DL model to detect bone marrow particles and cellular trails in WSIs and to classify suspect bone marrow cells.

Prostate cancer is mostly diagnosed using histopathological images; however, other diagnostic tools are also sometimes used. The spread and advancement of prostate cancer is evaluated using the Gleason grading system, which measures how abnormal the prostate cells appear in a cell biopsy. Li et al. (2020) used three different branches as convolution kernels (atrous spatial pyramid pooling, parallel branch, and standard) to extract multimodal information, segment the prostate cells, and perform Gleason grading. Duran-Lopez et al. (2020) proposed a custom-made CNN with convolution, batch normalization, and ReLU layers to diagnose prostate cancer from WSIs. Kott et al. (2021) trained and tested the pre-made ResNet architecture to classify each patch as benign or malignant and check the Gleason grade (4 or 5) if they are malignant. Hassan et al. (2022) classified ultrasound images using various pre-trained CNN models – MobileNet V2 DLAs achieved 99% accuracy. Furthermore, they classified MRI images using a modified VGG-16 CNN where the last layer was replaced with a RF classifier. Lastly, Vente et al. (2021) segmented prostate cells from MRI slices using a five-layered 2D-UNet CNN model; they also incorporated zonal information into the model.

DLAs exist for the diagnosis of ovarian cancers from MRIs, histopathological images, ultrasound, gene expression, and cytological images. Wu et al. (2018) used a pre-trained AlexNet CNN architecture for ovarian cancer diagnosis from cytological images. Jian et al. (2021) proposed a multiple-instance CNN (MICNN) with modality-based attention (MA) and contextual MIL pooling layer to diagnose ovarian cancer from multimodal MRIs. Kasture et al. (2021) diagnosed histopathological images with nearly 85% accuracy using a pre-trained VGG-16 CNN model. Ghoniem et al. (2021) used an LSTM network for feature extraction and a CNN classifier for ovarian cancer diagnosis using data from gene expression, copy number variations (CNVs), and histopathological images. Finally, Zhang et al. (2019) utilized a pre-made GoogleLeNet transfer learning CNN for uniform local binary pattern (ULBP) feature extraction from ultrasound images. The ULBP features were then classified using a RF classifier.

Diagnosis of colorectal cancer usually takes place using endoscopic images or using histopathological images from the tissue samples (biopsy) acquired using the endoscopic procedure. Karhan and Akal (2020) and Tsai and Tao (2020) used histopathological images and ResNet architectures for colorectal cancer diagnosis. The former used a ResNet-18 architecture, gray-level co-occurrence matrix, and local binary pattern features, while the latter used a ResNet-50 architecture, which yielded higher accuracy. Zhou et al. (2021) also used a ResNet architecture and modified it for diagnosis using hematoxylin and eosin-stained WSIs. Wang et al. (2021) segmented and detected colorectal polyps in endoscopic images using multi-task real-time deep neural network (MRDNN). Detection of colorectal polyps aids in the early diagnosis of colorectal cancer. The network is composed of skip-connection, up-sampling, down-sampling, and convolution layers, and it also performs encoding and decoding.

Similarly, Zhang et al. (2017) detected and classified hyperplastic and adenomatous colorectal polyps with the help of a pre-existing CNN architecture "CaffeNet".

Skin lesion images and microscopic images of skin cells acquired using non-invasive procedures aid in skin cancer diagnosis. Adegun and Virri (2020) detected melanoma in skin lesion images using a deep convolutional architecture consisting of encoder-decoder networks and softmax classifiers. Goyal et al. (2020) segmented noisy skin lesion images by combining DeeplabV3+ and mark R-CNN architectures. Jiang et al. (2021) utilized a deep residual attention network composed of convolutional, max-pooling, deep residual attention, global summation pooling, and fully connected dense layers to diagnose skin cancer using histopathological images. Ali et al. (2021) classified skin lesion images using a DCNN model that utilizes sigmoid layers for weight updation, backpropagation for fine tuning, and Adam optimizer for gradient descent. Lastly, Adla et al. (2021) modified the CapsNet architecture and replaced the last few layers with an encoder-decoder architecture for feature extraction and

TABLE 1.2
Most Notable DLAs for Each Cancer Type Considered in Our Study

Cancer Type	Deep Learning Architecture	Diagnostic Tool Used	Classification Accuracy	Reference
Brain	Custom-made 16-layered CNN	MRIs	98.7%	Sultan et al. (2019)
Breast	Custom-made CNN with a TLSTM layer and other conventional layers	HER2-stained pathological images	98.33%	Saha et al. (2018)
Leukemia	Hybrid CNN consisting of MobileNetV2 and the ResNet18 framework	Microscopic blood cell images	99.39% and 97.18% in two datasets	Das et al. (2021)
Lung	Fast fully CNN	WSIs	97.30%	Wang et al. (2020)
Lymphoma	Image processing operations for pre-processing and CNN for classification	Eosin-stained WSIs	95% for image prediction and 100% for set-by-set prediction	Achi et al. (2019)
Myeloma	Custom-made CNN model	Microscopic blood cell images	94.17%	Gehlot et al. (2021)
Prostate	Custom-made CNN model	WSIs	99.98%	Duran-Lopez et al. (2020)
Ovarian	GoogleLeNet for feature extraction followed by RF for classification	Ultrasound images	99.15%	Zhang et al. (2019)
Colorectal	Multi-task real-time deep neural network	Endoscopic images	98.86%	Wang et al. (2021)
Skin	Modified CapsNet CNN model	Dermoscopic images	98.5%	Adla et al. (2021)

classification of pre-processed dermoscopic images. Pre-processing involved noise reduction and hair removal. The most notable DLAs and their classification accuracies for each of the cancer types considered in our study are presented in Table 1.2.

1.4   RESULTS AND DISCUSSION

CAD systems were designed using a variety of diagnostic aids, and a pie chart representing the percentage of different diagnostic tools is shown in Figure 1.1. Nearly 37% of the DLAs utilize histopathological images and WSIs as input, and the next commonly used ones include MRI scans, microscopic blood cell and blood smear images, skin lesion images, CT scans, ultrasound, and endoscopic images. A small percentage of other diagnostic tools are also used as shown in Figure 1.1.

The size of the dataset used influences the model's accuracy. A sufficiently large dataset is mandatory for proper training and validation. Larger datasets give better results. However, due to a lack of available data, some models have utilized only small-sized datasets. Many researchers have faced issues in data collection as a large number of these datasets and the medical images acquired from hospitals consist of encrypted DICOM files, which are not easily accessible or processed. A unified dataset consisting of medical images from different sources would help in this regard. Data augmentation is an effective method to increase the number of images in the datasets; several researchers considered in our study have used data augmentation to enhance the performance of their model. Some data augmentation techniques include addition of noise, rotating, cropping, and filtering the images, etc. Figure 1.2 represents the percentage of different dataset sizes utilized by different DLAs considered in our study. Nearly 60% of the researchers have used over 1,000 images, and 23% have used less than 500 images. The size of the dataset discussed in the pie chart is the dataset size before performing data augmentation. The dataset is split for training, validation, and testing in different ratios. The most commonly used split ratios

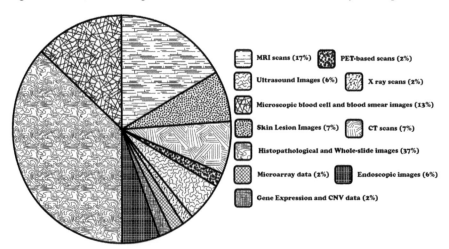

FIGURE 1.1   Pie chart representing the percentage of different diagnostic tools utilized by the DLAs considered in our study.

by researchers in our study are 80-10-10, 70-15-15, and 70-20-10. Different splits provide differing results for different models, and therefore, it would be optimal to try these three ratios before deciding, as a data split that provides the best results for one model might not work well in another model.

Nearly 90% of the papers surveyed are based on CNN-based classifiers, while 4% are based on ANNs and the rest are based on an autoencoder, GAN, and MRDNN. CNNs are found to be most effective in diagnosing medical images, are simple to construct and use, and are therefore most widely used. Twenty-three out of 48 models have yielded a classification accuracy over 95%, and 35 models yielded an accuracy over 90%. Some models have also achieved 100% sample-wise detection accuracy even if they have slightly lower image-wise detection accuracy. Figure 1.3 represents the spread of classification accuracies achieved by different DLAs considered in our study. Out of all the pre-made CNN architectures available, ResNet and VGG16 CNN models have provided the best results for medical images and have been widely used. Other metrics commonly used for the evaluation of DLAs include sensitivity, specificity, and F1 score. Similarity coefficients are also used to evaluate segmentation algorithms, where dice similarity coefficient and kappa similarity coefficient are most commonly used. Adding ML layers such as SVM or RF as the last layer of the CNN has also significantly found to increase accuracies. Overfitting is a common problem faced by DLAs, and the addition of dropout layers has helped mitigate the same.

As most of these DLAs are already highly accurate, future research can involve expansion of such models for use in hospitals. Most of these models surveyed are also yet to be tested on real-time data from hospitals, which is an integral step.

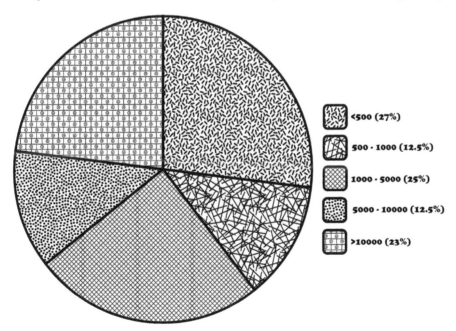

FIGURE 1.2 Pie chart representing the dataset size of different datasets utilized in the DLAs considered in our study.

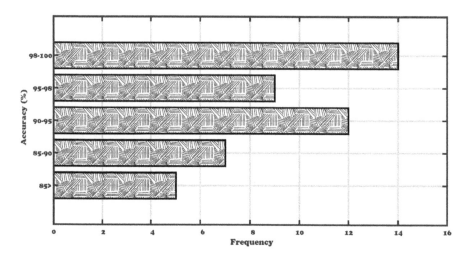

FIGURE 1.3   Bar graph representing the classification accuracies of the DLAs considered in our study.

The development of open-source platforms to submit medical image data would also greatly aid researchers develop and test DLAs as they would have more data to work with. DLAs can also be developed to predict the occurrence of cancers using data from electronic health records (EHRs) and blood test results as these tests are cheaper and are also undertaken by patients on a more regular basis, and therefore, models that would automatically detect abnormalities from patient data would be very helpful for early diagnosis.

1.5   CONCLUSION

In this chapter, we surveyed recent DLAs utilized for the detection and diagnosis of brain, breast, lung, prostate, ovarian, colorectal, skin cancers, lymphoma, leukemia, and myeloma. Of all the DLAs available, CNNs are most widely used with 90% of our survey adopting CNN-based models. The inputs used are mostly medical images, with histopathological and whole-slide images being the most popular (37%), followed by MRI scans (17%) and microscopic blood cell and blood smear images. Nearly half of the DLAs studied boast accuracies over 95%, which indicates the high potential of these methods for use as diagnostic aids. The high accuracies of the DL-based diagnostic methods available warrant the expansion and further testing of these techniques for commercial use. Hospitals, clinicians, radiologists, and patients will greatly benefit with the implementation of such highly accurate CAD systems. The unique properties of the CNNs utilized by various researchers in their DLAs are discussed along with their limitations, recommendations, and directions for future research.

REFERENCES

Aboelenein, N.M., Songhao, P., Koubaa, A., Noor, A. & Afifi, A. (2020). HTTU-net: Hybrid two track U-net for automatic brain tumor segmentation. *IEEE Access*, 8, 101406–101415.

Achi, H. E., Belousova, T., Chen, L., Wahed, A., Wang, I., Hu, Z., Kanaan, Z., Rios, A., & Nguyen, A. (2019). Automated diagnosis of lymphoma with digital pathology images using deep learning. *Ann. Clin. Lab. Sci.*, 49(2), 153–160.

Adegun, A.A. & Viriri, S. (2020). Deep learning-based system for automatic melanoma detection. *IEEE Access*, 8, 7160–7172.

Adla, D., Reddy, G.V.R., Nayak, P. & Karuna, G. (2021). Deep learning-based computer aided diagnosis model for skin cancer detection and classification. *Distrib. Parallel Databases.* https://doi.org/10.1007/s10619-021-07360-z

Alhinai, N. (2020). Chapter 1 - Introduction to biomedical signal processing and artificial intelligence. In W. Zgallai (Eds.), *Developments in Biomedical Engineering and Bioelectronics, Biomedical Signal Processing and Artificial Intelligence in Healthcare* (pp. 1–28). Academic Press.

Ali, M.S., Miah, M.S., Haque, J., Rahman, M.M., & Islam, M.K. (2021). An enhanced technique of skin cancer classification using deep convolutional neural network with transfer learning models. *Mach. Learn. Appl.*, 5, Article 100036.

Anilkumar, K.K., Manoj, V.J. & Sagi, T.M. (2021). Automated detection of B cell and T cell acute lymphoblastic leukaemia using deep learning. *IRMB*, 43(5), 1–9.

Apalla, Z., Nashan, D., Weller, R.B., & Castellsagué, X. (2017). Skin cancer: Epidemiology, disease burden, pathophysiology, diagnosis, and therapeutic approaches. *Dermatol. Ther.,* 7(1), 5–19.

Belyadi, H. & Haghighat, A. (2021). Chapter 1 - Introduction to machine learning and python. In H. Belyadi & A. Haghighat (Eds.), *Machine Learning Guide for Oil and Gas Using Python* (pp. 1–55). Gulf Professional Publishing.

Boldú, L., Merino, A., Acevedo, A., Molina, A. & Rodellar, J. (2021). A deep learning model (ALNet) for the diagnosis of acute leukaemia lineage using peripheral blood cell images. *Comput. Meth. Prog. Bio.*, 202, Article 105999.

Borley, N. & Feneley, M.R. (2009). Prostate cancer: Diagnosis and staging. *Asian J. Androl.*, 11(1), 74–80.

Bradley, S.H., Kennedy, M. & Neal, R.D. (2019). Recognising lung cancer in primary care. *Adv. Ther.*, 36(1), 19–30.

Buckner, J.C., Brown, P.D., O'Neill, B.P., Meyer, F.B., Wetmore, C.J. & Uhm, J.H. (2007). Central nervous system tumors. *Mayo Clin. Proc.*, 82(10), 1271–1286.

Castellino, R.A. (2005). Computer aided detection (CAD): An overview. *Cancer Imaging*, 5(1), 17–19.

Chanal, P.M., Kakkasageri, M.S. & Manvi, S.K.S. (2021). Chapter 7 - Security and privacy in the internet of things: Computational intelligent techniques-based approaches. In S. Bhattacharyya, P. Dutta, D. Samanta, A. Mukherjee & I. Pan (Eds). *Recent Trends in Computational Intelligence Enabled Research* (pp. 111–127). Academic Press.

Chen, C., Wang, Y., Niu, J., Liu, X., Li, Q. & Gong, X. (2021). Domain knowledge powered deep learning for breast cancer diagnosis based on contrast-enhanced ultrasound videos. *IEEE Trans. Med. Imaging*, 40(9), 2439–2451.

Cooper, G.M. (2000). The development and causes of cancer. In *Cell: A Molecular Approach.* 2nd edition. Sinauer Associates.

Das, P. K. & Meher, S. (2021). An efficient deep convolutional neural network based detection and classification of acute lymphoblastic leukemia. *Expert Syst. Appl.*, 183, Article 115311.

Davis, A.S., Viera, A.J. & Mead, M.D. (2014). Leukemia: An overview for primary care. *Am. Fam. Physician*, 89(9), 731–738.

Dilley, J., Burnell, M., Gentry-Maharaj, A., Ryan, A., Neophytou, C., et al. (2020). Ovarian cancer symptoms, routes to diagnosis and survival - Population cohort study in the 'no screen' arm of the UK collaborative trial of ovarian cancer screening. *Gynecol. Oncol.*, 158(2), 316–322.

Doi, K. (2007). Computer-aided diagnosis in medical imaging: Historical review, current status and future potential. *Comput. Med. Imaging Graph.*, 31(4–5), 198–211.

Doubeni, C.A., Doubeni, A.R. & Myers, A.E. (2016). Diagnosis and management of ovarian cancer. *Am. Fam. Physician*, 93(11), 937–944.

Duran-Lopez, L., Dominguez-Morales, J.P., Conde-Martin, A.F., Vicente-Diaz, S. & Linares-Barranco, A. (2020). PROMETEO: A CNN-based computer-aided diagnosis system for WSI prostate cancer detection. *IEEE Access*, 8, 128613–128628.

Feng, Y., Zhang, L. & Mo, J. (2020). Deep manifold preserving autoencoder for classifying breast cancer histopathological images. *IEEE/ACM Trans. Comput. Biol. Bioinform.*, 17(1), 91–101.

Frank, E., Zhen, Y., Han, F., Shailesh, T. & Matthias, D. (2020). An introductory review of deep learning for prediction models with big data. *Front. Artif. Intell. Appl.*, 3, Article 4.

Ge, C., Gu, I.Y.H., Jakola, A.S. and Yang, J. (2020). Enlarged training dataset by pairwise GANs for molecular-based brain tumor classification. *IEEE Access*, 8, 22560–22570.

Gehlot, S., Gupta, A. & Gupta, R. (2021). A CNN-based unified framework utilizing projection loss in unison with label noise handling for multiple myeloma cancer diagnosis. *Med. Image Anal.*, 72, Article 102099.

Gerecke, C., Fuhrmann, S., Strifler, S., Schmidt-Hieber, M., Einsele, H. & Knop, S. (2016). The diagnosis and treatment of multiple myeloma. *Dtsch. Ärztebl.*, 113(27–28), 470–476.

Ghoniem, R.M., Algarni, A.D., Refky, B. & Ewees, A.A. (2021). Multi-modal evolutionary deep learning model for ovarian cancer diagnosis. *Symmetry*, 13(4), Article 643.

Gonbadi, F.B., & Khotanlou, H. (2019). Glioma brain tumors diagnosis and classification in MR images based on convolutional neural networks. *9th International Conference on Computer and Knowledge Engineering*, Mashhad, Iran, 1–5.

Goyal, M., Oakley, A., Bansal, P., Dancey, D. & Yap, M.H. (2020). Skin lesion segmentation in dermoscopic images with ensemble deep learning methods. *IEEE Access*, 8, 4171–4181.

Hamilton, W. (2010). Cancer diagnosis in primary care. *Br. J. Gen. Pract.*, 60(571), 121–128.

Hassan, M.R., Islam, M.F., Uddin, M.Z., Ghoshal, G., Hassan, M.M., Huda, S. & Fortino, G. (2022). Prostate cancer classification from ultrasound and MRI images using deep learning based explainable artificial intelligence. *Future Gener. Comput. Syst.*, 127, 462–472.

Hassanpour, S.H., & Dehghani, M. (2017). Review of cancer from perspective of molecular. *J. Cancer Res. Pract.*, 4(4), 127–129.

Haq, A.U., Li, J.P., Saboor, A., Khan, J., Zhou, W., Jiang, T., Raji, M.F. & Wali, S. (2020). 3DCNN: Three-layers deep convolutional neural network architecture for breast cancer detection using clinical image data. *17th International Computer Conference on Wavelet Active Media Technology and Information Processing*, Chengdu, China, 83–88.

Huff, J. (1993). Chemicals and cancer in humans: First evidence in experimental animals. *Environ Health Perspect.*, 100, 201–210.

Ibrahim, D.M., Elshennawy, N.M. & Sarhan, A.M. (2021). Deep-chest: Multi-classification deep learning model for diagnosing COVID-19, pneumonia, and lung cancer chest diseases. *Comput. Biol. Med.*, 132, Article 104348.

Ismael, S.A.A., Mohammed, A. & Hefny, H. (2020). An enhanced deep learning approach for brain cancer MRI images classification using residual networks. *Artif. Intell. Med.*, 102, Article 101779.

Jaffe, E.S. (2019). Diagnosis and classification of lymphoma: Impact of technical advances. *Semin. Hematol.*, 56(1), 30–36.

Jian, J., Xia, W., Zhang, R., Zhao, X., Zhang, J., Wu, X. Li, Y., Qiang, J. & Gao, X. (2021). Multiple instance convolutional neural network with modality-based attention and contextual multi-instance learning pooling layer for effective differentiation between borderline and malignant epithelial ovarian tumors. *Artif. Intell. Med.*, 121, Article 102194.

Jiang, S., Li, H. & Jin, Z. (2021). A visually interpretable deep learning framework for histopathological image-based skin cancer diagnosis. *IEEE J. Biomed. Health. Inform.*, 25(5), 1483–1494.

Jones, O.T., Ranmuthu, C., Hall, P.N., Funston, G. & Walter, F.M. (2020). Recognising skin cancer in primary care. *Adv. Ther.*, 37(1), 603–616.

Karhan, Z. & Akal, F. (2020). Comparison of tissue classification performance by deep learning and conventional methods on colorectal histopathological images. *Med. Technol. Natl. Congr.*, 2020 Medical Technologies Congress, Antalya, Turkey, 1–4.

Kasture, K.R., Sayankar, B.B. & Matte, P.N. (2021). Multi-class classification of ovarian cancer from histopathological images using deep learning - VGG-16. *2nd Global Conference for Advancement in Technology*, Bangalore, India, 1–6.

Koo, M.M., von Wagner, C., Abel, G.A., McPhail, S., Rubin, G.P. & Lyratzopoulos, G. (2017). Typical and atypical presenting symptoms of breast cancer and their associations with diagnostic intervals: Evidence from a national audit of cancer diagnosis. *Cancer Epidemiol.*, 48, 140–146.

Kott, O., Linsley, D., Amin, A., Karagounis, A., Jeffers, C., Golijanin, D., Serre, T. & Gershman, B. (2021). Development of a deep learning algorithm for the histopathologic diagnosis and gleason grading of prostate cancer biopsies: A pilot study, *Eur. Urol. Focus.*, 7(2), 347–351.

Kumar, D., Jain, N., Khurana, A., Mittal, S., Satapathy, S.C., Senkerik, R. & Hemanth, J.D. (2020). Automatic detection of white blood cancer from bone marrow microscopic images using convolutional neural networks. *IEEE Access*, 8, 142521–142531.

Lemjabbar-Alaoui, H., Hassan, O.U., Yang, Y.W. & Buchanan, P. (2015). Lung cancer: Biology and treatment options. *Biochimica. et. Biophysica. acta.*, 1856(2), 189–210.

Li, D., Bledsoe, J.R., Zeng, Y., Liu, W., Hu Y., Bi, K., Liang, A. & Li, S. (2020). A deep learning diagnostic platform for diffuse large B-cell lymphoma with high accuracy across multiple hospitals. *Nat. Commun.*, 11, Article 6004

Li, Y., Huang, M., Zhang, Y., Chen, J., Xu, H., Wang. G. & Feng, W. (2020). Automated gleason grading and gleason pattern region segmentation based on deep learning for pathological images of prostate cancer. *IEEE Access*, 8, 117714–117725.

Lippi, M., Gianotti, S., Fama, A., Casali, M., Barbolini, E., et al. (2020). Texture analysis and multiple-instance learning for the classification of malignant lymphomas. *Comput. Meth. Prog. Bio.*, 185, Article 105153.

Merriel, S., Funston, G. & Hamilton, W. (2018). Prostate cancer in primary care. *Adv. Ther.*, 35(9), 1285–1294.

Mitra, S., Ganguli, S. & Chakrabarti, J. (2018). Chapter 1 – Introduction. In J. Chakrabarti & S. Mitra (Eds.), *Translational Epigenetics, Cancer and Noncoding RNAs* (pp. 1–23). Academic Press.

Mohan, G. & Subashini, M.M. (2019). Chapter 4 - Medical imaging with intelligent systems: A review. In A.K. Sangaiah (Eds.), *Deep Learning and Parallel Computing Environment for Bioengineering Systems* (pp. 53–73). Academic Press.

Nazari, E., Farzin, A. H., Aghemiri, M., Avan, A., Tara, M., & Tabesh, H. (2020). Deep learning for acute myeloid leukemia diagnosis. *J. Med. Life.*, 13(3), 382–387.

Ozdemir, O., Russell, R.L. & Berlin, A.A. (2020). A 3D probabilistic deep learning system for detection and diagnosis of lung cancer using low-dose CT scans. *IEEE Trans. Med. Imaging*, 39(5), 1419–1429.

Padala, S.A., Barsouk, A., Rawla, P., Vakiti, A., Kolhe, R., Kota, V. & Ajebo, G.H. (2021). Epidemiology, staging, and management of multiple myeloma. *Med. Sci.,* 9(1), Article 3.

Pambuk, C.I.A., & Muhammad, F.M. (2018). Cancer cause: Biological, chemical and physical carcinogens. *Merit Res. J. Med. Med. Sci.*, 6(9), 303–306.

Prakash, S.S., & Visakha, K. (2020). Breast cancer malignancy prediction using deep learning neural networks. *Second International Conference on Inventive Research in Computing Applications*, Coimbatore, India, 88–92.

Prusty, R.K., Begum, S., Patil, A., Naik, D.D., Pimple, D.S. & Mishra, G. (2020). Knowledge of symptoms and risk factors of breast cancer among women: A community-based study in a low socio-economic area of Mumbai, India. *BMC Women's Health*, 20(1), Article 106.

Rajkumar, S.V. & Kumar, S. (2016). Multiple myeloma: Diagnosis and treatment. *Mayo Clin. Proc.*, 91(1), 101–119.

Saha, M. & Chakraborty, C. (2018). Her2Net: A deep framework for semantic segmentation and classification of cell membranes and nuclei in breast cancer evaluation. *IEEE Trans. Image Process.*, 27(5), 2189–2200.

Sairamya N.J., Susmitha, L., George, S.T. & Subathra, M.S.P. (2019). Chapter 12 - Hybrid approach for classification of electroencephalographic signals using time–frequency images with wavelets and texture features. In D.J. Hemanth, D. Gupta & V.E. Balas (Eds.), *Intelligent Data-Centric Systems, Intelligent Data Analysis for Biomedical Applications* (pp. 253–273). Academic Press.

Saladi, R.N. & Persaud, A.N. (2005). The causes of skin cancer: A comprehensive review. *Drugs Today*, 41(1), 37–53.

Sanju & Kumar, A. (2021). Classification of multiple myeloma cancer cells using convolutional neural networks and transfer learning. *Asian Conference on Innovation in Technology*, Pune, India, 1–6.

Shah, R., Rosso, K. & Nathanson, S.D. (2014). Pathogenesis, prevention, diagnosis and treatment of breast cancer. *World J. Clin. Oncol.*, 5(3), 283–298.

Shephard, E.A., Neal, R.D., Rose, P.W., Walter, F.M. & Hamilton, W. (2016). Symptoms of adult chronic and acute leukaemia before diagnosis: Large primary care case-control studies using electronic records. *Br. J. Gen. Pract.*, 66(644), 182–188.

Smith, D., Ballal, M., Hodder, R., Soin, G., Selvachandran, S.N. & Cade, D. (2006). Symptomatic presentation of early colorectal cancer. *Ann. R. Coll. Surg. Engl.*, 88(2), 185–190.

Soffritti, M., Minardi, F. & Maltoni, C. (2003). Chapter 21 - Physical carcinogens. In D.W. Kufe, R.E. Pollock & R.R. Weichselbaum (Eds.), *Holland-Frei Cancer Medicine*, 6th edition.

Steinbuss, G., Kriegsmann, M., Zgorzelski, C., Brobeil, A., Goeppert, B., Dietrich, S., Mechtersheimer, G., & Kriegsmann, K. (2021). Deep learning for the classification of non-Hodgkin lymphoma on histopathological images. *Cancers*, 13(10), Article 2419.

Sultan, H.H., Salem, N.M. & Al-Atabany, W. (2019). Multi-classification of brain tumor images using deep neural network. *IEEE Access*, 7, 69215–69225.

Syrykh, C., Abreu, A., Amara, N., Siegfried, A., Maisongrosse, V., Frenois, F.X. et al. (2020). Accurate diagnosis of lymphoma on whole-slide histopathology images using deep learning. *Digit. Med.*, 3, Article 63.

Tan, T., Li, Z., Zangani, F.G., Ouyang, Q., Tang, Y., Hu, Z. & Li, W. (2018). Optimize transfer learning for lung diseases in bronchoscopy using a new concept: Sequential fine-tuning. *IEEE J. Transl. Eng. Health Med.*, 6, 1–8

Tehsin, S., Zameer, S. & Saif, S. (2019). Myeloma cell detection in bone marrow aspiration using microscopic images. *11th International Conference on Knowledge and Smart Technology*, Phuket, Thailand, 57–61.

Tsai, M.J. & Tao, Y.H. (2020). Deep learning techniques for colorectal cancer tissue classification. *14th International Conference on Signal Processing and Communication Systems*, Adelaide, Australia, 1–8.

Vente, C.D., Vos, P., Hosseinzadeh, M., Pluim, J. & Veta, M. (2021). Deep learning regression for prostate cancer detection and grading in Bi-parametric MRI. *IEEE. Trans. Biomed. Eng.*, 68(2), 374–383.

Vyshnav, M.T., Sowmya, V., Gopalakrishnan, E.A., Variyar, S., Menon, V.K. & Soman, K. (2020). Deep learning based approach for multiple myeloma detection. *11th International Conference on Computing, Communication and Networking Technologies*, Kharagpur, India, 1–7.

Wang, C., Huang, S., Lee, Y., Shen, Y., Meng, S., Jeff & Gaol, L. (2022). Deep learning for bone marrow cell detection and classification on whole-slide images. *Med. Image Anal.*, 75, Article 102270.

Wang, S., Yin, Y., Wang, D., Lv, Z., Wang, Y. & Jin, Y. (2021). An interpretable deep neural network for colorectal polyp diagnosis under colonoscopy. *Knowl. Based Syst.*, 234, Article 107568.

Wang, W., Liu, F., Zhi, X., Zhang, T. & Huang, C. (2021). An integrated deep learning algorithm for detecting lung nodules with low-dose CT and its application in 6G-enabled internet of medical things. *IEEE Internet Things J.*, 8(7), 5274–5284.

Wang, X., Chen, H., Gan, C., Lin, H., Dou, Q., Tsougenis, E., Huang, Q., Cai, M. & Heng, P. (2020). Weakly supervised deep learning for whole slide lung cancer image analysis. *IEEE Trans. Cybern.*, 50(9), 3950–3962.

Wilson, C.B. (1979). Current concepts in cancer: Brain tumors. *N. Engl. J. Med.*, 300(26), 1469–71.

Wu, M., Yan, C., Liu, H. & Liu, Q. (2018). Automatic classification of ovarian cancer types from cytological images using deep convolutional neural networks. *Biosci Rep.*, 38(3), Article BSR20180289.

Zhang, L., Huang, J. & Liu, L. (2019). Improved deep learning network based in combination with cost-sensitive learning for early detection of ovarian cancer in color ultrasound detecting system. *J. Med. Syst.*, 43, Article 251.

Zhang, R., Zheng, Y., Mak, T.W.C., Yu, R., Wong, S.H., Lau, J.Y.W. & Poon, C.C.Y. (2017). Automatic detection and classification of colorectal polyps by transferring low-level CNN features from nonmedical domain. *IEEE J. Biomed. Health Inform.*, 21(1), 41–47.

Zhou, C., Jin, Y., Chen, Y., Huang, S., Huang, R., Wang, Y., Zhao, Y., Chen, Y., Guo, L. & Liao, J. (2021). Histopathology classification and localization of colorectal cancer using global labels by weakly supervised deep learning. *Comput. Med. Imaging Graph.*, 88, Article 101861.

Zinzani, P.L. (2005). Lymphoma: Diagnosis, staging, natural history, and treatment strategies. *Semin. Oncol.*, 32(1), 4–10.

2 Cancer Data Pre-Processing Techniques

Jyotismita Chaki
Vellore Institute of Technology

CONTENTS

DOI: 10.1201/9781003277002-2

2.1   INTRODUCTION

Cancer data is considered to be of high quality if it satisfies the requirements of its planned usage. Good-quality cancer data preparation is the essential part when automation in cancer disease recognition is concerned. Cancer data quality is determined by a variety of factors. These qualities are as follows: completeness, accuracy, consistency, timeliness, relatability, and interpretability. The cancer data you want to mine is incomplete (it loses attribute values or some characteristics of interest, or it only contains aggregate data), noisy or inaccurate (it contains errors or values that differ from the anticipated), and inconsistent (e.g., comprising inconsistencies in the dataset).

There are numerous reasons for inaccurate cancer data (having incorrect attribute values). The data collection instruments utilized could be defective [1]. There could have been the computer or human errors during the data entry process. When the patient does not want to disclose information about other diseases, they may purposefully enter incorrect data values for some vital fields, such as writing incorrect disease names in the place of any other disease suffering. (This is referred to as disguised missing data.) Data transmission inconsistencies can also happen. There could be technological constraints, such as a small buffer size for synchronization of data transfer and usage. Incorrect data can also be caused by inconsistencies in nomenclature or data codes, as well as inconsistent formats for input fields such as dates. Duplicate tuples necessitate data cleaning as well.

Incomplete cancer data can happen for a variety of reasons. Patient information for the medicine intake data, for example, may not always be obtainable. Other information may be excluded simply because it was not deemed crucial at the time of admission. Relevant information may not be recorded because of a misinterpretation or equipment failure. Data that contradicted other recorded data may have been removed. Moreover, the recording of the patient's medical history or changes to the data may have gone unnoticed. Missing data may have to be inferred, especially for tuples with missing values for some attributes.

Machines prefer to process information that is neat and tidy – they read data as 1s and 0s [2]. As a result, calculating structured data such as whole numbers and percentages is simple. Unstructured data, such as text and images, must first be cleaned and formatted before being analyzed. When training deep learning models with data sets, the phrase "garbage in, garbage out" is frequently used. This means that if user trains their model with poor or "dirty" data, they'll end up with the wrong, poorly trained model that won't be appropriate for the analysis.

Good, pre-processed data is even more crucial than the most powerful and advanced deep learning algorithms, to the point where deep learning models trained on faulty data may be harmful to the analysis they're attempting to perform, resulting in "garbage" results [3–5]. Users will set themselves up for a much more accurate degradation process if users properly pre-process and clean the data. Researchers frequently hear about the significance of "data-driven decision making," but if these decisions are based on inaccurate data, they are simply bad decisions.

Cancer data pre-processing has three objectives in general [6]. First is the need to reduce the impact of data acquisition and biological artifacts. Second is the need to validate statistical assumptions and transform the data to conform to these assumptions. Three, to achieve sensitivity in group analysis and validity, the need is to standardize the location of disease regions across different subjects.

The organization of this chapter is as follows: Section 2.2 discusses about the cancer types; data collection modes are included in Section 2.3; Section 2.4 reports the common pre-processing techniques, which are applicable for the cancer data; and lastly, Section 2.5 concludes this chapter.

2.2   CANCER TYPES

Cells are the basic building blocks of the human body. Cells divide and grow to produce new cells as the body requires them [7]. Cells usually die when they become too old or damaged. Then, new cells replace them. Cancer develops when genetic changes disrupt this orderly process. Cells begin to proliferate uncontrollably. These cells can combine to form a mass known as a tumor. A tumor can be malignant or benign. A malignant tumor can grow and spread to other parts of the body. A benign tumor can grow but does not spread. Some types of cancer do not form a tumor. In this section, some cancer types are discussed.

2.2.1   CERVICAL CANCER

Cervical cancer develops in the cells that line the cervix, which is the lower part of the uterus (womb) [7]. The cervix links the uterus body (the upper portion where the fetus grows) to the vagina (birth canal). Cancer develops when cells in the body begin to proliferate uncontrollably.

2.2.2   LIVER CANCER

Liver cancer is a potentially fatal disease and one of the fastest increasing cancer types [8]. Primary and secondary liver cancer are the two types. Primary cancer begins in the liver. Secondary cancer spreads from another part of the body to the liver.

2.2.3 BREAST CANCER

Breast cancer is a disease in which the cells in the breast proliferate uncontrollably. There are various types of breast cancer [9]. The type of breast cancer is determined by which cells in the breast develop into cancer. Breast cancer can start in any part of the breast. A breast is composed of three major components: ducts, lobules, and connective tissue. The majority of breast cancers start in the lobules or ducts. Breast cancer can spread outside of the breast via lymph and blood vessels.

2.2.4 LUNG CANCER

Lung cancer starts in the lungs and can spread to lymph nodes or other organs, including the brain [9]. Cancer from other organs can spread to the lungs as well. Lung cancers are typically classified into two types: small cell and non-small-cell (including adenocarcinoma and squamous cell carcinoma). These types of lung cancer development are treated in different ways. Non-small-cell lung cancer outnumbers small cell lung cancer.

2.2.5 COLORECTAL CANCER

Colorectal cancer is a condition in which cells in the colon or rectum proliferate uncontrollably [9]. In short, it is known as colon cancer. The colon is also known as the large bowel or large intestine. The rectum is the passage between the colon and the anus. Polyps, or abnormal growths, can form in the colon or rectum.

2.2.6 ORAL CANCER

The broad term for cancer that affects the inside of the mouth is oral cancer (mouth cancer) [8]. Oral cancer can appear as a common problem with the lips or mouth, such as white patches or bleeding sores. The distinction between a common problem and potential cancer is that these changes do not disappear. Oral cancer, if left untreated, can spread from the mouth and throat to other parts of the head and neck.

2.3 DATA COLLECTION MODES

Cancer data collection begins with identifying cancer patients who have been diagnosed or treated in hospitals, radiology departments, outpatient clinics, doctors' offices, surgical centers, laboratories, surgical centers, or other providers (such as pharmacists) who detect or treat cancer patients. In this section, some widely used data collection modes are discussed.

2.3.1 Magnetic Resonance Imaging (MRI) Data

The MRI produces cross-sectional images of the internal organs. However, MRI images are created using strong magnets rather than radiation [7]. An MRI scan takes cross-sectional slices (views) of the body from various angles as if the patient were looking at a slice of their body from the front, side, or above their head. MRI images soft tissue parts of the body that are sometimes difficult to see with other imaging tests. Some cancers can be found and managed to identify using MRI. MRI can also be used to look for signs that cancer has spread from where it began to another part of the body. MRI images can also assist doctors in the planning of treatments such as surgery or radiation therapy. MRI data is generally collected for the recognition of cervical cancer, oral cancer, liver cancer, and breast cancer.

2.3.2 Computed Tomography (CT) Scan Image Data

To examine structures inside the body, healthcare professionals use computed tomography, also known as a CT scan [8]. A CT scan creates images of a cross-section of the body using X-rays and computers. It takes pictures of different organs, allowing medical professionals to see the body in great detail. CT scan data is generally collected for the recognition of cervical cancer, oral cancer, liver cancer, colorectal cancer, and lung cancer.

2.3.3 X-ray Image Data

An X-ray is a quick, painless test that generates images of the structures within the body [10]. X-ray beams pass through the body and are absorbed differently depending on the density of the material through which they pass. On X-rays, dense materials like bone and metal appear white. The air in the lungs appears black. Fat and muscle appear as grayscale images. Chest X-rays can reveal evidence of pneumonia, tuberculosis, or lung cancer. Mammography is a type of X-ray test that is used to examine breast tissue. X-ray data is generally collected for the recognition of liver cancer, lung cancer, oral cancer, colorectal cancer, and breast cancer.

2.3.4 Ultrasound Image Data

An ultrasound machine generates sonograms by emitting high-frequency sound waves that travel through your body [8]. Echoes are created when sound waves bounce off organs and tissues. The machine converts these echoes into real-time images of organ structure and movement, as well as blood flow through blood vessels. The images are viewable on a computer screen. Ultrasound is excellent for capturing images of soft tissue diseases that do not show up well on X-rays. Ultrasound data is usually collected for the recognition of liver cancer and oral cancer.

2.3.5   GENE EXPRESSION DATA

Cancer genes are operationally defined by their altered expression, which results in an abnormal phenotype in a significant subset of cancers [11]. The altered expression may help or hinder the initiation or progression of a neoplasm, as oncogenes do, or it may inhibit it, as tumor suppressor genes do. Only mutated genes have traditionally been considered as candidate cancer genes, but cancer phenotypes are caused by altered gene expression, and there is no simple 1:1 relationship between mutated genes and cancer phenotypes. Gene expression data is generally collected for the recognition of cervical cancer, liver cancer, and lung cancer.

2.3.6   TEXT DATA

Cancer-related information can be found in various types of medical reports in a clinical setting [12]. Electronic medical records (EMRs) are very helpful for TM – electronic documents that may describe demographic information, medical history, medication, and known allergies, laboratory test results, radiology images, and so on. Pathology and imaging reports, in particular, are useful for documenting cancer-related information. A pathology report describes the findings of a microscopic examination of cells and tissues following a biopsy or surgery. It typically includes patient information, a description of how cells appear under a microscope, and a diagnosis. This information is then used by clinicians to help them make treatment decisions. Imaging reports (or radiology reports) serve the same purpose as diagnostic reports in that they convey a specialist interpretation of images and relate it to the patient's signs and symptoms. Further categorization can be done based on the type of imaging technique used, with each having its reporting standards or guidelines, such as X-ray imaging reports (including chest radiography and mammography reports), CT scan reports, and MRI reports. Text data is frequently collected for the recognition of cervical cancer and oral cancer.

2.4   COMMON PRE-PROCESSING TECHNIQUES APPLICABLE FOR CANCER DATA

Pre-processing refers to all of the transformations performed on raw data before feeding it to the deep learning or machine learning algorithm. For example, training a convolutional neural network on raw images will almost certainly result in poor classification performance. Pre-processing is also important for accelerating training (for instance, scaling and centering techniques).

2.4.1   MRI DATA

In this section, some pre-processing techniques for the MRI data are discussed.

2.4.1.1   Intensity Inhomogeneity Correction

A common issue encountered in the development of such computer-aided diagnostic tools is the correction of intensity inhomogeneity (IIH) in MR images [13].

The following are some of the most popular mathematical models for describing IIH: (i) low-frequency framework, which presumes the IIH to be a random process or a random variable and recovers the IIH map through low-pass filtering; (ii) hyper-surface framework, which conforms the IIH map by a smooth function, the parameters of which are generally collected through regression; (iii) statistical framework, which presumes the IIH to be a random process or a random variable and recovers the IIH map through parameter analysis.

2.4.1.2   Registration

MR scanning can result in misaligned images that necessitate image registration [14]. Because MR scanning is much slower than CT scanning, MR slices within the same image sequence are more likely to be offset from one another. While slice-level registration is needed when handling 3D images in a single channel, image-level registration is also needed when processing multiple modalities simultaneously. Image fusion or domain adaptation between MR images acquired utilizing different field of view throughout separate retrospective studies could be a critical instance.

2.4.1.3   Segmentation

After pre-processing, an image is segmented into disparate, nonoverlapping regions with varying degrees of homogeneity in their texture features [15]. The goal in cancer patients would be to delineate the region of interest (ROI) containing distinguishing features. Segmentation techniques have evolved and are classified in various ways. There are three types of segmentation, each with varying degrees of computer-aided automation: manual, supervised, and unsupervised. Manual segmentation, which is completely computer-aided, needs the skills of a neuroradiologist to draw a periphery around the enclosing the pathology. The user provides input to the algorithm, instructing it on how to conduct and what constraints to follow. The unsupervised segmentation method, which necessitates no user input, is the most difficult. Connected threshold, Region-growing algorithms, Otsu's segmentation, Neighbourhood connected segmentation, Watershed algorithm, Confidence connected, and others are the most frequently used segmentation methods.

2.4.1.4   Slice Timing Correction

To construct an organ volume, a frequent sample is constructed from multiple slices of the organ during each repetition time [6]. But even so, since those are acquired sequentially, each slice is generally sampled at various time points, and so even though the organ volume can be treated as being scanned at a single time point, this is generally not the case, so the top of the organ volume may be sampled a second or two later than the bottom, and this is something need to be corrected. As a result, slice time correction shifts each voxel's time series so that they seem to have been sampled concurrently. As a result, temporal interpolation and other methods can be used to correct this. Using temporal interpolation, the amplitude of the MR signal is estimated at the start of each information from nearby time points. To interpolate it, sinc functions or linear spline can be used. Conversely, phase shift and Fourier methods can be used to slide the time course by applying a phase shift to the time course's Fourier transform. Both methods are equally effective.

2.4.1.5 Motion Correction

Organ motion is a serious issue in cancer imaging, and even minor movements of the organ during an experiment can be a significant cause of error if not handled properly [6]. When trying to analyze a time series associated with a single voxel, it represents the same region of the organ at each time point. Nevertheless, if the patient moves their organ, one voxel that was in this position may now be in a completely different area due to the organ motion, which needed to be avoided. As a result, this is generally correctable through a process known as rigid body transformation. In this case, it can be assumed that the organ is a rigid body that can move and attempt to correct for this movement. And this can be done in general, to find the best possible alignment between an input image and some target image. To align the two images, one must be transformed so that it lies on top of the other. And in this case, a rigid body transformation can be used.

2.4.1.6 Nuisance Variable Removal

The MRI data includes both signal and noise [16]. Organ motion etc are among the noise components. Independent component analysis (ICA) can be used to eliminate the noise components. ICA is a technique for separating MRI signals into spatially ICs. The computed ICs are further categorized into noise and signal components based on spatial and temporal characteristics. There are automatic methods for classifying ICs, but their performance is not always consistent.

2.4.1.7 Filtering

Filtering-based methodologies are the most traditional, simple, and computationally light of the four categories [15]. Filtering eliminates elements that meet or do not meet a predefined threshold. The noise eliminated from MR images corresponds to artifacts at low frequencies. Moreover, because filtering is imperfect, there is a high likelihood of removing valid signals when using low-pass methods, as well as the possibility of creating new artifacts known as edge effects. Although research has been conducted to mitigate edge effects, the overall result still demonstrates a biased field. When analyzing brain tumor images, it is critical to correctly identify structural differences that change as the disease progresses.

Homomorphic filtering and homomorphic unsharp masking are the two main classical filtering methods that are still used today. The image is first log-transformed before being transformed into the frequency domain. The bias field is then removed using a low-pass filter, with the corrected image being the difference between the bias and original images. This biased field image is commonly referred to as the background image. The same operations are performed by homomorphic unsharp masking, but the image is not log-transformed.

2.4.1.8 Spatial Smoothing

Spatial smoothing produces blurred data by calculating the weighted average over neighboring voxels with a Gaussian kernel [16]. The kernel's full width at half maximum (FWHM) is typically set to be twice the voxel size. Spatial smoothing has the advantage of reducing noise, but it can also reduce signal intensity. As a result, when using spatial smoothing, researchers must proceed with caution.

2.4.2   CT Scan Image Data

In this section, some pre-processing methods for the CT scan data are discussed.

2.4.2.1   Denoising

Patient movements, beam hardening, low resolution, scanner malfunction, intrinsic low-dose radiation, and metal implants are the most common sources of image disturbance [14]. The literature addresses each of these disturbances separately. In general, images can be denoised into two categories: frequency and spatial.

2.4.2.2   Interpolation

There is a preferred choice for equal physical spacing for the input images, as is usually the case for object detection and segmentation [14]. To avoid center-specific or reconstruction-dependent findings, it is preferable to keep the resolution constant. Images are typically interpolated in the XY plane and/or the z-direction based on the desired physical spacing or voxel number. Cubic-spline and B-spline are better-convolving functions for resampling images because they perform similarly to an ideal low-pass filter. An incorrect resampling step can harm subsequent registration and processing, such as lowering the resolution below the expected size of detectable objects.

2.4.2.3   Registration

Image registration entails a spatial transformation to align a floating image's area of interest with a reference image [14]. In radiology, medical image registration is assessed in two ways: (i) slice-level registration in an image due to patient movements during the scan and (ii) image-level registration to have comparably aligned images in a training dataset. Before denoising and interpolation, the first registration type may be required only in certain CT images produced by slow scanning. The latter type of image registration can help traditional machine learning tools learn space-variant features for classification or segmentation. Deep learning algorithms can be trained to learn features that are insensitive to affine transformations or even different perspectives and illuminations. However, registration may be useful to facilitate training in complex problems. Furthermore, there may be scenarios where registered images are required as input for deep neural networks. Poorly registered pairs of MR and CT scans in training, for example, harm the quality of synthetic CT generation.

2.4.2.4   Normalization

Linear transformation can be used to force two critical points (smallest and largest values) to be mapped to (0, 255) or (0, 65,535), respectively, to squeeze or stretch the CT data intensity values so that they effectively fit into the offered range of input images (8 or 16 bits) monotonically [14]. Typically, normalization can be performed at the institution or dataset level (utilizing the minimum and maximum pixel values among all the patients). Alternatively, for certain application areas, CT images can be normalized at the patient or slice level.

2.4.3   X-ray Image Data

In this section, some pre-processing techniques for the X-ray data are discussed.

2.4.3.1 Adaptive Contrast Enhancement

Adapted improvement-controlled contrast was created to address the issues of saturation artifacts, over-enhancement, and mean brightness of the data [17].

   a. Histogram equalization: Histogram equalization is a subset of the broader class of histogram remapping techniques. Because of its speed and effectiveness, histogram equalization is widely used to improve the contrast of X-ray images. The histogram is a gray-level function that indicates the gray level of each pixel. As a result, the gray nonlinear transform will enhance the contrast ratio by adjusting the accumulation function, and the gray in the small range will be transformed in the entire field.
   b. Adaptive histogram equalization: When compared to whole histogram equalization, AHE has the advantage of better local contrast. However, the AHE must compute the local histogram and accumulate the distribution function for each pixel, which is extremely computationally demanding. Furthermore, the AHE is sensitive to noise.
   c. Contrast-limited adaptive histogram equalization: The AHE increases image contrast while also increasing noise. In some cases, enhancement causes image distortion in a detail area, affecting how clinicians examine the enhanced image. We must increase image contrast while also limiting the magnified noise. Thus, limiting the contrast function to AHE in each block will result in the generation of a transform function. What percentage of the contrast will be restricted? Each image block requires preliminary adjustments. Then, to limit the gray-level probability density, the limit function can be defined and modify the exceeded histogram.

2.4.3.2 Region Localization

Region localization (RL) is the assessment of image boundaries that enclose objects of interest with a coarse level of precision [18]. RL is useful for assisting human experts in the rapid display and review of images (independent of its use in initializing a segmentation process). For instance, with an algorithm that can quickly and reliably identify the spine region with a marked line passing, this region of interest can be automatically zoomed on the display, even if the orientation and location of the spine vary significantly in these images. Provided a line passing through the image, this method assumes that a line passing through the most amount of organ structure in the image will lie over a large portion of the affected area.

2.4.4 Ultrasound Image Data

In this section, some pre-processing methods for the ultrasound data are discussed.

2.4.4.1 Deblurring

When no information about the distortion (blurring) is known, the blind deconvolution algorithm can be used effectively [19]. The algorithm restores both the image and the point spread function (PSF) at the same time. Each iteration employs the accelerated, damped Richardson-Lucy algorithm. Additional optical system (e.g., camera) characteristics can be used as input parameters to improve the quality of image restoration. PSF constraints can be passed in via a user-defined function.

2.4.4.2   Resolution Enhancement

By combining the low-resolution images, a high-resolution image is created [20]. Apodization is another technique used by ultrasound scanners to reduce side lobes and enhance resolution by using aperture weighing functions. Another method is compounding that can enhance resolution since combining images taken from different angles causes the PSF to become more isotropic and uniform across the image. Shadowing can be reduced in terms of artifacts because structures obscured by high reflectors appear when the ultrasound beam comes from a different direction. Compounding is classified into three types: frequency compounding, spatial compounding, and strain compounding. Frequency compounding is the process of combining images acquired at different frequencies. It can be used in transmit mode by employing multiple sources at various frequencies. There are various methods for spatial compounding. The ultrasound beam can be electronically steered to different angles, and the images captured from these different angles are then combined. The sample or transducer can be rotated to obtain images from multiple angles, which are then registered (aligned) before compounding. Images can also be obtained by moving the transducer laterally or by combining lateral and angular displacements. Using external forces that produce three-dimensional tissue motion, the strain compounding approach generates different strain states. When only lateral and axial movements are corrected, the acquired images have a different speckle appearance due to out-of-plane motion. The resolution of these images can be improved by combining them.

2.4.4.3   Denoising

In general, ultrasound images have a low signal-to-noise ratio. There are three main reasons for this. First, ultrasound scanners utilize pulsed signals, which have a short time duration and thus a broad frequency spectrum. As a consequence, various noise sources can influence the signals. Second, the signals' coherent nature causes speckle noise. Third, sound waves are extremely distorted when they travel via tissues. As a result, ultrasound images endure the noise. The noise adaptive fuzzy switching median filter is dependable for salt-and-pepper noise reduction [21]. This filtering component employs fluffy logic to manage vulnerability caused by noise in the extracted local information. A speckle reduction anisotropic reduction filter is utilized to reduce speckle noise. It acts as an edge detector in the affected speckled image, returning higher values for high-contrast regions and lower values for low-contrast regions. By protecting sharp edges, the median filter outperforms the mean filter. It essentially swaps every pixel value by the center of the force level in that pixel's area. The Wiener filter lowers the level of noise in a signal. The signal received is compared to a noiseless signal. It is a linear non-adaptive filter. It provides effective results in removing noise from ultrasound images. It is determined by statistical methodology.

2.4.5   Gene Expression Data

In this section, some pre-processing techniques for the gene expression [22] data are discussed.

2.4.5.1   Scale Transformations

Because ratios are asymmetrical, scale transformations such as log transformation can be applied to the dataset. The user has the option of selecting the preferred base for log-transforming the dataset.

2.4.5.2   Management of Missing Values

Patterns with an excessive number of unknown ratios can be deleted, and there are several options for imputing the remaining ones. For standard hierarchical clustering methods, where all calculations are focused on a distance matrix, an overabundance of missing values can be an issue. If two patterns have insufficient points in common, the distance between them is undefined, and clustering fails. Furthermore, other methods, such as principal component analysis, are incapable of dealing with missing values. Imputation for these values can avoid these issues, but it may still be necessary to eliminate some patterns beforehand if there is insufficient data.

2.4.5.3   Replicate Handling

Replicate handling consists of two steps: one for removing inconsistent replicates and another for merging the remaining ones.

2.4.6   Text Data

In this section, some pre-processing techniques for the text data [1] are discussed.

2.4.6.1   Data Cleaning

Data cleaning routines "clean" the data by completing missing values, smoothing noisy data, identifying and removing outliers, and resolving inconsistencies. Users are unlikely to trust the results of any data mining if they believe the data is contaminated. Furthermore, dirty data can confuse the mining procedure, resulting in untrustworthy output. Although most mining routines include methods for dealing with imperfect or noisy data, these procedures are not always robust. They may instead focus on avoiding overfitting the data to the function being modeled. As a result, running the data through some data cleaning routines is a useful preprocessing step.

2.4.6.2   Data Reduction

Data reduction produces a much smaller representation of the data set while producing the same (or nearly the same) analytical results. Dimensionality and numerosity reduction are two data reduction strategies.

Data encoding strategies are used in dimensionality reduction to acquire a reduced or "compressed" representation of the original data. Data compression methods (such as principal component analysis and wavelet transforms) and attribute subset selection (e.g., eliminating irrelevant attributes) are two examples (e.g., where a subset of more beneficial attributes is extracted from the original set). Data are replaced by alternative, smaller representations in numerical reduction using parametric models (such as log-linear or regression models) or non-parametric models (such as with data aggregation, histograms, sampling, clusters, etc.).

2.4.6.3   Normalization
The cancer data to be analyzed is normalized or scaled to a narrower range, such as [0.0, 1.0]. For example, the data may include the attribute's age and some test values. The test value is typically assigned much higher or lower values than age. As a result, if the attributes are left unnormalized, output (cancer detection) can be unreliable.

2.4.6.4   Discretization and Concept Hierarchy Generation
Discretization and concept hierarchy generation, in which raw data values for attributes are replaced by ranges or higher conceptual levels, can also be useful. For example, raw age values could be replaced with higher-level concepts like youth, adult, or senior. Discretization and concept hierarchy generation are powerful data mining tools because they enable data mining at multiple levels of abstraction.

2.5   CONCLUSIONS
Cancer data pre-processing is utilized to depict complex structures with features, discretize continuous features, binarize attributes, convert discrete features to continuous features, and deal with missing and unknown feature values. Various techniques can be useful in data pre-processing, which can be dependent on the data modality. Text documents, images, and graphs, for example, cannot be utilized directly as inputs for deep learning algorithms. They must be described using derived features like a bag of words (for text documents), various statistics (for graphs and images), or dimensionality reduction techniques like the principal component analysis. When using deep learning methods that cannot deal with continuous features, discretization of continuous features is required. Continuous feature cells are represented with non-overlapping sub-interval indices. Discretization algorithms must determine both the optimal number of sub-intervals and their boundaries. When using deep learning methods that can only deal with two-valued (binary) features, feature binarization is required. Using two-interval discretization, continuous features are binarized. Discrete features are binarized by creating a binary feature for each original feature value or by creating a binary feature for each possible split of feature values into two spatially separated subsets. Depending on the cancer data collection modality, different types of pre-processing techniques can be used. For MRI, the mostly used data pre-processing techniques are IIH correction, registration, segmentation, slice timing correction, motion correction, nuisance variable removal, filtering, and spatial smoothing. Denoising, interpolation, registration, and normalization are mainly used as the CT scan data pre-processing techniques. For X-ray data, histogram equalization, adaptive histogram equalization, contrast-limited adaptive histogram

equalization, and RL are widely used pre-processing techniques. Deblurring, resolution enhancement, and denoising are some pre-processing techniques used for ultrasound data. For gene expression data, scale transformations, management of missing values, and replicate handling are widely used pre-processing techniques. Data cleaning, data reduction, normalization, discretization, and concept hierarchy generation are used as the text pre-processing techniques. Many other pre-processing techniques are used to process other types of cancer data. In the future, all those techniques will be studied.

REFERENCES

1. Data preprocessing (http://hanj.cs.illinois.edu/cs412/bk3/03.pdf).
2. Data pre-processing (https://monkeylearn.com/blog/data-preprocessing/).
3. Chaki, J. (2022). Two-fold brain tumor segmentation using fuzzy image enhancement and DeepBrainet2. 0. *Multimedia Tools and Applications, 81,* 1–27.
4. Chaki, J. (2022). Brain MRI segmentation using deep learning: background study and challenges. In *Brain Tumor MRI Image Segmentation Using Deep Learning Techniques* (pp. 1–12). MA: Academic Press.
5. Chaki, J. (Ed.). (2021). *Brain Tumor MRI Image Segmentation Using Deep Learning Techniques.* MA: Elsevier.
6. Pre-processing techniques (https://www.coursera.org/lecture/functional-mri/module-13-pre-processing-of-fmri-data-CRpFc).
7. Cervical cancer (https://www.cancer.org).
8. Cancer data and their modalities (https://my.clevelandclinic.org/).
9. Breast cancer (https://www.cdc.gov).
10. Mayo clinic (https://www.mayoclinic.org/).
11. Sager, R. (1997). Expression genetics in cancer: shifting the focus from DNA to RNA. *Proceedings of the National Academy of Sciences, 94*(3), 952–955.
12. Spasić, I., Livsey, J., Keane, J. A., & Nenadić, G. (2014). Text mining of cancer-related information: review of current status and future directions. *International Journal of Medical Informatics, 83*(9), 605–623.
13. Hou, Z. (2006). A review on MR image intensity inhomogeneity correction. *International Journal of Biomedical Imaging, 2006,* 1–11.
14. Masoudi, S., et al. (2021). Quick guide on radiology image pre-processing for deep learning applications in prostate cancer research. *Journal of Medical Imaging, 8*(1), 010901.
15. Vadmal, V., Junno, G., Badve, C., Huang, W., Waite, K. A., & Barnholtz-Sloan, J. S. (2020). MRI image analysis methods and applications: an algorithmic perspective using brain tumors as an exemplar. *Neuro-Oncology Advances, 2*(1), vdaa049.
16. Park, B. Y., Byeon, K., & Park, H. (2019). FuNP (fusion of neuroimaging preprocessing) pipelines: a fully automated preprocessing software for functional magnetic resonance imaging. *Frontiers in Neuroinformatics, 13,* 5.
17. Wu, S., Zhu, Q., Yu, S., Li, Q., & Xie, Y. (2013). Multiscale X-ray image contrast enhancement based on limited adaptive histogram equalization. In *Proceedings of the Fifth International Conference on Internet Multimedia Computing and Service* (pp. 231–236), China.
18. Koonsanit, K., Thongvigitmanee, S., Pongnapang, N., & Thajchayapong, P. (2017). Image enhancement on digital x-ray images using n-clahe. In *2017 10th Biomedical Engineering International Conference (BMEICON)* (pp. 1–4). IEEE, Japan.

19. Abdallah, Y. M. Y., Algaddal, A. S., & Alkhir, M. A. (2015). Enrichment of ultrasound images using contrast enhancement techniques. *International Journal of Science and Research (IJSR)*, *4*(1), 2381–2385.
20. Ortiz, S. H. C., Chiu, T., & Fox, M. D. (2012). Ultrasound image enhancement: a review. *Biomedical Signal Processing and Control*, *7*(5), 419–428.
21. Sawant, A., & Kulkarni, S. (2022). Ultrasound image enhancement using super resolution. *Biomedical Engineering Advances*, *3*, 100039.
22. Herrero, J., Díaz-Uriarte, R., & Dopazo, J. (2003). Gene expression data preprocessing. *Bioinformatics*, *19*(5), 655–656.

3 A Survey on Deep Learning Techniques for Breast, Leukemia, and Cervical Cancer Prediction

N Jothiaruna and Anny Leema A
Vellore Institute of Technology

CONTENTS

3.1 INTRODUCTION

Cancer is the second most dangerous disease in the world disrupting the procedures of blood cell formation. We find three major proportions of blood cells, mainly (i) RBC (red blood cell), (ii) WBC (white blood cell), and (iii) platelets. RBCs carry oxygen to various parts of the body, WBCs fight against bacteria, and platelets take care of bleeding issues. Most middle-aged women are affected by breast cancer, and more than 7 million women are affected by cancer around the world [1]. If we identify cancer in an early stage, it is curable. Leukemia is a type of cancer that mainly affects kids and adults. It is taking place in bone marrow and starts producing abnormal WBC. Some of the patients are affected due to genes and environment, and in some cases, it is difficult to predict exactly what causes leukemia. Cervical cancer affects the lower part of the uterus, and most women worldwide are suffering from this type of cancer. PAP (Papanicolaou) smear screening and HPV vaccine are the

DOI: 10.1201/9781003277002-3

preventive measures used at an earlier stage. At the time of cervical cancer, abdominal pain and filthy-smelling white discharge indication will be there.

This type of disease is caused mainly by sexually transmitted infection, many sexual partners, earlier-age sexual, smoking, etc [2]. Early detection and providing treatment at the appropriate time mitigate its severity and reduce human loss. The overall knowledge of leukemia [3] and cervical cancer [4] was low among the people. The image processing technique is used to process the image and extract the feature in an image shown in Figure 3.1; Deep Learning (DL) technology gives robust performance results [5]. The role of DL is very important in the early detection of cancerous cells, and it is being widely implemented. Hence, in this paper, survey was done on various DL and image processing techniques used for the prediction and diagnosis of cancer at an earlier stage.

3.1.1 BREAST CANCER

Prediction of breast cancer in old days is very difficult but today with the techniques and algorithms of DL, the results are predicted very correctly using various techniques. After the advancements in the technology of AI, our objective is to develop a breast cancer prediction model using various DL techniques. These models can predict any deviations in the normal pattern. The Machine Learning (ML) model was built using various techniques like K nearest neighbor (KNN), naive Bayes, decision tree, support vector machine (SVM), and Random Forest. The performance

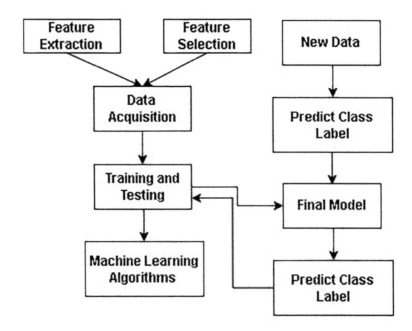

FIGURE 3.1 Architecture diagram for leukemia, cervical, and breast cancer prediction applying ML techniques.

is analyzed using various measures like accuracy, precision, and recall. Some of the factors associated with breast cancer are age, family history, vitamin D deficiency, overweight, smoking and drinking habit, daily food style, etc [6].

3.1.2 LEUKEMIA [7]

Leukemia is a type of blood cancer mainly affecting the bone marrow, altering the production of WBCs. WBC fights against bacteria aiding in the production of healthy cells. Each cell has its Hayflick limit, which in the case of leukaemia would lose its control on producing a number of immature blood cells. Two stages of cancers are (i) acute and (ii) chronic. Acute is a fast-growing disease and is difficult to cure. Chronic is a slow-growing disease and can be cured. This type mainly affects children and adults due to abnormalities in genes and some other idiopathic reasons. Figure 3.2 describes the classification types like acute myeloid leukemia (AML), acute lympho-cytic leukemia (ALL), chronic myeloid leukemia (CML), and chronic lymphocytic leukemia (CLL). In leukemia, it will produce too much immature WBC, which is the main factor. Morphological change is the main factor when normal cell changes to a cancerous cell, and another fraction of a number of unhealthy cell count will be high. Figure 3.3 shows the cancerous cell and its morphological changes.

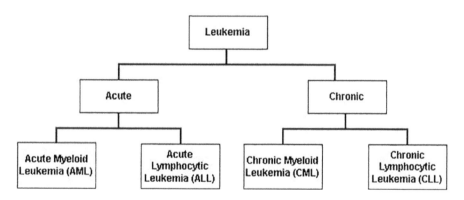

FIGURE 3.2   Classification of leukemia types.

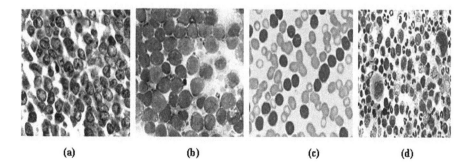

FIGURE 3.3   (a) ALL (b) AML (c) CLL (d) CML.

3.1.3 CERVICAL CANCER

Cervical is a type of cancer from the cervix [8]. Uncontrollable production of cells is the main factor for cancer. In the cervix, two types of cells will be present: endocervix and exocervix. Endocervix is the primary type of the cervix, which connects to the uterus and is enclosed by the cell. Exocervix presents outside the uterus and is enclosed with squamous cells. Two types of cervical cancer are (i) squamous cell carcinoma and (ii) adenocarcinoma. For differentiating each cancer cell, microscope is used. Figure 3.4 shows the squamous cell carcinoma and adenocarcinoma. Here, squamous cell carcinoma is mostly affected by 90% of women suffering from this cancer [1]. It develops outside of the uterus (exocervix cell). Adenocarcinoma develops in the endocervix cells; it is very rare. A mix of both cancer types develop in both endocervix and exocervix cells.

3.2 LITERATURE SURVEY

3.2.1 DEEP LEARNING METHODS FOR LEUKEMIA PREDICTION

The decision tree technique was introduced for finding the non-immature leukemia cells by flow cytometry data. To eliminate the overfitting node, lasso algorithm is carried out. This algorithm is mainly used for reducing the weight features [9]. Microarray data is a challenging factor because of less number of sample size and more features. A hybrid method is proposed using the stacked auto encoder (AE) technique, SVM, and then convolution neural network (CNN) is used for classification of cancer cell [10]. For leukemia and prostate cancer, a new method called the support vector sampling technique (SVST) was proposed to identify specific genes and sensitivity. Also, if more numbers of the genes are selected, it gives better performance results in both leukemia and prostate cancer [11]. To classify leukemia cells, algorithms and SVM are used. To reduce the size of the dataset, the SVM-RFE technique is used, which removes the unrelated gene. Then for differentiating the correlated gene, fast correlation-based filter (FCBF) is used [12]. Table 3.1 describes the research carried out by different authors and the accuracy obtained by implementing various methods.

Algorithms like naive Bayes [13], SVM [15], KNN, and decision tree are used for finding all types of leukaemia cancer [14,16]. To measure the effectiveness of the model for these approaches, fivefold cross-validation was used [17]. A prediction algorithm is used to diagnose acute leukemia and allogeneic hematopoietic stem cell transplantation (also HSCT) is used. ADTree algorithm is an alternate prediction algorithm that is proposed to give the virtuous prediction result [18]. Detection of known diseases and unknown disease processes is carried out here. To classify the candidate gene, new method called OCSVM (one-class classification support vector machine) is proposed to diagnose AML cancer [19]. Statistical feature artificial neural network (ANN) is used for partitioning the blast cell and for a microscopic image. Initially, the region of interest (ROI) is used for segmenting the negative (non-ROI) and non-negative (ROI). ANN is mainly used for identifying the positive and negative cells in the microscopic image. In the statistical features, a genetic algorithm is used to segment the WBC in an image [20].

TABLE 3.1
Survey about Leukemia

Author	Type	Methodology Used	Drawbacks	Accuracy
Rehman, Abbas, et.al.	Acute lymphoblastic leukemia	A bone marrow image is taken as input, which is segmented for accurate extraction of features. Classification is performed using convolution neural network.	Segmentation of overlapping cells could be done to improve the accurate prediction of the disease.	97.78%
Pradeep Kumar Das, Sukadev Meher	Acute lymphoblastic leukemia	The hybrid transfer learning method is applied to classify ALL using MobileNet-V2 and ResNet-18 by splitting the dataset in two ways: training 70% and testing 30%, and training 50% and testing 50%.	Splitting the data as training 50% and testing 50% provides improper detection of cells.	97. 18%
Nizar Ahmed, Altug Yigit, Zerrin Isik, et.al.	Acute lymphoblastic leukemia	Microscopic blood images are taken; image augmentation and image transformation are performed with several techniques and applied to the convolution neural network algorithm.	Preprocessing should be done to remove blood stains in an image to accurate detection of diseases.	81%
Sarmad Shafique, MS and Samabia Tehsin	Acute lymphoblastic leukemia	AlexNet pre-trained model is used to classify the diseases; to improve prediction accurately, different augmentation techniques are used.	Deep learning models can be used to get better results by adding a dataset.	96.06%
Moraes, L. O., Pedreira	Chronic lymphoid leukemias	Bone marrow samples are taken from mature lymphoid leukemia patients; a decision tree is applied; to avoid overfitting, Lasso technique is used.	Advanced techniques can be used.	95%

MFC (multicolor flow cytometry) technique is used to identify the MRD (minimal residual diseases) such as AML and MDS (myelodysplastic syndrome) [21]. The image processing technique is used to identify blast cells in a microscopic image. K-means clustering and panel selection are used for segmenting the cells; then, different morphologically identifying process is carried out both in public and in private data. Classification is done using neural network and decision tree method [22]. Classification is done using MLP (multilayer perceptron) and SFAM (simplified fuzzy ARTMAP) to segment the WBC in ALL and AML. For the training process, Levenberg-Marquardt (LM) and Bayesian regulation (BR) algorithms are used. BR gives a good result by comparing it with LM [23].

To distinguish the types of WBCs, a segmentation technique is used. HSI color space is used to segment the region of WBC by 3D ellipsoid. For backpropagation, MLP technique works well [24]. To differentiate ALL and AML in gene expression data, ANN is used. It is mainly used for classification purposes. This process is validated by tenfold cross-validation and leave-one approach [25]. To predict AML, M3-type simulated handling and neural network technique is used. A good heuristic algorithm is simulated handling. Here, the OTSU method is used to detect the coordinates for removing unwanted pixels in it, and the clustering method is performed [26].

3.2.2 MACHINE LEARNING METHODS FOR CERVICAL CANCER PREDICTION

Deep CNN is used for classifying cervical cancer in the cytological image [27]. Increasing the training sample size is done by flipping (horizontally and vertically), resizing, and rotating (90, 180 degrees) the image. Preprocessing is done by applying a Gaussian high-pass filter and edge sharpener [18]. Survey has been taken on Hmong and Mien hill women's around 450 members through a pap test (Papanicolaou test) and they found that every person has less than or greater than four partners [28]. Using Fourier transform, normal and abnormal cervical cells can be automatically detected by a pap 2D image. In the frequency spectrum, they have divided cells into subsections by using the center of the radius and found the mean value for each subsection. For classification, they used KNN, SVM, Random Forest, and adaptive boosting (Ada Boost). By comparing other algorithms, SVM gives higher classification results [29]. Table 3.2 indicates different authors' research done using ML and DL concepts.

For the detection of cervical cells by segmenting the cervical image into several pieces, they used the SVM technique in CNN. It showed higher accuracy than another algorithm. But instead of segmenting the image into several pieces, they would have examined the image by pixels, which could be given a higher accuracy rate [30]. To segment an overlapping cell in a cytoplasm and nuclei, a multistep-level set (LVS) technique is used. Region-based and edge-based Gaussian filter methods are used at an initial stage, and the LVS technique is applied after the initial step.

Here, clump segmentation gives a good result compared to nuclei segmentation. In nuclei segmentation, it gives a good outcome but it gives more failure also [31]. Edge cutting and ensemble learning techniques are used to identify and classify cervical cancer. Using Pap smear screening and liquid-based cytology, they identified the cell within the cervical cell and classified those cells. Finally, clustering is done for both normal and abnormal cells. By improving the cell extraction and segmentation, the accuracy is higher [32]. The classification and segmentation methods are used for identifying cervical cells; for testing purposes, Harley Pap smear dataset is used. Initially, the R-CNN segmentation technique is used to separate the regions and then finally classify the segmented cell regions. The performance

TABLE 3.2
Survey on Cervical Cancer

Author	Methodology Used	Drawbacks	Accuracy
Wu Miao., Chuanbo Yan	Deep convolution neural network is used to classify the cancerous cell. By applying the augmentation technique, the accuracy level improved by 3.85%.	Pathologist is insufficient.	93.33%
Allehaibi, K. H. S., Nugroho	Mask R-CNN segmentation method is applied to the whole cell; deep R-CNN is used as classifier. In this model, there is no need for preprocessing because of Mask R-CNN.	The model consumes more time when compared to other models.	98.1%
Jiayi Lu, Enmin Song, et.al.	To improve the performance of the prediction, data correction is used, and to enhance the robustness, gene assist module is used. The ensemble method is used to classify the diseases.	The model should concentrate more on distinctive data.	83.16%
Wen Wu, Hao Zhou	Malignant cancer is diagnosed using support vector machine (SVM)-based approaches. Compared with another method, SVM-PCA (principle component analysis) gives better results.	Computational cost is high.	92.46%
Chankong, T	A pap smear image is used to classify cervical cancer using Fourier spectral features. Here, the frequency spectrum is separated into the radial direction and angle direction, and performance is evaluated using SVM.	Performance can be improved using a set of spectral features.	94.38%

measure for segmentation used precision, recall, and ZSI, and for classification F1 score, accuracy, sensitivity, specificity, and h-mean [33]. C-MLP (cascaded multi-layered perceptron) and ELM (extreme learning machine) are the two techniques proposed for classifying the cervical cell. For input, cell features were used output LSIL (low-squamous intraepithelial lesion) or HSIL (high-squamous intraepithelial lesion). C-MLP gives better accuracy in performance than the ELM technique [34]. A new ensemble technique is used to identify the risk of cervical cancer by using some algorithms like SVM, KNN, decision tree, and logistic regression. They have concluded that by comparing other methods, DL gives better results [35].

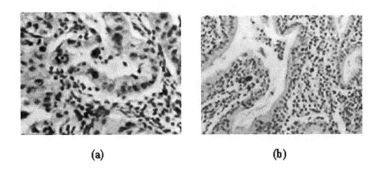

(a)   **(b)**

FIGURE 3.4   (a) Squamous cell carcinoma (b) Adenocarcinoma.

An SVM is used for classifying malignant tumors and benign tumors. Also, SVM-based approaches like support vector machine-recursive feature elimination (SVM-RFE) and support vector machine-principal component analysis (SVM-PCA) are used to classify the tumor because they give better result than others [36]. Using CNN prediction, the classification of cancerous cells is proposed. To classify the image, ELM technique is used, and other techniques like MLP and AE are also used to classify the abnormal cell [37]. Using the Bayesian algorithm, detection of tumor cells and automatic segmentation are processed. Segmentation is done mainly by the extraction of the boundary region in a magnetic response (MR) based on non-rigid conversion, and it avoids issues like tumor deterioration and influences on nearby muscles [38]. A Pap smear image processing dataset is taken, and by using a shape-based technique, only nuclei are segmented in a Pap smear image. After segmenting, using the watershed approach, overlapping cytoplasm was taken separately [39]. For the feature selection process, a random forest algorithm is used [30].

3.2.3   Deep Learning Methods for Breast Cancer Prediction

Three different datasets are collected, and detailed differences are found between the three datasets by feature selection algorithms. Limiting the threshold improves the correlation value, and the different types of classifiers are employed. Each attribute has its own behavior, and it plays an important role in the prediction. In this project, Random Forest gives the best classification results compared to others. The correlation factor helps to achieve a better accuracy compared to other feature selection methods, which have low correlation values [40].

SEER (Surveillance, Epidemiology, and End Results) dataset contains all cancer details for the past 30 years. The data for processing was prepared and the non-cancer data in the dataset was rejected; then, the attribute selection process has been carried out by the chi-squared selection process [41]. Extensible Breast Cancer Prognosis Framework includes risk assessment, survivability, and recurrence. It improves the performance of SVM classifiers with representative feature subset selection. With feature selection and the AdaBoost algorithm, accuracy of the classifier is enhanced. The results also include cross-validation to evaluate the performance [42].

The Wisconsin dataset, which has 11 features and 699 instances, is taken to predict the breast cancer results. The evaluation parameters are accuracy, sensitivity, specificity, and tenfold cross-validation. SVM, C4.5, and K-NN are the comparative models to find the accuracy of the prediction [43]. Muhammad Shahbaz predicted breast cancer by collecting samples of bone marrow from acute leukemia patients. Each sample is trained, and it contains more number of human gene expressions spotted on a DNA microarray; they identify the address of each gene location and measure the intensity of the spot from that they perform the classifiers and predict the results. They can improve the prediction by reducing the number of attributes listed in the dataset. It can also be done by principal component analysis [44].

The WCRS from Wisconsin dataset has 9 features and 699 instances used to predict the breast cancer results. ANN is the comparative model used to find the accuracy of the prediction [45]. M.F. Akay obtained the Wisconsin dataset, which has 9 features and 683 instances considered to predict the breast cancer results. SVM combined with feature selection is the comparative model to find the accuracy of the prediction [46]. The Wisconsin dataset has 9 features and 683 instances which are taken to predict the breast cancer results. The evaluation parameters are tenfold cross-validation. Logistic regression, decision trees, Bayes net, Random Forest, ANN, RBFN, and Rotation Forest are the comparative models used to find the accuracy of the prediction [47].

The name of the dataset is Breast Cancer Wisconsin (Diagnostic) Dataset. The dataset has 569 instances, a multivariate dataset, which is applicable for classification. It has 32 attributes, including radius, smoothness, concavity, texture, etc. The output labels are malignant and benign. The datasets are going to be trained and tested. If the data are better trained, the result will be in a more accurate manner. Generally, the results are dependent on how the data are trained. If the data is not trained well, the accuracy level will decrease. We have applied the various supervised ML classification techniques like Random Forest, Naïve Bayes, decision tree, SVM, and KNN to find the performance of each classifier to predict the cancerous cell. The performance of these techniques is analyzed using the metrics precision, recall, accuracy score, and confusion matrix. The architecture diagram of the proposed system is shown in Figure 2.1. The dataset is imported from the sklearn website package. The dataset is split into training and test datasets with proper proportions.

3.3   CONCLUSION

This chapter describes the cancerous cell in leukemia, breast, and cervical cancer. Many techniques like ML, DL, and CNN are used to diagnose and classify cancer cells. The main issue in cancer is generating infinite abnormal cells. Using cell count, we can predict the stage of cancer. WBCs will fight infection and will generate healthy cells but in leukemia cancer, it won't fight infection; instead, it will produce multiple unhealthy cells. If cell count is increasing more and more, then it leads to a dangerous situation for a person's health. Cervical cancer produces multiple abnormal cells, and the cell won't fight with infection. Many kids are suffered from leukemia cancer, so for its prevention, earlier detection is good. Predicting cancer at an earlier stage is better to cure it easily. Deep learning techniques perform better when detecting cancerous cells. In the future, the research gap identified is to solve the overlapping issues to predict accurately.

REFERENCES

1. Travis, R. C., Reeves, G. K., Green, J., Bull, D., Tipper, S. J., Baker, K., & Million Women Study Collaborators. Gene–environment interactions in 7610 women with breast cancer: prospective evidence from the Million Women Study. *The Lancet*, 375(9732), 2143–2151 (**2010**).
2. Bleyer, A. Young adult oncology: the patients and their survival challenges. *CA: A Cancer Journal for Clinicians*, 57(4), 242–255 (**2007**).
3. Rehman, A., Abbas, N., Saba, T., Rahman, S. I. U., Mehmood, Z., & Kolivand, H. Classification of acute lymphoblastic leukemia using deep learning. *Microscopy Research and Technique*, 81(11), 1310–1317 (**2018**).
4. Ali, C. I., Makata, N. E., & Ezenduka, P. O. (2016). Cervical cancer: a health limiting condition. Gynecol Obstet (Sunnyvale), 6(378), 2161–0932 (**2016**).
5. Anwar, S. M., Majid, M., Qayyum, A., Awais, M., Alnowami, M., & Khan, M. K. Medical image analysis using convolutional neural networks: a review. *Journal of medical systems*, 42(11), 1–13 (**2018**).
6. Do, M. H., Lee, S. S., Jung, P. J., & Lee, M. H. Intake of fruits, vegetables, and soy foods in relation to breast cancer risk in Korean women: a case-control study. *Nutrition and Cancer*, 57(1), 20–27 (**2007**).
7. Nazari, E., Farzin, A. H., Aghemiri, M., Avan, A., Tara, M., & Tabesh, H. Deep learning for acute myeloid leukemia diagnosis. *Journal of Medicine and Life*, 13(3), 382 (**2020**).
8. Fernandes, K., Chicco, D., Cardoso, J. S., & Fernandes, J. Supervised deep learning embeddings for the prediction of cervical cancer diagnosis. *PeerJ Computer Science*, 4, e154 (**2018**).
9. Moraes, L. O., Pedreira, C. E., Barrena, S., Lopez, A., & Orfao, A. A decision-tree approach for the differential diagnosis of chronic lymphoid leulleukemias peripheral B-cell lymphomas. *Computer Methods and Programs in Biomedicine*, 178, 85–90 (**2019**).
10. Kiliçarslan, S., Adem, K., & Çelik, M. Diagnosis and classification of cancer using hybrid model based on relief and convolutional neural network. *Medical Hypotheses*, 137, 109577 (**2020**).
11. Chen, A. H., & Lin, C. H. A novel support vector sampling technique to improve classification accuracy and to identify key genes of leukemia and prostate cancers. *Expert Systems with Applications*, 38(4), 3209–3219 (**2011**).
12. Kavitha, K. R., Gopinath, A., & Gopi, M. Applying improved SVM classifier for leukemia cancer classification using FCBF. In *2017 International Conference on Advances in Computing, Communications and Informatics ICACCI*, pp. 61–66. IEEE, Udupi, India (**2017**).
13. Rehman, A., Abbas, N., Saba, T., Rahman, S. I. U., Mehmood, Z., & Kolivand, H. Classification of acute lymphoblastic leukemia using deep learning. *Microscopy Research and Technique*, 81(11), 1310–1317 (**2018**).
14. Das, P. K., & Meher, S. An efficient deep convolutional neural network based detection and classification of acute lymphoblastic leukemia. *Expert Systems with Applications*, 183, 115311 (**2021**).
15. Ahmed, N., Yigit, A., Isik, Z., & Alpkocak, A. Identification of leukemia subtypes from microscopic images using convolutional neural network. *Diagnostics*, 9(3), 104 (**2019**).

16. Shafique, S., & Tehsin, S. Acute lymphoblastic leukemia detection and classification of its subtypes using pretrained deep convolutional neural networks. *Technology in Cancer Research & Treatment*, 17 (**2018**), doi: 10.1177/1533033818802789.
17. Li, P., Wang, X., Liu, P., Xu, T., Sun, P., Dong, B., & Xue, H. Cervical lesion classification method based on cross-validation decision fusion method of vision transformer and densenet. *Journal of Healthcare Engineering*, 3241422 (**2022**).
18. Fuse, K., Uemura, S., Tamura, S., Suwabe, T., Katagiri, T., Tanaka, T., & Kuroha, T. Patient-based prediction algorithm of relapse after all-HSCT for acute Leukemia and its usefulness in the decision-making process using a machine learning approach. *Cancer Medicine*, 8(11), 5058–5067 (**2019**).
19. Vasighizaker, A., Sharma, A., & Dehzangi, A. A novel one-class classification approach to accurately predict disease-gene association in acute myeloid leukemia cancer. *PloS one*, 14(12), e0226115, (**2019**).
20. Al-jaboriy, S. S., Sjarif, N. N. A., Chuprat, S., & Abduallah, W. M. Acute lymphoblastic leukemia segmentation using local pixel information. *Pattern Recognition Letters*, 125, 85–90 (**2019**).
21. Ko, B. S., Wang, Y. F., Li, J. L., Li, C. C., Weng, P. F., Hsu, S. C., ... Liu, J. H. Clinically validated machine learning algorithm for detecting residual diseases with multicolor flow cytometry analysis in acute myeloid leukemia and myelodysplastic syndrome. *EBioMedicine*, 37, 91–100 (**2018**).
22. Negm, A. S., Hassan, O. A., & Kandil, A. H. A decision support system for Acute Leukaemia classification based on digital microscopic images. *Alexandria Engineering Journal*, 57(4), 2319–2332 (**2018**).
23. Nasir, A. A., Mashor, M. Y., & Hassan, R. Classification of acute leukemia cells using multilayer perceptron and simplified fuzzy ARTMAP neural networks. *The International Arab Journal of Information Technology*, 10(4), 1–9, (**2013**).
24. Su, M. C, Cheng, C.Y., Wang, P. C. A neural-network-based approach to white blood cell classification. *The Scientific World Journal*, 2014, 796371–796371 (**2014**).
25. Dwivedi, A. K. Artificial neural network model for effective cancer classification using microarray gene expression data. *Neural Computing and Applications*, 29(12), 1545–1554 (**2018**).
26. Adjouadi M, Ayala M, Cabrerizo M, Zong N, Lizarraga G, & Rossman M. Classification of leukemia blood samples using neural networks. *Annals of Biomedical Engineering*, 38(4), 1473–1482 (**2010**).
27. Wu, M., Yan, C., Liu, H., Liu, Q., & Yin, Y. Automatic classification of cervical cancer from cytological images by using convolutional neural network. *Bioscience Reports*, 38(6), BSR20181769, (**2018**).
28. Kuntasorn, S., Anuwatnonthakate, A., & Apidechkul, T. Prevalence and factors associated with abnormal cervical cell among the Hmong and Mien hill tribe women in Pha Yao province, Thailand. *Siriraj Medical Journal*, 71(3), 220–227 (**2019**).
29. Chankong, T. Automatic classifying of cervical cells using Fourier spectral features. In *2018 4th International Conference on Green Technology and Sustainable Development (GTSD)*, pp. 759–762, IEEE, Ho Chi Minh City, Vietnam (**2018**).
30. Allehaibi, K. H. S., Nugroho, L. E., Lazuardi, L., Prabuwono, A. S., & Mantoro, T. Segmentation and classification of cervical cells using deep learning. *IEEE Access*, 7, 116925–116941 (**2019**).
31. Yusoff, I. A., Isa, N. A. M., Othman, N. H., Sulaiman, S. N., & Jusman, Y. Performance of neural network architectures: cascaded MLP versus extreme learning machine on cervical cell image classification. In *10th International Conference on Information Science, Signal Processing and their Applications (ISSPA)*, pp. 308–311. IEEE, Kuala Lumpur, Malaysia (**2010**).

32. Lu, J., Song, E., Ghoneim, A., & Alrashoud, M. Machine learning for assisting cervical cancer diagnosis: an ensemble approach. *Future Generation Computer Systems,* 106, 199–205 (**2020**).

33. Wu, W., & Zhou, H. Data-driven diagnosis of cervical cancer with support vector machine-based approaches. *IEEE Access,* 5, 25189–25195 (**2017**).

34. Ghoneim, A., Muhammad, G., & Hossain, M. S. Cervical cancer classification using convolutional neural networks and extreme learning machines. *Future Generation Computer Systems,* 102, 643–649 (**2020**).

35. Lu, C., Chelikani, S., Jaffray, D. A., Milosevic, M. F., Staib, L. H., & Duncan, J. S. Simultaneous nonrigid registration, segmentation, and tumor detection in MRI guided cervical cancer radiation therapy. *IEEE Transactions on Medical Imaging,* 31(6), 1213–1227 (**2012**).

36. Win, K. P., Kitjaidure, Y., Hamamoto, K., & Myo Aung, T. Computer-assisted screening for cervical cancer using digital image processing of pap smear images. *Applied Sciences,* 10(5), 1800 (**2020**).

37. Basha, S. M., Rajput, D. S., & Iyengar, N. Ch. A novel approach to perform analysis and prediction on breast cancer dataset using R. *International Journal of Grid Distributed Computing,* 11(2), 41–54, (**2018**).

38. Angarita, F. A., Chesney, T., Elser, C., Mulligan, A. M., McCready, D. R., & Escallon, J.Treatment patterns of elderly breast cancer patients at two Canadian cancer centres. *European Journal of Surgical Oncology,* 41(5), 625–634, (2015).

39. Huang, Y. L., Wang, K. L., & Chen, D. R. Diagnosis of breast tumors with ultrasonic texture analysis using support vector machines. *Neural Computing & Applications,* 15(2), 164–169 (**2006**).

40. Samulski, M., Karssemeijer, N., Lucas, P., & Groot, P. Classification of mammographic masses using support vector machines and Bayesian networks. In *Medical Imaging (2007): Computer-Aided Diagnosis* International Society for Optics and Photonics, Vol. 6514, p. 65141J, San Diego, CA, United States 2007.

41. Shabhaz, M., Faruq, S., Shaheen, M., & Masood, S. A. Cancer diagnosis using data mining technology. *Life Science Journal,* 9(1), 308–313 (**2012**) (ISSN: 1097-8135).

42. Adeena, K. D., & Remya, R. Extraction of relevant dataset for support vector machine training: a comparison. In *2015 International Conference on Advances in Computing, Communications and Informatics (ICACCI)*, pp. 222–227. IEEE, Kochi, India (**2015**).

43. Prathibhamol, C. P., & Ashok, A. Solving multi label problems with clustering and nearest neighbor by consideration of labels. In *Advances in Signal Processing and Intelligent Recognition Systems*, Thampi, S., Bandyopadhyay, S., Krishnan, S., Li, KC., Mosin, S., Ma, M (eds.), pp. 511–520. Springer, Cham (**2016**).

44. Amrane, M., Oukid, S., Gagaoua, I., & Ensari̇, T. Breast cancer classification using machine learning. In *2018 Electric Electronics, Computer Science, Biomedical Engineerings' Meeting (EBBT)*, pp. 1–4, Istanbul, Turkey (**2018**).

4 An Optimized Deep Learning Technique for Detecting Lung Cancer from CT Images

M. Vanitha, R. Mangayarkarasi,
M. Angulakshmi, and M. Deepa
Vellore Institute of Technology

CONTENTS

4.1   INTRODUCTION

Lung cancer is the most common cancer in many countries. The main cause of lung cancer is smoking. In earlier days, lung cancer is diagnosed through histologic techniques. In the literature, many researchers made an attempt to detect lung cancer using machine learning techniques where they depend on feature engineering heavily. Due to the invention introduced in hardware and software, the availability of high-end computing devices with Artificial Intelligence techniques greatly facilitates the physician in predicting disease impact precisely. In the literature, many researchers presented various practices to detect lung cancer through CT scan images.

One of the biggest revolutions in computer vision is convolutional neural networks (CNNs) presented in ImageNet challenge in the year 2012. Lung cancer detection and classification problem find whether the cancerous nodules are in the image or not. Image repositories like the Lung Image Database Consortium image collection

DOI: 10.1201/9781003277002-4

(LIDC-IDRI) and Clinical Proteomic Tumour Analysis Consortium Lung Squamous Cell Carcinoma (CPTAC-LSCC) greatly influence the prediction through software.

Image segmentation techniques are found to be the most promising in classifying the lung nodules. Such methods are a kind of hit-and-trial approach that purely relies on a specific single image. Thus, alleviating the drawbacks of such methods, CNNs have been used to extract the features followed by classification. Such architecture yields result with high accuracy in most computer vision tasks. Another type of neural network architecture is deep learning, which has been used for the candidate lung cancer classification task. Deep learning models produce better results than the conventional methods. The proposed work is not only meant for classifying lung cancer, but also could be used to detect and classify other biomedical images.

The motivation by the classification performance of CNN helped to propose a method for the classification of lung cancer from CT images. The basic problem statement deals with the classification and recognition of pulmonary nodules from the input lung CT images. The recognition phase deals with whether the pulmonary nodules located in an image are a nodule or not a nodule.

CNNs are preferred to simulate the proposed work to classify lung cancer. An architecture using a selective searching approach has been used in this work for the recognition of lung nodules, which is more efficient than the normal window searching approach. Classification problems find some hindrances due to the availability of minimal data and overfitting of the training datasets. This kind of problem may lead to biased decision in the classification of lung cancer. Such action has been controlled by the technique called data augmentation (making very small transformations like rotating the image by a small angle to create new images), cropping the image, attention modeling, etc. Thus, it brings sufficient data for the classification task. Hence, the proposed method applied data augmentation such as translation, reflection, and intensity alteration, which are performed to overcome overfitting.

The contribution of the proposed work is to classify lung cancer using the CNN with an effective selective search approach, which increases the accuracy of the method. Dataset with synthetically modified data using data augmentation helps to increase the relevant data in the datasets to get better performance of convolution neural network. The proposed method with convolution neural network and data augmentation decreases the overfitting problem and increases the effectiveness of the system to classify lung cancer from CT images.

This chapter is organized as follows: Literature survey is specified in Chapter 2. The CNN is explained in Chapter 3. The proposed CNN architecture is specified in Chapter 4. The explanation of experimental analysis is specified in Chapter 5. Finally, conclusion and proposed work are specified in Chapter 6.

4.2 LITERATURE REVIEW

Jiang et al. [1] suggested a different approach for pre-processing the CT images of the lung before fed into CNN-based classification model. Results are better. In 2D images, objects can overlap, so this may lead to have a high number of false positives. Xiaojie Huang et al. [2] proposed 3D CNN to detect lung nodules using 3D cubes of

CT scans of the lung. Since 3D images give a better insight about objects, the CNN 3D works relatively well compared to the 2D CNN.

Shewaye et al. [3] presented a technique to classify pulmonary nodules as malignant or a normal through CT images. Geometry and histogram details were used to get the insight about the image characteristics of pulmonary nodules. Jia Ding et al. [4] proposed a framework consists of two stages, in the first stage, a region based convolution neural network is envisioned to detect the candidate axis slices. Then in the second phase of the framework 3D based Deep convolutional neural network is included to reduce the false positive rate. The proposed model is experimented on Lung Nodule Analysis 2016 (LUNA 2016) dataset. Suzan et al. [5] proposed a method based on bags of features (BoF) for the classification of lung cancer. The image dataset was taken from The Cancer Imaging Archive (TICA). The authors used the scale-invariant feature transform (SIFT) for extracting the features. A bag of features was used to quantize the coefficients into a codebook, and then, this codebook was fed as the K-Nearest Neighbor classifier. The efficacy of the

TABLE 4.1

State of the Art Methods for Lung Cancer Prediction

Authors	Techniques	Dataset/Images	Remarks
Alam et al. [21]	Multistage lung cancer detection through SVM is tested	UCI MLDb	Obtains 97% in detection and 87% in prediction
Kakeda et al. [22]	Features extracted through CAD system are used to train ANN model	Image database consists of 274 radiographs and 323 lung nodules	Results using CAD images are better than without CAD images
Lakshmanaprabu et al. [16]	Presents an optimized deep NN model	Model trained with 50 CT images	Obtains 94.56% classification accuracy
Ausawalaithong et al. [23]	Presents an automated lung cancer using DenseNet-121	Chest X-ray 14 and JSRT	Produces 74.58% as a classification accuracy
Haarburger et al. [24]	Lung cancer prediction using ResNet18 and CNN	Lung1 dataset-TCIA	Proposed system excels with the mean c-index 0.623 while comparing with other state-of-the-art method
Causey et al. [25]	Presents a deep learning model DeepScreener upon low-dose CT images	TCIA-1449 CT images	Obtains 82% as classification accuracy, and greatly reduces the false-positive rate.
Toğaçar et al. [26]	Lung cancer prediction at early stage using CNN	CT Images	Detection rate is 99.51%
Mahadevaswamy et al. [27]	Lung cancer prediction using KNN algorithm	1021 data samples have 23 attributes from data.world	Obtains 95.8% as a classification accuracy

system is measured using area under the curve (AUC) metric. Table 4.1 depicts the various state-of-art methods available for predicting lung cancer. Mohammad Tariqul Islam et al. [6] have used the image classification frameworks VGGNet, ResNet, and AlexNet. The authors consider the probabilities of classification from different architectures. The datasets used were the Indiana chest JSRT dataset, X-ray dataset, and Shenzhen dataset.

Anirudh et al. [7] suggested a method based on 3D CNNs to extract the features for the detection of nodules. The demerit associated with the 3D-CNN is that they demand 3D labels, which are costlier than the 2D labels. The proposed solution requires only a point label that can be used to train the CNN. The proposed approach reduces the rate of false positives with weak labels.

Botong Wu et al. [8] made lung nodule diagnosis, and prediction of the malignancy level is done simultaneously. The proposed framework learns the high-level features from the bottom of the U-net architecture and image segmentation.

Song et al. [9] used various deep neural networks to classify the lung cancer images. The proposed neural networks were trained with the CT images from the LIDC-IDRI database. The CNN network gave the result with an accuracy of 84.15%, a sensitivity of 83.96%, and a specificity of 84.32%.

Sergece et al. [10] proposed high-level image representation discriminant compact features at the beginning of the deep CNN and classified medical images with binary labels. The method experimented on dataset 2017 (KDSB2017).

Salaken et al. [11] proposed a deep autoencoder-based model to learn the features as well as to classify the same. The results obtained through the deep learning architectures perform significantly better than those through other classifiers.

Cengil et al. [12] implemented lung nodule classification of SPIE-AAPM-LungX data using CT images. The drawback of this method is that the used image dataset was quite small.

Causey et al. [13] proposed a new algorithm "DeepScreener," which is applied on the CT image dataset from the National Lung Screening Trial (NLST) cohort. The algorithm does not require lung nodule annotation to make a prediction. It uses multitask features and consecutive slices to determine whether a nodule is cancerous.

Wang et al. [14] introduced the "Central Focused Convolutional Neural Networks (CF-CNN)" model, which is used to perform segmentation of lung nodules. It experimented on the LIDC-IDRI database and Guangdong General Hospital (GDGH). The proposed method achieved a high segmentation performance of 80.02% and 82.15% on the GDGH and LIDC databases, respectively.

3D multipath VGG network was proposed by Tekade et al. [15], and they evaluated on 3D cubes, which are extracted from the LIDC-IDRI database, LUNA 2016, and Kaggle Data Science bowl (2017) datasets.

Lakshmanaprabu et al. [16] used linear discriminate analysis (LDA) and optimal deep neural network (ODNN) models for analyzing the lung cancer images. The proposed framework uses LDR for dimensionality on lung cancer images to classify malignant or normal.

BAT algorithm was proposed by Rattan et al. [17] to enhance the performance of the system. In order to achieve better accuracy for classifying the malignant images, artificial neural network is used by these authors. Abadi et al. [18] proposed a method based on a radial basis function network to classify malignant or benign cancer. Sarker et al. [19] diagnosed lung cancer using the features like tumor location, volume, and shape, and their accuracy was 95.68%.

4.3 DESIGN APPROACH AND DETAILS

This chapter deals with the whole pipelining, which is used in our work. It will consist of the details of training and making the network. Also, the architectures used and the data preparation strategy that is being used in this chapter have also been discussed here. The block diagram of the proposed method is shown in Figure 4.1. First, the images are extracted from the dataset, and then, the data augmentation is performed. Here, translation, rotation, and flipping are done as per data augmentation. Classification of lung cancer from images is made using CNN.

4.3.1 BASIC CNNs

CNN is the most conjoint deep learning algorithm in order to find patterns in images. It is related to the neural networks of the human brain, the trainable biases and weights of neurons present in the CNNs. Several inputs are received by each neuron. The weighted sum of the inputs is calculated. The output is generated upon passing the weighted sum to an activation function. The variance between the other neural networks and CNN is that CNN has convolutional layers. There were multiple layers present in CNN, and it has four major categories of layers. They are pooling layer, fully connected layer, convolutional layer, and output layer. The multiplication of a set of weights with the input is the task involved in convolution, and it is a linear operation. This set of weights is called a kernel or filter [20].

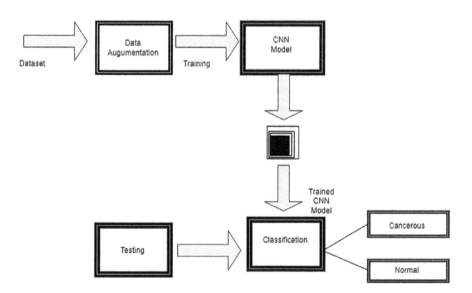

FIGURE 4.1 Block diagram of the proposed method.

4.3.2 Convolutional Layer and Sub-Sampling Method

There is no full association between the input and the output of the same layer, for the multilayer perception. In addition, this perception is entirely different from the sparse connectivity of a convolutional layer. There is a connection between neurons of adjacent layers, and the sparse connection exploits the spatial correlation. Since the typical CNN layer of convolutional filter is simulated diagonally through the intact in the graphic arena, we can extract the same feature no matter what position it is extracted and the reason we replicate the filter. To make the learning process easier and more efficient, it is required to minimalize the number of constraints. Sub-sampling layer identifies a local averaging and a sub-sampling. In order to minimize the output sensitivity and alterations, the determination of the feature map is taken into account. The kernel size of LeNet-5 network has a 2×2; each element figures the average of the four inputs and multiplies it with a trainable quantity and then adds a trainable bias.

4.4 PROPOSED CNN ARCHITECTURE

In the proposed method, we have used CNN architecture with an input layer by one, hidden layers of four, and an output layer of one. The input image is resized to the dimension of 222*22*1 for processing. Maximum pooling layer and batch normalization layer are performed for each layer. Downsampling of the image or reducing the size of the image is done in maximum pooling. The output of each layer is normalized using a batch normalization layer to increase the speed of the training process. Relu is an activation function used across all layers. The sizes of the kernel and pool layers are 3*3 and 2*2, respectively.

4.4.1 Data Augmentation

The following section explains about data augmentation performed to decrease the overfitting problem. First, the images from the dataset have been extracted in TIFF form, and image normalization is performed by dividing it by 255. Image resize is performed. Data augmentations such as rotation, flipping, and translation are performed to get more details of the dataset. Rotation of the image is performed as per equation 4.2. All of the transformation is affine transformation of the original image that takes the form:

$$y = W x + b \tag{4.1}$$

The rotation scheme rotates the image around its center via mapping each pixel (x, y) of an image to (x', y') with the following transformation:

$$\begin{pmatrix} x' \\ y' \end{pmatrix} = \begin{pmatrix} \cos\theta & -\sin\theta \\ \sin\theta & \cos\theta \end{pmatrix} \begin{pmatrix} x \\ y \end{pmatrix} \tag{4.2}$$

We define the horizontal flip by switching I value to its opposite, as flipping is done as per equation 4.3:

$$\begin{pmatrix} I' \\ Q' \end{pmatrix} = \begin{pmatrix} -I \\ Q \end{pmatrix},$$

(4.3)

and define the vertical flip is done as per equation 4.4 by switching the Q value to its opposite, as,

Layer (type)	Output Shape	Param #
conv2d_1 (Conv2D)	(None, 222, 222, 32)	320
max_pooling2d_1 (MaxPooling2	(None, 111, 111, 32)	0
batch_normalization_1 (Batch	(None, 111, 111, 32)	128
conv2d_2 (Conv2D)	(None, 109, 109, 64)	18496
max_pooling2d_2 (MaxPooling2	(None, 54, 54, 64)	0
batch_normalization_2 (Batch	(None, 54, 54, 64)	256
conv2d_3 (Conv2D)	(None, 52, 52, 64)	36928
max_pooling2d_3 (MaxPooling2	(None, 26, 26, 64)	0
batch_normalization_3 (Batch	(None, 26, 26, 64)	256
conv2d_4 (Conv2D)	(None, 24, 24, 96)	55392
max_pooling2d_4 (MaxPooling2	(None, 12, 12, 96)	0
batch_normalization_4 (Batch	(None, 12, 12, 96)	384
conv2d_5 (Conv2D)	(None, 10, 10, 32)	27680
max_pooling2d_5 (MaxPooling2	(None, 5, 5, 32)	0
batch_normalization_5 (Batch	(None, 5, 5, 32)	128
dropout_1 (Dropout)	(None, 5, 5, 32)	0
flatten_1 (Flatten)	(None, 800)	0
dense_1 (Dense)	(None, 128)	102528
dense_2 (Dense)	(None, 2)	258

Total params: 242,754
Trainable params: 242,178
Non-trainable params: 576

FIGURE 4.2 Network structure information for the proposed CNN.

$$\begin{pmatrix} I' \\ Q' \end{pmatrix} = \begin{pmatrix} -I \\ -Q \end{pmatrix},$$

$$(4.4)$$

Overfitting is the main problem with deep artificial neural networks. Overfitting occurs when dealing network with too many parameters and many iterative circles. Data augmentation helps to battle overfitting by representing the data that specifies the true pattern. Initially, from the original image size of 256×256, random patches of 224×224 size are mined. Then, translation and reflection of the image are performed. Then, the intensities of the RbG channels of the image are altered. Whenever the hidden neuron is activated with a possibility of 0.5%, it contributes to forward and backpropagation. The architecture shared weight each time it represented a new input pattern, but at the same time they sampled a new architecture. Hence, better performance of overfitting is obtained as it reduces neuron correlation. The proposed architecture of CNN is specified in Figure 4.2.

4.5   EXPERIMENTAL ANALYSIS

The proposed lung cancer prediction framework is being tested on LICR/IDRI. The LIDC/IDRI dataset consisted of 1,010 patients, and the LUNA dataset has data of 888 patients. The Kaggle dataset only provides whether a patient has cancer. These datasets provide information about the location and size of the nodules as separate annotation files along with the dicom images. However, these datasets didn't provide any information on whether a nodule was cancerous. We will use the 5th dataset Lung nodule malignancy by K Scott Mader. The dataset contains images in TIFF format. The malignancy score is given for each of the tiles in the dataset (0 is healthy and 1 is malignant). It has around 100 images sampled from the LUNA, 16 competition. The data augmentation done to the image is specified in Figure 4.3.

The proposed method performance is calculated by the following metrics:

i. *Accuracy*

This measure is computed by the overall predictions divided by the entire number of samples, which is given in the equation (4.5):

$$\text{Accuracy} = \frac{\text{TPos} + \text{TNeg}}{\text{TPos} + \text{TNeg} + \text{FPos} + \text{FNeg}}$$

$$(4.5)$$

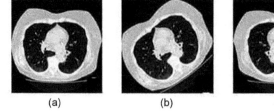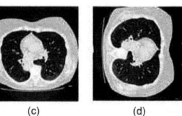

(a)	(b)	(c)	(d)

FIGURE 4.3   (a) Original image (b) Rotation at 45° (c) Flipped image (d) Rotation at 90°.

where TPos—true positive, TNeg—true negative, FPos—false positive, and FNeg—false negative

ii. *Sensitivity*

It is well defined as the amount of definite positives that are correctly identified as positives by the model, which is given in equation (4.6):

$$Sensitivity = \frac{TPos}{TPos + FNeg} \qquad (4.6)$$

iii. *Specificity (TPR)*

It is the ability of the classifier to detect negative results, which is calculated as given in equation (4.7):

$$TPR = \frac{TNeg}{TNeg + FPos} \qquad (4.7)$$

iv. *Precision (P)*

This is the measure of relevant instances that are retrieved, which is determined as given in equation (4.8):

$$P = \frac{TPos}{TNeg + FPos}. \qquad (4.8)$$

4.5.1 PARAMETER SETTING

The KNN uses Euclidean distance to measure distance between two points. K is set as 5 for K value in KNN. For SVM, the c parameter is set as 1,000 and the kernel is set as 'rbf'. The degree of SVM is set to three, and gamma is set to Auto. In the case of naïve Bayes, nonparametric naïve Bayes has been implemented for the proposed method. In the case of histogram-based classification, features are extracted from the image and plotted using the histogram. LeNet network with single-channel image with size 32*32*1 is applied. A filter of size 5×5 and 1 with stride is used for LeNet. The output volume result is set to 28×28 size. CNN applied learning rate as105, dropout rate as 0.1, batch size as 3, hidden-layer size as 32, and number of epochs as 100.

From Table 4.2, it is identified that the proposed architecture with augmentation gives better results. The proposed method also gives better results compared to other machine learning techniques, namely, SVM, etc. Generally, in deep learning, a large dataset is very significant as many images help to progress training accuracy. A strong algorithm may produce less accuracy with a small number of data. But weaker-long algorithms with more numbers of data can produce significant accuracy. Moreover, CNN produces optimal results for balanced datasets than for unbalanced datasets. Without including new images to the training dataset, the number of images can be increased by image augmentation. Variations of original images are created by image augmentation. It is achieved in the proposed method by performing

TABLE 4.2

Comparison of Proposed Method with Other Methods

Models	Accuracy	Sensitivity	Specificity	Precision	F_1
KNN	0.757	0.833	0.897	0.852	0.857
SVM	0.864	0.902	0.905	0.859	0.865
Naïve Bayes	0.888	0.931	0.943	0.877	0.874
3D CNN [2]	0.800	0.892	.0921	0.895	0.861
Histogram-based classification [3]	0.883	0.931	0.945	0.896	0.879
Region-based CNN [4]	0.91	0.961	0.963	0.902	0.865
LeNet	0.94	0.972	0.984	0.971	0.910
CNN	0.970	0.982	0.983	0.987	0.956
CNN (with data augmentation with rotation, flipping, and translation)	0.982	0.988	0.991	0.921	0.972

rotations, flips, and translations on CT lung images to increase the accuracy of the proposed method. Another problem is overfitting. Data augmentation helps to reduce overfitting. It refers to a very high variance function during modeling the training output. More diverse data of data augmentation helps to reduce overfitting. Thus, in the proposed method, data augmentation reduces overfitting and increases accuracy for the detection of lung cancer using CT images.

4.6　CONCLUSION

A method has been proposed to detect lung cancer from CT using CNNs. The data augmentations were performed to increase the number of images in the dataset and to reduce the overfitting of data for lung cancer detection. The proposed method provides accuracy of 98% compared to other available methods. The publicly available dataset for lung cancer LIDC-IDRI images is used for experimental analysis. Even though data augmentation increases the performance of the system, it has significant drawbacks such as more training time, high computational costs due to transformation, and additional memory costs. In future work, the above-specified drawbacks of data augmentation will be reduced for lung cancer detection from CT images.

REFERENCES

1. Jiang, H., Ma, H., Qian, W., Gao, M., & Li, Y. (2017). An automatic detection system of lung nodule based on multigroup patch-based deep learning network. *IEEE Journal of Biomedical and Health Informatics, 22*(4), 1227–1237.
2. Huang, X., Shan, J., & Vaidya, V. (2017). Lung nodule detection in CT using 3D convolutional neural networks. In *2017 IEEE 14th International Symposium on Biomedical Imaging (ISBI 2017)* (pp. 379–383), IEEE, Melbourne, Australia.

3. Shewaye, T. N., & Mekonnen, A. A. (2016). Benign-malignant lung nodule classification with geometric and appearance histogram features. *arXiv preprint arXiv:1605.08350.*

4. Ding, J., Li, A., Hu, Z., & Wang, L. (2017). Accurate pulmonary nodule detection in computed tomography images using deep convolutional neural networks. In *International Conference on Medical Image Computing and Computer-Assisted Intervention* (pp. 559–567). Springer, Cham.

5. Suzan, A. M., & Prathibha, G. (2017). Classification of benign and malignant tumors of lung using bag of features. *International Journal Scientific& Engineering Research*, *8*(3), 1–4.

6. Islam, M. T., Aowal, M. A., Minhaz, A. T., & Ashraf, K. (2017). Abnormality detection and localization in chest x-rays using deep convolutional neural networks. *arXiv preprint arXiv:1705.09850.*

7. Anirudh, R., Thiagarajan, J. J., Bremer, T., & Kim, H. (2016). Lung nodule detection using 3D convolutional neural networks trained on weakly labeled data. In Georgia D. Tourassi; Samuel G. Armato III (eds), *Medical Imaging 2016: Computer-Aided Diagnosis* (Vol. 9785, p. 978532). International Society for Optics and Photonics, United States.

8. Wu, B., Zhou, Z., Wang, J., & Wang, Y. (2018, April). Joint learning for pulmonary nodule segmentation, attributes and malignancy prediction. In *2018 IEEE 15th International Symposium on Biomedical Imaging (ISBI 2018)* (pp. 1109–1113). IEEE, Washington, D.C.

9. Song, Q., Zhao, L., Luo, X., & Dou, X. (2017). Using deep learning for classification of lung nodules on computed tomography images. *Journal of Healthcare Engineering*, *2017*, 1–7.

10. Serj, M. F., Lavi, B., Hoff, G., & Valls, D. P. (2018). A deep convolutional neural network for lung cancer diagnostic. *arXiv preprint arXiv:1804.08170.*

11. Salaken, S. M., Khosravi, A., Khatami, A., Nahavandi, S., & Hosen, M. A. (2017, April). Lung cancer classification using deep learned features on low population dataset. In *2017 IEEE 30th Canadian Conference on Electrical and Computer Engineering (CCECE)* (pp. 1–5). IEEE, Canada.

12. Cengil, E., & Çinar, A. (2018). A deep learning based approach to lung cancer identification. In *2018 International Conference on Artificial Intelligence and Data Processing (IDAP)* (pp. 1–5). IEEE, Malatya, Turkey.

13. Causey, J. L., Zhang, J., Ma, S., Jiang, B., Qualls, J. A., Politte, D. G., ... Huang, X. (2018). Highly accurate model for prediction of lung nodule malignancy with CT scans. *Scientific Reports*, *8*(1), 1–12.

14. Wang, S., Zhou, M., Liu, Z., Liu, Z., Gu, D., Zang, Y., ... Tian, J. (2017). Central focused convolutional neural networks: Developing a data-driven model for lung nodule segmentation. *Medical image analysis*, *40*, 172–183.

15. Tekade, R., & Rajeswari, K. (2018). Lung cancer detection and classification using deep learning. In *2018 Fourth International Conference on Computing Communication Control and Automation (ICCUBEA)* (pp. 1–5). IEEE. Pune, India.

16. Lakshmanaprabu, S. K., Mohanty, S. N., Shankar, K., Arunkumar, N., & Ramirez, G. (2019). Optimal deep learning model for classification of lung cancer on CT images. *Future Generation Computer Systems*, *92*, 374–382.

17. Rattan, S., Kaur, S., Kansal, N., & Kaur, J. (2017). An optimized lung cancer classification system for computed tomography images. In *2017 Fourth International Conference on Image Information Processing (ICIIP)* (pp. 1–6). IEEE, Himachal Pradesh, India.

18. Abadi, A. M., Wutsqa, D. U., & Pamungkas, L. R. (2017). Detection of lung cancer using radiograph images enhancement and radial basis function classifier. In *2017 10th International Congress on Image and Signal Processing, BioMedical Engineering and Informatics (CISP-BMEI)* (pp. 1–6). IEEE, China.

19. Sarker, P., Shuvo, M. M. H., Hossain, Z., & Hasan, S. (2017). Segmentation and classification of lung tumor from 3D CT image using K-means clustering algorithm. In *2017 4th International Conference on Advances in Electrical Engineering (ICAEE)* (pp. 731–736). IEEE, Independent University, Bangladesh.

20. Reddy, S., Faruq, M. S. U., & Lakshmi, K. R. (2016). Image segmentation by using linear spectral clustering. *Journal of Telecommunications System & Management*, *5*(3), 1–5. https://www.hilarispublisher.com/open-access/image-segmentation-by-using-linear-spectral-clustering-2167-0919-1000143.pdf.

21. Alam, J., Alam, S., & Hossan, A. (2018, February). Multi-stage lung cancer detection and prediction using multi-class svm classifie. In *2018 International Conference on Computer, Communication, Chemical, Material and Electronic Engineering (IC4ME2)* (pp. 1–4). IEEE. Rajshahi, Bangladesh.

22. Kakeda, S., Moriya, J., Sato, H., Aoki, T., Watanabe, H., Nakata, H., ... Doi, K. (2004). Improved detection of lung nodules on chest radiographs using a commercial computer-aided diagnosis system. *American Journal of Roentgenology*, *182*(2), 505–510.

23. Ausawalaithong, W., Thirach, A., Marukatat, S., & Wilaiprasitporn, T. (2018). Automatic lung cancer prediction from chest X-ray images using the deep learning approach. In *2018 11th Biomedical Engineering International Conference (BMEiCON)* (pp. 1–5). IEEE. Chiang Mai, Thailand.

24. Haarburger, C., Weitz, P., Rippel, O., & Merhof, D. (2019). Image-based survival prediction for lung cancer patients using CNNS. In *2019 IEEE 16th International Symposium on Biomedical Imaging (ISBI 2019)* (pp. 1197–1201). IEEE. Venice, Italy.

25. Causey, J. L., Guan, Y., Dong, W., Walker, K., Qualls, J. A., Prior, F., & Huang, X. (2019). Lung cancer screening with low-dose CT scans using a deep learning approach. *arXiv preprint arXiv:1906.00240*.

26. Toğaçar, M., Ergen, B., & Cömert, Z. (2020). Detection of lung cancer on chest CT images using minimum redundancy maximum relevance feature selection method with convolutional neural networks. *Biocybernetics and Biomedical Engineering*, *40*(1), 23–39.

27. Mahadevaswamy, U. B., Siddhanti, S. R., Bhumika, S. M., & Mounashree, B. (2021). A real time application for lung cancer prediction using machine learning. In *2021 2nd International Conference on Communication, Computing and Industry 4.0 (C2I4)* (pp. 1–6). IEEE, Bangalore, India.

5 Brain Tumor Segmentation Utilizing MRI Multimodal Images with Deep Learning

C. Chellaswamy and P. Thiruvalar Selvan
SRM TRP Engineering College

S. Markkandan
Vellore Institute of Technology

T. S. Geetha
Sriram Engineering College
Vellore Institute of Technology, Chennai Campus

CONTENTS

5.1 INTRODUCTION

Brain tumors are among the more dangerous cancers on the universe. Glioma is by far a frequent type of principal brain malignancy, which develops when glial units within spinal cord as well as brain become cancerous. Glioma has multiple histology and carcinogenic stages, and glioblastoma sufferers have a median survival duration of less than 14 months following identification [1]. Magnetic resonance imaging (MRI), a renowned congenital method that provides a vast and variable quantity of anatomical distinctions for every scanning technique, is commonly utilized by clinical practitioners for the detection of cerebral lesions [2]. Physical human segmentation and interpretation of anatomical MRI data of cerebral lesions, on the other hand, are difficult, and it is a long time-acquiring activity that can currently be performed only by expert cerebral radiotherapists [3,4]. As a result, cerebral lesion delineation that is both automated and sturdy might exert a considerable influence on brain tumor identification and therapy. This could possibly aid in early detection and therapy of brain illnesses like Alzheimer's disease, schizophrenia, and dementia. Physicians can use a computed node automatically for tumor segmentation for success in the progress of the treatment and assistance in getting critical data relating to the size, placement, and geometry of lesions (especially augmenting tumor central portions and complete malignant territories) [5].

There are a number of variations among the malignancy and surrounding healthy neighboring tissue that make treatment a difficult job. Dimension, skew area (unfavorable distortion owing to faulty data gathering), placement, and contour are all factors in the feasibility of classification in clinical scanning assessment [5]. As in research, numerous algorithms have shown help in any attempt to determine precise as well as economical borderline contours of cerebral lesions in clinical data. There are three types of models to choose from: (i) The enrollment and label identity merging of numerous healthy cerebral guidebooks with a novel picture source is the basis of multi-atlas registration (MAS) methods. Such MAS techniques have been rarely effective in coping on scenarios which demand rapidity due to the challenges in establishing typical cerebral guidebooks and the requirement of significant amount of guidebooks [6]. (ii) Manually defined characteristics are used primarily in neural network models in handling various issues (or pre-set characteristics). Retrieval of some crucial details within the source image with the employment of a characteristic retrieval method is seen as the first phase with a sort of segmentation, followed by an exclusionary network for distinguishing malignancy from healthy cells [7,8]. Neural network models in use typically combine manually defined parameters alongside a variety of classifiers, like random forest as well as support vector machine [9]. They have provided approaches and techniques for gathering attributes, edge-related information, and various relevant data, which typically utilize more duration. Furthermore, the function of these approaches has been rather miserable when diagnostic borders distinguishing normal membrane and malignancy are blurry or ambiguous. (iii) Deep learning methods dynamically identify key information. In a variety of industrial fields, including pedestrian identification [10], voice identification and interpretation [11], even cerebral lesion dissection [12], these techniques have shown remarkable outcomes.

Zhang et al. introduced the TSBTS system (task-structured brain tumor segmentation system), which investigates all the assignment framework architecture and the task-task architecture to replicate specialists' competence. The assignment framework architecture finds different malignancy areas through the measurement of modal density information of different types, which depict unique clinical traits, while the task-task architecture associates the greatest unique region with single portion of the malignancy plus utilizes this to locate other component nearby [13].

An approach for describing valuable aspects via cognitive information shift between various modal datasets has been used in Ref. [14]. They employed a generative adversarial network (GAN) learning strategy for harvesting underlying features within the input of any model for assistance in providing information shift. To tackle the problem of uneven information in clinical cerebral capacity, Zhou et al. developed a One-pass MultiTask Network (OM-Net) [15]. OM-Net employs both global and task-peculiar variables to acquire discriminative and collaborative attributes. OM-Net is strengthened through a combination of knowledge-based education and exchange of information through education in the virtual media. In addition, the implementation of cross-task-guided attention (CGA) module is done for communication of forecast findings among activities. A combined regional and universal ambient data is concurrently under the deep CNN framework suggested by Havaei et al. This method involves the incorporation of a straightforward yet effective feature harvesting strategy [16]. An AssemblyNet model is used for 3D entire-brain MRI segmentation that leverages the legislative choice of notion [17]. This legislative system is capable of resolving unknown issues, making difficult judgments, and obtaining an appropriate agreement. AssemblyNet uses a consensus casting method through exchange of information between surrounding U-Nets. The issue of inadequate learning samples is addressed by such a system.

Cerebral scans statistics is skewed because tumors are tiny in comparison with the balance of the skull. Conventional systems are skewed against the heavily portrayed category as a result of this description, and learning a deep network frequently results in poor genuine positive ratios. Conventional deep learning algorithms have also complicated architecture, making them moment-acquiring. The authors have developed a sophisticated pre-processing method for meeting the aforementioned fundamental challenges and for the elimination of a large quantity of irrelevant data in our research that yielded encouraging outcomes albeit with current deep learning algorithms, without employment of a complicated deep learning algorithm for the identification of the tumor's position and harvest attributes due to the employment of this method, which results in a duration-acquiring procedure with a significant error incidence. In addition, the pre-processing phase in this technique reduces overfitting concerns by decreasing the amount of the area of focus. A cascade CNN technique is also used following the pre-processing phase for satisfactory collection of combined regional and universal information. A unique distance-wise concentration method employed within the CNN structure provides resilience to render this system against changes in lesion mass and position.

5.2   MATERIAL AND METHODS

This section provides a description of the pre-processing method, various slices of tumor representation, and the expected area of the tumor used in this study. Three cerebral modes (fluid-attenuated inversion recovery (Flair), T1-contrasted (T1C), and, T2-weighted (T2)) have been used. An in-depth description of the technique is provided in the following chapter.

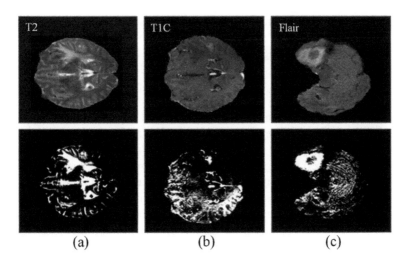

FIGURE 5.1 Examples of three different MRI modalities and their corresponding normalized Z-score (a) T2, (b) T1C, and (c) FLAIR.

5.2.1 PRE-PROCESSING

Despite several current deep learning algorithms that employ the entire image for the extraction of essential characteristics, the authors have just made an analysis of a small portion from data to obtain critical elements. The real negative outcomes are considerably reduced by deleting these needless unhelpful sections. Use of an extremely deep convolutional network through the employment of this approach can be avoided. Integration of three cerebral modes, notably fluid attenuated inversion recovery (Flair), T1-contrasted (T1C), and T2-weighted (T2), has been seen providing reliable ultimate segmentation reliability. Z-score standardization has been applied across the various modes for rendering the MRI dataset better homogenous as well as for the removal of the impact of asymmetry (particularly with the FLAIR mode). When applied to a clinical cerebral imaging, the result is a fuzzy grouping image having a nil average with unity variance. In just the brain area, the authors performed the process through the removal of the average and splitting with the typical variation (hardly a backdrop). This process was carried out separately with every person's brain size. Figure 5.1 depicts several examples of the four source modes as well as the standardization outcomes for each.

5.2.2 TUMOR REPRESENTATION IN EACH SLICE

In this research, the authors have discovered a continuous rise or diminish in subsequent cuts in the mass and form. During the first slicing, the appearance of a tiny lesion was seen in any feasible area of the picture. The cancer would then persist in just the identical area within the picture in subsequent slicing, although it would grow in mass [18]. Following this, once the optimum mass was attained, the lesion

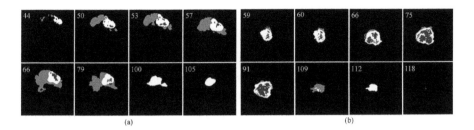

FIGURE 5.2 Ground truth of five different slices. The slice number is present inside of each slice. (a) Brats18_TCIA02_377_1 and (b) Brats18_2013_23_1.

began to shrink until absolutely eradicated. The authors' pre-processing approach has been built around this notion.

Figure 5.2 shows the ground truth of five different slices used in this study. The fundamental rationale for adopting the four brain modes indicated above is that they have distinct properties for spotting certain regions of the lesion. Furthermore, location of these three components in any of the four modes was found required for the location of cancer and integration for the formation of a cohesive body. Consequently, with every mode, the primary objective was to detect single section of the tumor.

5.2.3 FINDING THE EXPECTED AREA OF THE TUMOR

Development, disappearance, and a large tumor size in distinct slices were seen to be associated with multiple patients through examination of closer (Figure 5.2). The largest malignancies, as example, are shown in Figure 5.2a and b, correspondingly, under layers 80 and 55. Further noteworthy feature is that, to the best understanding of the authors, no substantial variation in the size of continuous slices and slight variation is observed in the size of the tumor. Through the use of the inquiry period, researchers have discovered the location of the developing and fading lesion as a difficult and tricky operation. However, it is never the case while seeking for the largest lesion within the picture. We take four key steps to locate the cancer region in each piece: (i) construct the Z-score-standardized visual by scanning all modes excluding the T1 image; (ii) bifolding the acquired image using the FLAIR, T2, and T1c criteria of 0.7, 0.7, and 0.9, accordingly; (iii) use a structural function to get rid of certain parts that are not important; (iv) blending of all bifolded pictures of FLAIR and T2; and (v) found required for making a fresh image followed by aggregation of the regions acquired out of every picture.

Prominence of the tumor in FLAIR and T2 pictures than adjacent areas of the skull makes the bifolding barrier factor greater than the average estimate (0.7 was the number chosen). T1ce photos also showed the tumor as substantially clearer than FLAIR and T2 pictures. As a result, utilization of a higher bifolding barrier factor was required (0.9 was the number we chose). Numerous healthy cells will be recognized as cancer entities when a low barrier factor for bifolding is specified [19]. The acquired data contain some cancer-like things, with the requirement of elimination of certain straightforward but accurate criteria in the subsequent phase.

Addition of restrictions was made to the bifolded T1c pictures for the determination of a bifold object as a constituent of the cancer or none. (i) Entities with a firmness exceeding 0.7, (ii) an entity with a size greater than 500 pixels, and (iii) the entity's primary shaft must be longer than 35 pixels in length. Each entity in the bifolded T1c picture that fails to meet these requirements is eliminated. Across all bifolded images, the established requirements (criteria) are identical, with the requirement to change anything for getting a decent outcome. Furthermore, choice of a number for each restriction over a broad range was made for eliminating the issue of employment of MRI pictures of varying dimensions and densities. Within BRATS 2018 sample, for example, the minimum entity dimension number was set at 500 pixels. Although utilizing a large range to pick an entity reduces precision, utilizing the additional criteria (rigidity and main shaft distance) allows one to successfully circumvent that difficulty.

The requirement of recognition of all bifold entities utilizing structural tools was seen for the production of bifold cancer picture and then combine them together. However, there is one more criterion that must be met prior integrating the bifolded T1c to the picture created from the bifold dot product of the FLAIR and T2 image. The influence of a bifold entity within the T1c pictures may be considered only when indeed the overlaying region is greater than 20 pixels, with a bifold entity within the picture derived via the bifold dot product of FLAIR and T2. The following stage is related to pinpointing of the position of the large tumor within the sections. With this objective, there is the requirement of discovered items, i.e., in fact, malignancies. Every malignant entity in successive layers was monitored for getting around that problem. This implies that when a cancer entity is discovered nearly in the identical position in consecutive layers with only a slight difference in dimensions, we may be certain that it is a legitimate tumor entity. Following the location of the genuine cancer entity in a layer, the next was a look for the largest entity on that identical region within most subsequent layers. Eventually, such entity could be extended via structural tools to encompass all probable lacking cancer locations. (This is what the authors refer to as the largest predicted region.) One could explore solely in this region for the malignancy and partition it in certain layers after discovering that entity as well as its placement. As a result of inclusion of all layers where the extent of the predicted regions varies somewhat beyond the anticipated layer-to-layer variation, we can generate a bifold overlay.

5.2.4 DEEP LEARNING ARCHITECTURE

Convolutional neural network (CNN) pipelines that constitute a variety of deep feed-forward artificial neural circuits have made significant advances in healthcare image analytics as well as treatment in history's artificial intelligence (AI) industries. The anatomical arrangement of the anthropoid brain's optical lobe, which utilizes the regional perceptron, influenced the architecture of a CNN paradigm. Its structure resembles with that of a neuron's network arrangement.

The CNN paradigm is not robust to spin and translation, and hence, fragmenting an entity could be shifted in the picture, which is a huge challenge. These are some of the main difficulties: With employing a CNN architecture in clinical imaging, the difficulty is the assessment duration, because several clinical purposes require quick replies for a reduction in the need for extra investigation and therapy. When confronted to a high-accuracy clinical imaging, the situation becomes considerably quite complex. As a result, utilization of 3D CNN network for the identification of tumors deploying typical gliding pane techniques does not yield a satisfactory outcome. This is quite troublesome when there are excellent dimensional pictures with a massive amount of 3D frame specimens for a study. The position, volume, alignment, and geometry of the lesion vary among individuals throughout every cerebral high-dimensional imaging, making it difficult to designate the tumor's prospective territory. Furthermore, screening a tiny portion of a picture instead of the entire frame is much more sensible.

With this objective in view, the authors initially defined the contour having a significant possibility of confronting the cancer, and deploy our CNN architecture toward that narrow zone, lowering processing expenses and enhancing network productivity. The main disadvantage of CNN models is the vagueness of differentiation results and the loss of spatial data generated by convolutional striding as well as pooling processes. Several sophisticated tactics have been used for an increase in segmentation precision and performance, including dilated convolution/pooling, skip connections, but also supplementary research and novel post-processing packages, notably hidden conditional random field and conditional random field. The employment of the elongated convolution technique results in the utilization of a broad perceptron minus the requirement of a pooling stack, which alleviates the concern of data erosion over the learning period. Incorporation of characteristics and feeding outcomes from earlier tiers to the current tier in the down-sampling phase, can help in gradual reinstatement of unaltered spatial resolution for skip connection. The attentive technique has recently been used in the case of deep learning and has demonstrated fine efficiency for a variety of computer imaging tasks such as occurrence segmentation, picture noise removal, human re-identification, image categorization, and so on.

5.2.5 Proposed Structure

A gradient CNN paradigm suggested in this research involves the incorporation of combined regional as well as worldwide data from several MRI modes. In addition, in four incoming modes, a distance-wise concentration strategy is presented to account for the influence of the brain lesion placement. Such distance-wise concentration method effectively provides the primary position characteristic of the image to the fully connected stack for solving overfitting concerns when compared to the self-co-attention technique, which uses several concurrent convolutional stages for discrimination among groups. Despite the wide use of numerous CNN-based systems in the past with multi-modality malignancy delineation, neither of it employs a mix of an attention-based technique and an area-expected methodology.

5.2.6 Distance-Wise Attention Module

The likelihood of discovering every pixel in the exploring phase can be found via contemplating the impact of disparity among the tumor's core and also the predicted region. To put it another way, recognition of the anticipated core (see Figure 5.3) enables

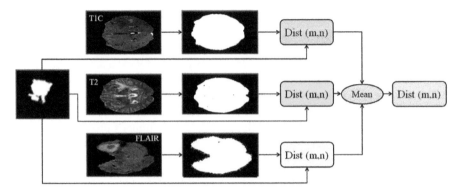

FIGURE 5.3   Estimation of distance using the three input modalities mask.

improved distinction across the three malignancy categories' pixels. For the purpose of identifying beneficial attributes, the distance-wise attention mechanism (DAM) package investigates distance-wise correlations within every layer of the four modes used. Provided a characteristic station array $K \in N^{H \times W \times R}$, $K = \{K_1, K_2, ..., K_R\}$, wherein $K_i \in R^{H \times W}$ denotes a station. The source channels, spatial elevation, and spatial expanse are represented by the constants R, H, and W, correspondingly. DAM can be defined as

$$\text{Dist}\,(m,\,n) = \frac{\sqrt[2]{(O_{cm} - O_{cn})^2 + (P_{cm} - P_{cn})^2}}{\text{No. of rows in the image}} \qquad (5.1)$$

where $O_c = (O_o + H_{obj})/2$ and $P_c = (P_o + Y_{obj})/2$. O_c and P_c denotes, respectively, the location of starting point in H_{obj} and the location of starting point in Y_{obj}. $H_{obj} = $ max arg(sum pixels == 1 in each row), $Y_{obj} = $ max arg(sum pixels == 1 in each column).

5.2.7   CASCADE CNN MODEL

Figure 5.4 illustrates the protocol for the cascade method suggested by the authors. Four modes have been employed to collect quite numerous high tumor characteristics conceivable: Flair, T1C, and T2. In addition, we sum up four equivalent normalized Z-score images of the four source modes to boost the dice rating of delineation outcomes by the elimination of introducing further tiers to the architecture.

There are zero requirements for a complicated deep structure like that in Ref. [10] due to the implementation of a robust pretreatment phase that removes around 80% of the irrelevant data out of every source images. There are minimal pixels for analysis by picking around 20% of the entire picture (that proportion is the average of the full layers of an individual) for every incoming mode and matching Z-score-standardized picture. Also, despite utilizing a deep CNN network, addressing the impact of the lesion's core on proper identification enhances the categorization outcome. For preventing the overfitting, a gradient CNN framework with eight source pictures is presented in this paper that incorporates the DAM unit at the channel's termination.

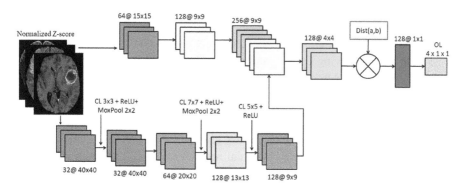

FIGURE 5.4 Proposed structure with DWA. The red and blue square inside the Z-score indicates the local and global patches. The DWA is included before the FCL.

This CNN algorithm incorporates two alternative paths that harvest regional and universal characteristics out from four source modes and the related Z-score-standardized pictures, as shown in Figure 5.4. The main purpose of the initial path is to identify pixels on the lesions' boundary (the universal feature), while the latter path's main objective is to mark every pixel within the lesion (the regional feature). A 40×40 slice (red frame) has been chosen out of every source image in the initial path for serving the system.

5.3 EXPERIMENTS

5.3.1 DATA AND IMPLEMENTATION DETAILS

The BRATS 2018 samples, which comprise multi-modal MRI pictures and individual's medical evidence containing varied diverse histologic subregions, various levels of toughness, with different outcome, were used for learning, verification, and evaluation of the workflow. Such multi-modal MR pictures, which are different from computed tomography (CT) pictures, contain measurements of 240×240×150 yet were medically produced utilizing a variety of magnetic field intensities, detectors, and regimens from a variety of organizations. The FLAIR, T1c, and T2 are three MRI patterns for learning, verification, and assessment.

These collections contain 75 LGG cases and 210 HGG cases that were arbitrarily partitioned into learning data (80%), verification data (10%), and assessment data (10%). In addition, neuroradiologists tagged images with malignant tags (necrosis, edema, non-improving malignancy, and improving malignancy are symbolized by 1, 2, 3, and 4, correspondingly. Likewise, a tissue with a score of nil is considered healthy). The third tag was not utilized. The empirical findings of the suggested architecture were obtained via MATLAB on an Intel Core i7-3.4 GHz, 15 MB Cache, 64 GB RAM, and GPU 1080Ti NVIDIA machine running on a 64-bit operating system. During the learning phase, the authors used Adaptive Moment Estimation (Adam) having a group length of 2, a load degradation of 10^{-5}, and a starting learning rate of 10^{-4}. We spent a whole of 13 hours learning and 7 seconds assessing each volume.

5.3.2 EVALUATION MEASURE

Parameters for the augmenting center (AC), tumor center (TC, comprising necrotic center with non-improving center), and total malignancy (TM, with all stages of tumor architecture) have been used in the evaluation of the success of the method. To calculate the overlaps among the actual reality and the forecasts, the Dice similarity coefficient (DSC) is used as an assessment tool. HAUSDORFF99, dice resemblance, and sensitivity were applied to achieve the research outcomes. The Hausdorff value is a measurement of the length across the expected and the surfaces of actual-reality regions. The convergence among the actual realities and the expectations is computed using a dice value as the assessment tool. The number of non-tumor pixels that are determined accurately is called specificity (real negative incidence). Sensitivity (also known as recall or real positive incidence) refers to the number of cancer pixels, which are estimated accurately. The following are the three standards:

$$\text{DICE}(N_a, N_p) = 2 * \frac{N_a \cdot N_p}{N_a + N_p} \tag{5.2}$$

$$\text{Sensitivity} = \frac{(N_a \cdot N_p)}{(N_p)} \tag{5.3}$$

5.3.3 EXPERIMENTAL RESULTS

The authors have used five different methods (multi-cascaded, cascaded random forests, cross-modality, task structure, and one-pass multi-task) for gaining a good understanding of tumor division efficiency and making quantitative and qualitative contrasts. Table 5.1 shows the quantitative outcomes for several types of the recommended architecture and also the inability of the CNN algorithm.

When a concentration component is incorporated to a two-path model eliminating the pre-processing approach, the segmentation outcomes improve throughout overall three attributes. Dice grades in three tumor locations improved from 0.261, 0.282, and 0.221 to 0.881, 0.8550, and 0.882 for finish, total, and central, correspondingly, after adopting the pre-processing strategy. In spite of just having a single-path CNN model (regional or universal parameters), the CNN approach provides a big boost for segmentation accuracy in all cancer areas, owing to the application of the pre-processing strategy. Furthermore, it has been discovered that applying the pre-processing technique has a greater impact than simply employing an attentiveness strategy. In similar terms, while engaging with a reduced portion of the source images recovered by the pre-processing technique, the suggested concentration strategy may be highly beneficial. The outperformance of regional features over universal features was seen from the contrast of regional and universal features.

Table 5.2 lists the Dice, sensitivity, and HAUSDORFF99 scores for each incoming picture utilizing all architectures. The greatest Dice, sensitivity, and lowest HAUSDORFF99 scores are indicated in bold for every category in Table 4.2.

TABLE 5.1

Evaluation Results of BRATS 2018 Dataset for Various Configurations

Method	Mean Sensitivity			Mean Dice Score		
	Enh	Whole	Core	Enh	Whole	Core
Two-route CNN	0.2644	0.2845	0.2383	0.2475	0.2509	0.219
Local-route CNN+Attention mechanism	0.3593	0.3683	0.3697	0.3409	0.3951	0.3849
Two-route CNN+Attention mechanism	0.4289	0.3802	0.3729	0.3904	0.396	0.3874
Global-route CNN+Attention mechanism	0.3284	0.338	0.3137	0.3385	0.2989	0.284
Pre-processing with local-route CNN	0.8635	0.8354	0.8635	0.879	0.8624	0.8489
Pre-processing with two-route CNN	0.8831	0.8698	0.8812	0.8943	0.9164	0.8532
Pre-processing with global-route CNN	0.7942	0.7998	0.7853	0.7562	0.7852	0.7564
Proposed method	0.9243	0.9375	0.8824	0.934	0.9405	0.9751

Table 4.2 shows that our technique can reach the maximum sensitivity scores in the Enh as well as entire tumor regions, with Ref. [10] achieving the maximum score in the central zone. Apparently, this is probably a negligible discrepancy among the HAUSDORFF99 readings when using the proposed CNN. With the overall three indicators, a considerable development in the Enh region was seen. Also, on the HAUSDORFF99 metric, it has the poorest scores in the total and central sections.

Several metrics help in significant enhancement while utilizing the suggested approach relative to the previous methods described. However, the sensitivity score in the central region employing [3,4] remains greater. These are three possible causes to the best of the authors' understanding. First, while implementing the four modes to the CNN framework, the suggested methodology devotes exceptional consideration to deleting inconsequential areas within them. Second, the approach investigates the broader environment malignancy segmentation through a combination of regional as well as universal information with varying amounts in convolutional stages. Third, the system can be skewed to an appropriate response group by taking into account the influence of the disparity among the tumor's core and the projected region. Furthermore, adoption of a CNN architecture helps in achievement of better optimistic efficiency and a reduction in total time when compared to the existing algorithms using massive systems. In addition, as demonstrated in Table 4.2, the suggested approach is quicker than the other evaluated approaches at fragmenting the lesion.

TABLE 5.2

Comparison between the Proposed Method and Other State-of-the-Art Method for the BRATS 2018 Dataset

Method	Mean Sensitivity			Mean Dice Score			HAUSDORFF99			Time (s)
	Enh	Whole	Core	Enh	Whole	Core	Enh	Whole	Core	
MCA	0.7435	0.874	0.7532	0.8748	0.7842	0.986	2.43	4.56	7.43	268
CRF	0.7621	0.8524	0.7834	0.8412	0.9043	0.8732	-	-	-	320
CMM	0.9154	0.7935	0.8436	0.9321	0.8563	0.8365	4.894	3.983	6.421	213
TSM	0.7942	0.8843	0.8358	-	-	-	3.526	5.853	9.32	198
OPMT	0.842	0.928	0.8631	-	-	-	2.91	4.841	6.843	279
Proposed	0.9213	0.9351	0.8695	0.9352	0.9453	0.986	1.764	1.593	2.397	112

Figure 5.5 shows the significant outcomes of the use of the authors' method on the BRATS 2018 dataset. Every zone has a common boundary with every adjacent zone, as illustrated. The boundary separating TC and augmenting locations within T1c pictures (third editorial) requires ready differentiation with a significant degree of precision while eliminating the usage of other modes owing to variations in score of TC and boosting regions. However, this is not the case while engaging with the malignant core's boundary, edema regions, or exacerbated edema regions. The aforementioned properties of each paradigm helps in observation of a reduction in exploring region assisting elimination of the requirement for a highly deep CNN architecture.

This system could harvest greater distinct environmental data from the malignancy and the cortex because of the inclusion of the DAM component, resulting in a superior segmentation outcome. Figure 5.6 depicts the enhanced segmentation as a consequence of the suggested technique's use of the DAM unit, notably in the boundary of contacting tumor regions. Figure 5.7 shows the correlation between the benchmark and the approach that demonstrates the efficiency of the suggested strategy in distinguishing across all four zones. The underlying reality for the four modes in the identical grid is shown in Figure 5.7. The multi-cascaded (Figure 5.7a) and cascaded random forests (Figure 5.7b) techniques are successful in identifying the edema region, but they are unable to recognize tiny areas of edema beyond the principal edema area.

The Cross-modality (Figure 5.7c) and One-Pass Multi-Task (Figure 5.7d) techniques show effectiveness in the recognition of tumor central and boosting regions, particularly in finding tumor central exterior and improving area's external boundary. The cross-modal approach is used for the exhibition of how certain distinct edema zones are bonded collectively in the ultimate fragmentation.

Implementation of the Cross-modality architecture, illustrated in Figure 5.7c, helps in achievement of the lowest segmentation efficiency for recognizing edema zones when contrasted to alternatives. This technique over-segments the edema regions, while it under-segments the malignant central locations. In comparison with Figure 5.7a–c, the One-Pass Multi-Task technique has a greater central agreement with the ground-truth, but it, nonetheless, has inadequate precision, notably in the

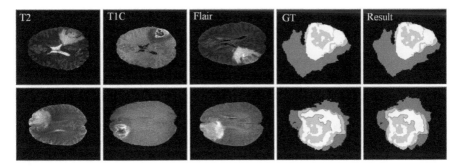

FIGURE 5.5 Brain cancer segmentation using the proposed method (yellow-enhanced region; red-core region; and blue-edema region).

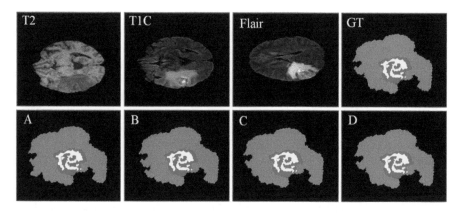

FIGURE 5.6   Comparison of the proposed structure by applying DAM (blue-edema region; yellow-enhanced region; and red-core region).

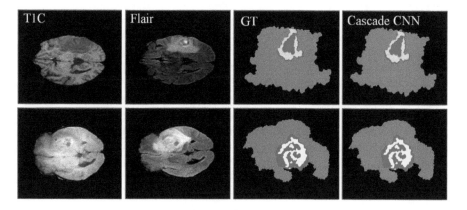

FIGURE 5.7   Comparison of the proposed structure by applying DAM (blue-edema region; yellow-enhanced region; and red-core region).

edema regions. According to the authors' findings, utilization of a consideration technique for prediction of the three separate zones of a cerebral tumor is an excellent way to assist experts and clinicians in assessing tumor levels, which is a popular issue in computer-aided diagnostic methods.

5.4   CONCLUSION

In this study, the authors have provided a novel brain cancer segmentation framework that takes advantage of the four MRI modes' description. It means that every modal has its own set of properties that assist the system differentiates across categories more effectively. A CNN algorithm (the best prevalent deep learning structure) has been shown providing achievement of efficiency comparable to person spectators by focusing just on a portion of the brain image around the tumor cells. Furthermore, a straightforward but effective gradient CNN framework has been suggested for capturing both regional and universal characteristics in two separate methods with variable patch dimensions. After a robust pre-processing strategy that extracts predicted region of the tumors, those patches have been chosen for supply of the system that their core is positioned within this location. Removal of a high number of irrelevant pixels from the image during the pre-processing stage helps in a reduction in the computing speed and capacity to make fast forecasts for categorizing the medical image. When contrasted to state-of-the-art methods, extensive trials have demonstrated the usefulness of the DAM in our algorithm, and also the extraordinary potential of our overall system.

Despite the superior outcomes enabled by the suggested approach, when contrasted to similar recently disclosed approaches, this method has limitations while dealing with tumor masses greater than one-third of the total cerebral volume. This is due to a decline in the feature harvesting efficiency with the size of the anticipated region of the tumor growing faster.

REFERENCES

1. Shumpei Morisawa, Kohei Jobu, Tomoaki Ishida, Kei Kawada, Hitoshi Fukuda, Yu Kawanishi, Taku Nakayama, Shinkuro Yamamoto, Naohisa Tamura, Mitsuhiro Takemura, Nao Kagimoto, Tsuyoshi Ohta, Noritaka Masahira, Hideo Fukuhara, Shun-ichiro Ogura, Tetsuya Ueba, Keiji Inoue, Mitsuhiko Miyamura, Association of 5-aminolevulinic acid with intraoperative hypotension in malignant glioma surgery, *Photodiagnosis and Photodynamic Therapy*, 37, 2022, 102657, https://doi.org/10.1016/j.pdpdt.2021.102657.
2. Mohamed T. Bennai, Zahia Guessoum, Smaine Mazouzi, Stéphane Cormier, Mohamed Mezghiche, A stochastic multi-agent approach for medical-image segmentation: Application to tumor segmentation in brain MR images, *Artificial Intelligence in Medicine*, 110, 2020, 101980, https://doi.org/10.1016/j.artmed.2020.101980.
3. Siddhesh Thakur, Jimit Doshi, Sarthak Pati, Saima Rathore, Chiharu Sako, Michel Bilello, Sung Min Ha, Gaurav Shukla, Adam Flanders, Aikaterini Kotrotsou, Mikhail Milchenko, Spencer Liem, Gregory S. Alexander, Joseph Lombardo, Joshua D. Palmer, Pamela LaMontagne, Arash Nazeri, Sanjay Talbar, Uday Kulkarni, Daniel Marcus, Rivka Colen, Christos Davatzikos, Guray Erus, Spyridon Bakas, Brain extraction on MRI scans in presence of diffuse glioma: Multi-institutional performance evaluation of deep learning methods and robust modality-agnostic training, *NeuroImage*, 220, 2020, 117081, https://doi.org/10.1016/j.neuroimage.2020.117081.
4. A. Khosravanian, M. Rahmanimanesh, P. Keshavarzi, S. Mozafari, Fast level set method for glioma brain tumor segmentation based on superpixel fuzzy clustering and lattice boltzmann method. *Computer Methods and Programs in Biomedicine*, 198, 2020, 105809, https://doi.org/10.1016/j.cmpb.2020.105809.
5. S. Bakas, Segmentation labels and radiomic features for the pre-operative scans of the TCGA-LGG collection. *Cancer Imaging Archive*, 2017, https://doi.org/10.7937/K9/TCIA.2017.GJQ7R0EF.
6. Nasser Mohamed Ramli, M. A. Hussain, Badrul Mohamed Jan, Bawadi Abdullah, Composition prediction of a debutanizer column using equation based artificial neural network model, *Neurocomputing*, 131, 2014, 59–76, https://doi.org/10.1016/j.neucom.2013.10.039.

7. M. Antonelli, et al. GAS: A genetic atlas selection strategy in multi-atlas segmentation framework. *Medical Image Analysis*, 52, 2019, 97–108. https://doi.org/10.1016/j.media.2018.11.007.

8. Zeynab Barzegar, Mansour Jamzad, WLFS: Weighted label fusion learning framework for glioma tumor segmentation in brain MRI, *Biomedical Signal Processing and Control*, 68, 2021, 102617, https://doi.org/10.1016/j.bspc.2021.102617.

9. Subba Rao Chalasani, T. S. Geetha, Chellaswamy Chellaiah, Arul Srinivasan, Optimized convolutional neural network-based multigas detection using fiber optic sensor, *Optical Engineering*, 60(12), 2021, 127108, https://doi.org/10.1117/1.OE.60.12.127108.

10. Q. V. Le, T. Mikolov, Distributed representations of sentences and documents. 2014, https://doi.org/10.1145/2740908.2742760.

11. H. Torabi Dashti, A. Masoudi-Nejad, F. Zare, Finding exact and solo LTR-retrotransposons in biological sequences using SVM. *Iranian Journal of Chemistry and Chemical Engineering*, 31(2), 2012, 111–116, https://doi.org/10.30492/IJCCE.2012.5998.

12. Jong-Myong Lee, Subarachnoid hemorrhage due to middle cerebral artery dissection mimicking aneurysm-case report, *Radiology Case Reports*, 17(7), 2022, 2537–2541, https://doi.org/10.1016/j.radcr.2022.04.020.

13. G. Chen, Q. Li, F. Shi, I. Rekik, Z. Pan, RFDCR: Automated brain lesion segmentation using cascaded random forests with dense conditional random fields. *Neuroimage*, 211, 2020, 116620. https://doi.org/10.1016/j.neuroimage.2020.116620.

14. A. Jalalifar, H. Soliman, M. Ruschin, A. Sahgal, A. Sadeghi-Naini, A brain tumor segmentation framework based on outlier detection using one-class support vector machine. In *Proceedings of the Annual International Conference of the IEEE Engineering in Medicine and Biology Society*, EMBS, 2020, vol. 2020, pp. 1067–1070, https://doi.org/10.1109/EMBC44109.2020.9176263.

15. D. Zhang, et al. Exploring task structure for brain tumor segmentation from multi-modality MR images. *IEEE Transactions on Image Processing*, 2020, https://doi.org/10.1109/TIP.2020.3023609.

16. D. Zhang, et al. Cross-modality deep feature learning for brain tumor segmentation. *Pattern Recognition*, 2020, https://doi.org/10.1016/j.patcog.2020.107562.

17. P. Coupé, et al. AssemblyNet: A large ensemble of CNNs for 3D whole brain MRI segmentation. *Neuroimage*, 219, 2020, 117026. https://doi.org/10.1016/j.neuroimage.2020.117026.

18. Zheng Huang, Yiwen Zhao, Yunhui Liu, Guoli Song, GCAUNet: A group cross-channel attention residual UNet for slice based brain tumor segmentation. *Biomedical Signal Processing and Control*, 70, 2021, 102958, https://doi.org/10.1016/j.bspc.2021.102958.

19. X. Zhao, et al. A deep learning model integrating FCNNs and CRFs for brain tumor segmentation. *Medical Image Analysis*, 43, 2018, 98–111. https://doi.org/10.1016/j.media.2017.10.002.

6 Detection and Classification of Brain Tumors Using Light-Weight Convolutional Neural Network

Sabyasachi Mukherjee and Arindam Biswas
Indian Institute of Engineering Science and Technology

Oishila Bandyopadhyay
Indian Institute of Information Technology

CONTENTS

6.1 INTRODUCTION

The formation of abnormal lump or mass in brain due to irregular growth of cells is termed as brain tumor (1). In recent times, brain tumor has become a serious cause of concern as around 3 lakhs of people worldwide are diagnosed with primary brain tumor every year. This has been a widely researched topic because of the severity and deadliness of the disease (2).

Apart from medical history and clinical examinations based on patient's symptoms, imaging of the brain is the most reliable medium for the detection of brain

DOI: 10.1201/9781003277002-6

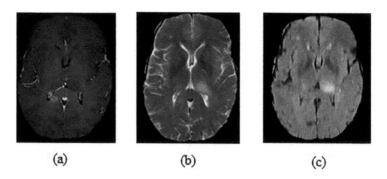

FIGURE 6.1   (a) T1C (b) T2 and (c) Flair MRI scans of brain.

tumor (3,4). Magnetic resonance imaging (MRI) and computed tomography (CT) are used to generate the detailed images to monitor the developments in brain. These images produce very accurate view of brain and help to diagnose tumor and other brain-related abnormalities. CT scan uses X-ray, which is potentially harmful for human body, whereas MRI is based on magnetic fields. Although CT is less expensive, MRI generates more detailed brain images. Clinical experts perform a detailed analysis of MRI to reveal the underlying condition of the brain. As these require high skill and time, the automated analysis of brain MRI and diagnosis of brain tumor is the need of the hour.

In this study, an automated process is designed to analyze brain MRI for the detection and classification of brain tumors. This process, being automated, is expected to help in the analysis of brain MRI in a timely and accurate manner. The need and sole dependence on human resource is also reduced a bit, making the whole process faster and resilient.

Out of various MRI modalities, T1C, T2, and flair types of MRI scans have been used for automated analysis (5). Although same region of brain is imaged, these different MRI modalities give independent information, which proves to be very useful. T1C, T2, and flair images of the same brain region show visibly different appearance of various tissue types (as shown in Figure 6.1). For example, the gray matter is darker in T1C, while it is brighter in T2. Exploring these differences among images of various types of MRI, the same tissue type can be analyzed in a different manner.

The primary objective of this study is to detect the presence of brain tumor and then classify brain tumor. This work proposes a light-weight convolutional neural network (CNN)-based architecture for the diagnosis and classification of brain tumor. The whole process comprises two major phases, namely, detection and classification phases.

6.2   RELATED WORKS

Computer-assisted brain tumor analysis has been very widely researched because of its importance in medical science domain. Even before the advent of deep learning, there were many attempts in brain tumor detection and segmentation using conventional image processing techniques. In recent years, researchers have proposed

TABLE 6.1

Summary of Recent Researches on Brain Tumor Classification

Author	Methodology
Toğaçar et al. (1,6)	Novel deep learning model that includes attention, hyper-column, and residual blocks
Rehman et al. (2,7)	Brain tumor extraction using 3D-CNN and use of pre-trained CNN for feature extraction
Saba et al. (3,8)	Concatenation of hand-crafted and VGG 19 features for tumor classification
Irsheidat et al. (4,9)	CNN-based brain tumor detection
Choudhury et al. (5,10)	Feature extraction by CNN and use of fully connected layer for classification
Sharif et al. (6,11)	Use of extreme learning model that is fed textural features for classification
Amin et al. (7,12)	Two-layer sparse autoencoder used for tumor detection
Amin et al. (8,13)	Deep LSTM model with four layers used for classification
Kalaiselvi et al. (9,14)	Five-layer CNN with stopping criteria and batch normalization used for classification
Rai et al. (10,15)	Less-layered less complex model based on U-net for tumor detection
Khan et al. (11,16)	CNN-based tumor classification with data augmentation and image processing techniques
Amin et al. (12,17)	Fusion of spatial and textural information among MRI modalities to extract tumor region, which is fed to CNN for classification
Kalaiselvi et al. (13,18)	Among various CNN models, best-performing model on Brats13 and WBA selected
Rajinikanth et al. (14,19)	Use of various deep learning architectures like VGG16, pre-trained models with SVM, etc
Ayadi et al. (15,20)	CAD system based on deep learning developed and evaluated on three different datasets

different CNN-based architectures such as 3D CNN-based model (7), VGG19 (8), deep LSTM (Long Short-Term Memory) model (13), five-layer CNN (14), U Net (15) etc. for the classification of brain tumor from brain MRI analysis. Most of these models have dense convolution layers with huge number of parameters. Increase in convolution layers demands high computation speed and increases the cost of the system. As the present work focuses on the state-of-the-art deep learning architectures, some of the recent works based on deep learning in the field of brain tumor analysis are summarized in Table 6.1.

6.3   DATASET DETAIL

Brain MRIs from two different datasets are used in this work. Three thousand (3,000) labeled MRI with 50% healthy and 50% diseased images are used to create the training and test dataset.

TABLE 6.2
Dataset Details

Dataset (Link)	Type of MRI	Number of Images	Type of Tumor	No. of Images
Brain tumor dataset (https://figshare.com/articles/ dataset/brain_tumor_dataset/1512427), Br35H (https://www.kaggle.com/ahmedhamada0/ brain-tumor-detection)	Diseased	1500	Meningioma Glioma Pituitary tumor	708 1,426 930
	Healthy	1500	NA	NA

Table 6.2 lists the datasets details from where MR images have been collected and used in this work. The diseased images available in this collection have MRI of three different types of brain tumors: meningioma, glioma, and pituitary tumor. It is evident that due to even distribution in the number of healthy and diseased images, there is a perfect balance although the tumor classification dataset suffers from class imbalance that needs to be addressed.

6.4 METHODOLOGY

Traditional CNNs need very high system requirements in terms of memory, storage, and processing capabilities. It is obvious that these CNNs with huge dataset prove to be very efficient. At the same time, there is a need for CNNs that will run in a computationally inexpensive environment and produce a satisfactory result. In this study, the concept of light-weight CNN is implemented using the concept of MobileNet V1 (21).

The complete process can be divided into two main phases. The presence of brain tumor is detected in the first phase, and in the second phase, classification of tumors takes place. For both segments, the concept of depth-wise separable convolution followed by point-wise convolution is applied. This type of convolution incurs much lesser computational cost while maintaining almost similar accuracy as with normal convolution.

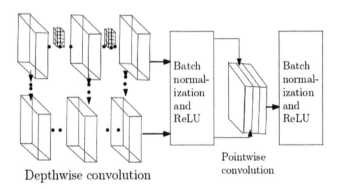

FIGURE 6.2 Convolution block (CB).

The proposed solution differs from MobileNetV1 in the following aspects:

- Lesser number of layers in the proposed architecture
- Lesser number of filters in the proposed architecture
- Smaller input image size
- Pre-processing with nonparametric nonuniform normalization retrospective correction function (N4BiasFieldCorrection) and data normalization

With the above modifications, the proposed solution needs relatively low-end system configurations to execute. The comparison of proposed solution along with MobileNet V1 and EfficientNet B0 (22) is discussed in Section 6.5.

6.4.1 DETECTION OF BRAIN TUMOR

This phase has utmost importance as this is the deciding factor for the presence of brain tumor in the MR scan. The dataset is well balanced between healthy images and MR scans with brain tumor. Using the concept of the depth-wise separable convolution block (CB) (as shown in Figure 6.2), the light-weight CNN is designed.

In this architecture, the input image size is taken as 100×100. This image is passed through a CB of 32 filters having size 3×3 first. A series of CB blocks having three blocks of 32 (all with stride 1), two blocks of 64 (one with stride 1 and another with stride 2), and two blocks of 128 (one with stride 1 and another with stride 2) filters have been applied. An average pooling block is used at the end for dimensionality reduction. A softmax activation function is used at the dense layer.

6.4.2 CLASSIFICATION OF BRAIN TUMOR

A similar light-weight CNN is used for identifying the type of tumor. Three types of brain tumors, namely, meningioma, glioma, and pituitary tumor MR scans, have been used for training and testing the setup. Since the difficulty level of this classification is more compared to the healthy and diseased brain MRI classification, more layers are added to the CNN-based model.

In this architecture, the input size is taken as 100×100. This image is passed through a CB of 32 filters having size 3×3. A series of CB blocks having three blocks of 32 (all with stride 1), three blocks of 64 (all with stride 1), two blocks of 128 (one with stride 1 and another with stride 2), and blocks of 256 (one with stride 1 and another with stride 2) filters have been applied. An average pooling block is used at the end for dimensionality reduction. A softmax activation function is used at the dense layer.

6.5 RESULTS AND DISCUSSIONS

The proposed architecture is trained with 80% images of the dataset. Figure 6.3 shows the confusion matrix generated using sample test dataset for the classification of healthy and diseased brain MRI.

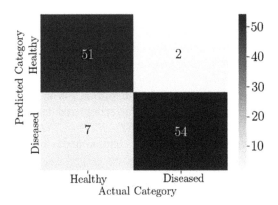

FIGURE 6.3 Confusion matrix of the classification of diseased and healthy MR scans (test set).

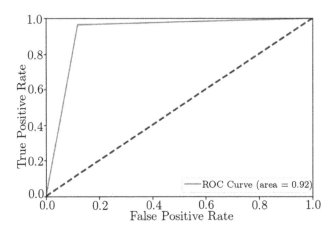

FIGURE 6.4 ROC curve of the classification of diseased and healthy MR scans.

The confusion matrix shows a considerable good result with very less incorrect classifications. The ROC curve for diseased and healthy brain MRI classification is shown in Figure 6.4. The AUC value of the proposed approach attains 0.92.

The diseased MRIs (80%) are used to train the model in the second phase to classify brain tumors in three categories: meningioma, glioma, and pituitary tumor.

Figure 6.5 shows the confusion matrix generated during brain tumor classification. The confusion matrix shows a very good result except for meningioma type of tumor. The micro-average AUC value of the approach is 0.96. In Figure 6.6, the class 0 ROC curve belongs to meningioma, class 1 ROC curve points to glioma, and ROC curve of pituitary tumor is represented by class 2.

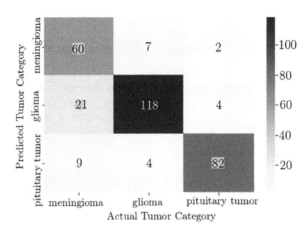

FIGURE 6.5   Confusion matrix of the classification of brain tumor types (test set).

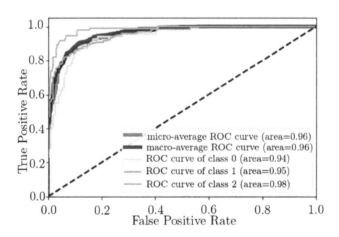

FIGURE 6.6   ROC curve of the classification of brain tumor types.

6.5.1 COMPARISON OF THE PROPOSED APPROACH WITH OTHER LIGHT-WEIGHT MODELS

Both the proposed models (used in phase 1 and phase 2, respectively) are similar in architecture. As the second one is much heavier than the first one, the comparison is shown with the second architecture with other light-weight CNN models. The main focus of this study is to design a minimal light-weight CNN that gives a satisfactory result in brain tumor detection and classification. The proposed solution achieves this goal with considerably smaller resource (Table 6.3).

TABLE 6.3

Comparison of the Proposed Approach with Other Light-Weight Models

Name of the Architecture	Total Number of Parameters (Million)	Number of Layers	Input Image Size
Proposed solution	0.3	12	100×100
MobileNet V1	4.2	28	224×244
EfficientNet B0	5.3	237	224×224

6.6   CONCLUSION

The main objective of this study is to design a low-cost CNN that can serve the purpose of brain tumor diagnosis from MR scan followed by the classification of the tumor. The proposed light-weight CNN does this job satisfactorily with an AUC value of 0.92 for tumor detection and an AUC value of 0.96 for tumor classification. Trained and tested with standard datasets of both the CNNs execute accurately. This study can further be extended to detect other brain-related diseases such as multiple sclerosis, brain hemorrhage, etc. Another area of further exploration can be the segmentation of brain MR scans using light-weight CNN.

REFERENCES

1. Primary brain tumours in adults. Lapointe, S., Perry, A., & Butowski, N. A. 2018, *The Lancet*.
2. Challenges to curing primary brain tumours. Aldape, K., Brindle, K. M., Chesler, L., Chopra, R., Gajjar, A., Gilbert, M. R., ... Gilbertson, R. J. 2019, *Nature Reviews Clinical Oncology*.
3. Brain tumor imaging. Brindle, K. M., Izquierdo-García, J. L., Lewis, D. Y., Mair, R. J., & Wright, A. J. 2017, *Journal of Clinical Oncology*.
4. Brain tumors. Herholz, K., Langen, K. J., Schiepers, C., & Mountz, J. M. 2012, *Seminars in Nuclear Medicine*.
5. Magnetic resonance imaging of meningiomas: a pictorial review. Watts, J., Box, G., Galvin, A., Brotchie, P., Trost, N., & Sutherland, T. 2014, *Insights into Imaging*.
6. BrainMRNet: Brain tumor detection using magnetic resonance images with a novel convolutional neural network model. Toğaçar, M., Ergen, B., & Cömert, Z. 2020, *Medical hypotheses*.
7. Microscopic brain tumor detection and classification using 3D CNN and feature selection architecture. Rehman, A., Khan, M. A., Saba, T., Mehmood, Z., Tariq, U., & Ayesha, N. 2021, *Microscopy Research and Technique*.
8. Brain tumor detection using fusion of hand crafted and deep learning features. Saba, T., Mohamed, A. S., El-Affendi, M., Amin, J., & Sharif, M. 2020, *Cognitive Systems Research*.
9. Brain tumor detection using artificial convolutional neural networks. Irsheidat, S., & Duwairi, R. 2020, *11th International Conference on Information and Communication Systems (ICICS)*. IEEE.
10. Brain tumor detection and classification using convolutional neural network and deep neural network. Choudhury, C. L., Mahanty, C., Kumar, R., & Mishra, B. K. 2020, *International Conference on Computer Science, Engineering and Application*.

11. Brain tumor detection based on extreme learning. Sharif, M., Amin, J., Raza, M., Anjum, M. A., Afzal, H., & Shad, S. A. 2020, *Neural Computing and Applications.*
12. Brain tumor detection by using stacked autoencoders in deep learning. Amin, J., Sharif, M., Gul, N., Raza, M., Anjum, M. A., Nisar, M. W., & Bukhari, S. A. C. 2020, *Journal of Medical Systems.*
13. Brain tumor detection: a long short-term memory (LSTM)-based learning model. Amin, J., Sharif, M., Raza, M., Saba, T., Sial, R., & Shad, S. A. 2020, *Neural Computing and Applications.*
14. Development of automatic glioma brain tumor detection system using deep convolutional neural networks. Kalaiselvi, T., Padmapriya, T., Sriramakrishnan, P., & Priyadharshini, V. 2020, *International Journal of Imaging Systems and Technology.*
15. 2D MRI image analysis and brain tumor detection using deep learning CNN model LeU-Net. Rai, H. M., & Chatterjee, K. 2021, *Multimedia Tools and Applications.*
16. Brain tumor classification in MRI image using convolutional neural network. Khan, H. A., Jue, W., Mushtaq, M., & Mushtaq, M. U. 2020, *Mathematical Biosciences and Engineering.*
17. Brain tumor classification based on DWT fusion of MRI sequences using convolutional neural network. Amin, J., Sharif, M., Gul, N., Yasmin, M., & Shad, S. A. 2020, *Pattern Recognition Letters.*
18. Deriving tumor detection models using convolutional neural networks from MRI of human brain scans. Kalaiselvi, T., Padmapriya, S. T., Sriramakrishnan, P., & Somasundaram, K. 2020, *International Journal of Information Technology.*
19. A customized VGG19 network with concatenation of deep and handcrafted features for brain tumor detection. Rajinikanth, V., Joseph Raj, A. N., Thanaraj, K. P., & Naik, G. R. 2020, *Applied Sciences.*
20. Deep CNN for brain tumor classification. Ayadi, W., Elhamzi, W., Charfi, I., & Atri, M. 2021, *Neural Processing Letters.*
21. Mobilenets: Efficient convolutional neural networks for mobile vision applications. Howard, A. G., Zhu, M., Chen, B., Kalenichenko, D., Wang, W., Weyand, T., ... & Adam, H. 2017, *arXiv preprint arXiv:1704.04861.*
22. Efficientnet: Rethinking model scaling for convolutional neural networks. Tan, M., & Le, Q. 2019, *International Conference on Machine Learning.*

7 Parallel Dense Skip-Connected CNN Approach for Brain Tumor Classification

*G. Yogeswararao, V. Naresh, R. Malmathanraj,
P. Palanisamy, and Karthik Balasubramanian*
National Institute of Technology

CONTENTS

7.1 INTRODUCTION

One of the most complicated organs in the human body is the brain. It is made up of millions of nerves, and each of these nerves communicates with multiple connections called synapses. The brain has multiple lobes – frontal, parietal, temporal, and occipital. Each of these lobes has different functions. The brain tumor is one of the most lethal forms of disease, due to the delicate and complex nature of the brain, thus increasing the difficulty in removing them. Tumors can exert extra pressure on the brain, thereby causing problems for the human body. There are multiple forms of brain tumor, but majority of them can be classified into "benign" or "malignant". Each of these types of tumors requires different kinds of treatment, and hence, it is very important to identify the correct nature of the tumor. As manually analyzing brain images for the presence of tumors is difficult and prohibitively time-consuming, the automated classification algorithms are required to identify brain tumors.

DOI: 10.1201/9781003277002-7

The deep learning approach plays a major role in image segmentation and classification since the architectures automatically learn image features from low to high level. The brain images are pre-processed using wavelet transform with different thresholds, and then, Support Vector Machine (SVM) has been used as a classifier to classify the tumor [1]. The brain tumor images that have been pre-processed using morphological operations and pixel subtraction followed by Otsus segmentation features are classified using probabilistic approach called naïve Bayes classifier [2]. The Convolutional Neural Network (CNN)-based tumor features followed by SVM classifier have been used to classify the brain tumor [3]. The brain tumor images have been classified using VGG16, ResNet, Inception, and ImageNet pre-trained transfer learning models [4]. Glioma and meningioma are potential life-threatening forms of brain tumors that can kill a patient if not diagnosed early enough [5]. The treatment options for brain tumors vary depending on the tumor location as well as size of the tumor and form. Because surgery has no harmful consequences on the brain, it is presently the most common therapy for brain tumors [6]. Rather than using typical feature extraction approaches, the ensemble of deep features has been fed to different machine learning (ML) classifiers to predict the tumors [7]. The MRI-based brain tumor has been classified using an ensemble of pre-trained deep learning features followed by ML classifiers [8].

This chapter focuses on the classification methods of these tumors, especially with the help of image processing and deep learning techniques. MRI images of the tumor from the dataset are downsized, for easier computation, and then classified using CNN.

The remains of this chapter are written further as follows: The proposed parallel dense skip-connected architecture is explained with block diagram in Section 7.2. The average classification accuracy and confusion matrix-based statistical performance measurements are reported in Section 7.3. Finally, Section 7.4 concludes this chapter.

7.2   PARALLEL DENSE SKIP-CONNECTED CNN (PDSCNN)

The proposed PDSCNN architecture consists of 45 layers with 4.09M parameters. The PDSCNN architecture comprises an input layer and K1n64 convolution layer followed by seven distinct parallel-shared input skip connection (DPSISC) blocks, 940 flattened layer along with two 256 fully connected layers and output layer. The block diagram of PDSCNN architecture is shown in Figure 7.1.

In order to design an effective and stable architecture, the skip connections have been used in recent times [9]. The internal blocks of parallel-shared input skip connection block (PSISC) and DPSISC are shown in Figure 7.2a and b.

Figure 7.2a shows the PSISC. The PSISC block consists of 64 channeled three 1×1 and three 3×3 convolution layers in the arranged manner, and also the

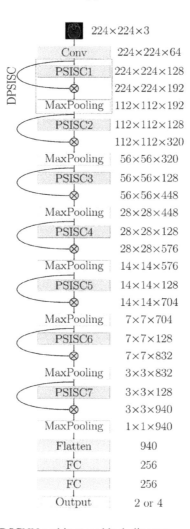

FIGURE 7.1 Proposed PDSCNN architecture block diagram.

input is dense skip to all six convolution layers. The PSISC block is always giving 128-channel output and maintaining the same input height and width. Figure 7.2b shows DPSISC block. The DPSISC consists of PSISC block with input skip connection followed by max-pooling. The max-pooling with pool size 2 is used in DPSISC block.

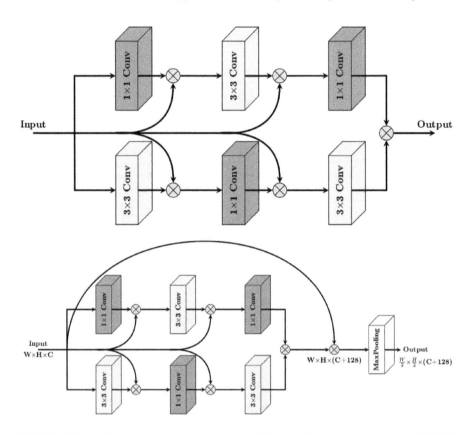

FIGURE 7.2 (a) Pictorial representation of parallel shared input skip connection (PSISC) block. (b) Pictural representation of distinct parallel shared input skip connection (DPSISC) block.

7.3 RESULTS AND DISCUSSION

7.3.1 NETWORK TRAINING PARAMETERS

In the present research work, the simulation results are conducted on a desktop computer equipped with Intel(R) Core (TM) i5–6500 CPU @ 3.20 GHz 3.19 GHz processor, 64-bit Operating System, 16.0 GB installed memory (RAM), and x64-based processor with Python 3.7 Jupyter notebook software. The input filter size for the architectures is $256 \times 256 \times 3$; the number of training epochs is set to 100; for both small 2C and large 2C datasets, the batch size is 16; and the learning rate is 0.001; Adam optimizer with $\beta_1 = 0.9$ and $\beta_2 = 0.999$ and Xavier kernel initializer are used.

7.3.2 BRAIN TUMOR MRI DATASET

In this chapter, we conducted a series of experiments on two publicly available brain MRI datasets for brain tumor classification. The brain MR image datasets are

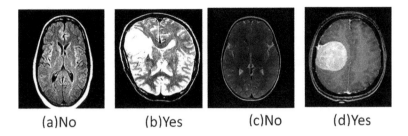

(a)No   (b)Yes   (c)No   (d)Yes

FIGURE 7.3 Samples of brain tumor MRI images (a) and (b) are large dataset, (c) and (d) are small dataset.

collected from the Kaggle database [10], and they have been given the names small 2C and large 2C. The small 2C dataset has 253 samples, with 155 of them containing cancers and the remaining 98 samples being tumor free. The large 2C database has 3,000 samples, 1,500 of which have tumors and 1,500 of which are tumor free. The samples of MRI brain images of small 2C and large 2C datasets are shown in Figure 7.3.

7.3.3 Tumor Identification Accuracies

In order to apprise the proposed PDSCNN architecture performances, in this chapter we conducted an experiment on two brain tumor datasets called small 2C and large 2C. The tumor identification accuracies of small 2C and large 2C are analyzed and compared with respect to the transfer learning and ensemble transfer learning networks. The training accuracy and loss curves of the proposed PDSCNN architecture are shown in Figure 7.4a and b, respectively.

The bar chart in Figure 7.5 shows the brain tumor identification accuracy of both small and large 2C tumor datasets.

From Figure 7.5a and b, we can see that the proposed PDSCNN architecture achieves higher tumor identification accuracy in both tumor datasets as compared to the existing networks. The tumor identification accuracy achieved 100% and 98.33% for the small 2C dataset and the large 2C datasets, respectively.

7.3.4 Confusion Matrices

The proposed PDSCNN architecture performances are evaluated with respect to confusion matrices. Figures 7.6 and 7.7 show the confusion matrices of both small 2C and large 2C datasets with respect to the proposed architecture. By using the confusion matrix, the statistical performance measurements, namely, accuracy, specificity, sensitivity, precession, and F-score, are calculated. Equations (7.1–7.5) are used to calculate the accuracy, specificity, sensitivity, precession, and F-score values.

$$K \in N^{H \times W \times R}, \quad K = \{K_1, K_2, ..., K_R\}, \tag{7.1}$$

$$K_i \in R^{H \times W} \tag{7.2}$$

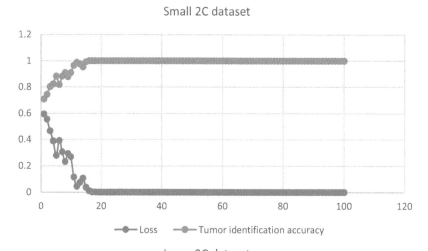

FIGURE 7.4 (a) Training accuracy and loss curves of small 2C tumor dataset with respect to the proposed architecture. (b) Training accuracy and loss curves of large 2C tumor dataset with respect to the proposed architecture.

$$\text{Dist}\,(m,\,n) = \frac{\sqrt[2]{\left(O_{cm} - O_{cn}\right)^2 + \left(P_{cm} - P_{cn}\right)^2}}{\text{No. of rows in the image}} \tag{7.3}$$

$$\text{DICE}\left(N_a,\,N_p\right) = 2 * \frac{N_a \cdot N_p}{N_a + N_p} \tag{7.4}$$

$$\text{Sensitivity} = \frac{\left(N_a \cdot N_p\right)}{\left(N_p\right)} \tag{7.5}$$

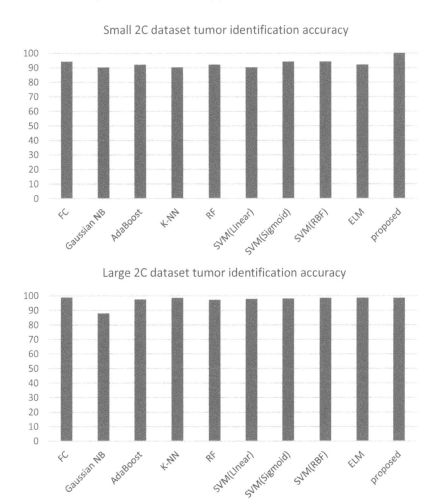

FIGURE 7.5 (a) Brain tumor identification accuracy of small 2C tumor dataset. (b) Brain tumor identification accuracy of large 2C tumor dataset.

where *TP* is true positive, *TN* is true negative, *FP* is false positive, and *FN* is false negative.

From the inference of Table 7.1, the statistical measurements scores are unity for small 2C dataset by using the proposed PDSCNN architecture. Accuracy of 98.33%, sensitivity of 97.93%, specificity of 98.70%, precession of 98.61%, and F-score of 98.20% are achieved for large 2C dataset by using the proposed PDSCNN architecture.

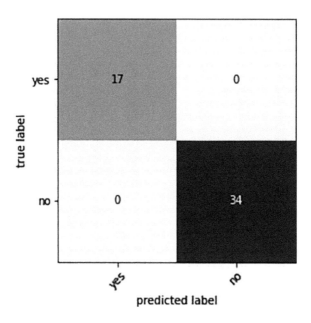

FIGURE 7.6 Confusion matrix of small 2C dataset using proposed PDSCNN architecture.

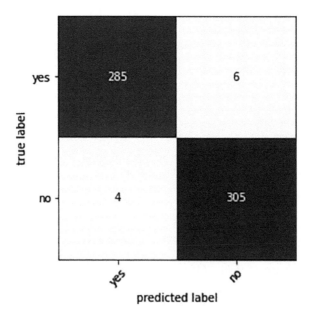

FIGURE 7.7 Confusion matrix of large 2C dataset using proposed PDSCNN architecture.

TABLE 7.1
Statistical Measurement Scores of Small 2C and Large 2C Datasets Using the Proposed PDSCNN Architecture

Statistical Measurements	Datasets	
	Small 2C	Large 2C
Accuracy	1.0000	0.9833
Sensitivity	1.0000	0.9793
Specificity	1.0000	0.9870
Precession	1.0000	0.9861
F-score	1.0000	0.9826

7.4 CONCLUSION

The normal and abnormal tumors of the brain are analyzed and classified in this chapter by using deep learning approach. The proposed deep learning approach called parallel dense skip-connected CNN architecture is used effectively to classify the brain tumors. The proposed PDSCNN architecture consists of 43 layers with parallel convolution and skip connections. The proposed architecture is tested with Kaggle dataset brain tumor small 2C and large 2C datasets. The brain tumor classification accuracy results of the PDSCNN architecture are superior as compared to conventional ML and the start-of-the-art deep learning networks. The skip connections and parallel convolution operation helps to reduce the redundant features, gradient vanishing problem, and number of parameters of the proposed architecture. This work can be further extended in the following direction: first, image segmentation can be used as pre-processing approach to identify the lesion part of the tumor to increase the classification accuracies. Second, fine-tune the proposed architecture to further increase the tumor identification accuracies with a smaller number of training parameters.

REFERENCES

1. M. Gurbină, M. Lascu and D. Lascu, "Tumor detection and classification of MRI brain image using different wavelet transforms and support vector machines." *2019 42nd International Conference on Telecommunications and Signal Processing (TSP)*, 2019, pp. 505–508, doi: 10.1109/TSP.2019.8769040.
2. H. T. Zaw, N. Maneerat and K. Y. Win, "Brain tumor detection based on Naïve Bayes classification." *2019 5th International Conference on Engineering, Applied Sciences and Technology (ICEAST)*, 2019, pp. 1–4, doi: 10.1109/ICEAST.2019.8802562.
3. S. K. Baranwal, K. Jaiswal, K. Vaibhav, A. Kumar and R. Srikantaswamy, "Performance analysis of brain tumour image classification using CNN and SVM." *2020 Second International Conference on Inventive Research in Computing Applications (ICIRCA)*, 2020, pp. 537–542, doi: 10.1109/ICIRCA48905.2020.9183023.

4. R. M. Prakash and R. S. S. Kumari, "Classification of MR brain images for detection of tumor with transfer learning from pre-trained CNN models." *2019 International Conference on Wireless Communications Signal Processing and Networking (WiSPNET)*, 2019, pp. 508–511, doi: 10.1109/WiSPNET45539.2019.9032811.

5. A.K. Anaraki, M. Ayati and F. Kazemi, "Magnetic resonance imaging-based brain tumor grades classification and grading via convolutional neural networks and genetic algorithms." *Biocybern. Biomed. Eng.* 2019, 39, 63–74.

6. R. Mehrotra, M.A. Ansari, R. Agrawal and R.S. Anand, "A transfer learning approach for AI-based classification of brain tumors." *Mach. Learn. Appl.* 2020, 2, 10–19.

7. Z. Ullah, M.U. Farooq, S.H. Lee and D. An, "A hybrid image enhancement based brain MRI images classification technique." *Med. Hypotheses* 2020, 143, 109922.

8. J. Kang, Z. Ullah and J. Gwak, "MRI-based brain tumor classification using ensemble of deep features and machine learning classifiers." *Sensors* 2021, 21, 2222, doi: 10.3390/s21062222.

9. Z. Wang et al., "Multi-memory convolutional neural network for video super-resolution." *IEEE Trans. Image Process.* 2019, 28, 5, 2530–2544, doi: 10.1109/TIP.2018.2887017.

10. N. Chakrabarty, "Brain MRI images for brain tumor detection dataset." Available online: https://www.kaggle.com/navoneel/brain-mri-images-for-brain-tumor-detection (accessed on 1 August 2020).

8 Liver Tumor Segmentation Using Deep Learning Neural Networks

Sumedha Vadlamani, Charit Gupta Paluri,
Jaydev Jangiti, and Sumit Kumar Jindal
Vellore Institute of Technology

CONTENTS

8.1 INTRODUCTION

According to Global Cancer Statistics [1], liver cancer has been a major cause of high death rate in most nations and is the fifth most prevalent malignancy among all cancers. For effective diagnosis and therapy, a reliable and accurate tumor segmentation method is required. Primary and secondary liver cancers are the two forms of

DOI: 10.1201/9781003277002-8

cancer seen in the liver. Malignant hepatoma [2] is one of the most diagnosed forms of cancer, which is equivalent for 80% of all occurrences. It is the third leading cause of cancer death, killing around 700,000 individuals each year throughout the world. Cirrhosis [3] caused by alcohol consumption, and the hepatitis B and C viruses are all substantial risk factors for primary liver cancer.

Liver treatment choices necessitate a precise diagnosis in order to analyze the size and location of tumors and make the optimal therapeutic treatment selection. The most often used imaging approach for liver cancer diagnosis is computed tomography (CT) scans, which provide a detailed anatomical information about the human body's abdominal organs [4]. A CT scan of the abdomen produces detailed cross-sectional pictures. The liver and its anti-tumorous portions are typically segmented from the rest of the CT image content, requiring extensive processing of these abdominal CT scan images. The intensity of the tumor and other contiguous tissues in the CT images was similar, making identification of the cancer regions in the scans challenging. As a result, in order to distinguish malignant tissue, these images must be analyzed and improved [5].

The existence of liver cancer can be detected in a CT scan by changes in pixel intensity when compared to the healthy liver in the surrounding area [6]. Manual segmentation of CT scan images in a clinical setting is challenging and time-consuming due to a variety of factors, including the liver organ's high flexibility in terms of form and volume between multiple patients. The fundamental characteristics of CT images include low contrast and fuzzy borders, making liver delineation challenging. Tumor segmentation is more complicated due to the minor observable variations between tumor and healthy tissues, especially around their boundaries [7]. Accurate and quick liver and tumor segmentation would aid liver surgery planning therapies by providing for subsequent estimate of tumor load and texture-based information. Furthermore, having a standardized and automated segmentation method would improve the accuracy of therapeutic response classification.

Machine learning (ML) and Artificial Intelligence (AI) have revolutionized the healthcare industry. With breakthrough innovations and technical solutions, the speed of prognosis of diseases and cures has been remarkable and faster than ever before. Artificial neural networks (ANNs), often known as neural networks, are a type of ML that form the foundation of deep learning approaches. Deep learning therefore is a subset of ML methods that uses representation learning and artificial neural networks [8]. Supervised, semi-supervised, and unsupervised learning are all possible options to provide AI-based solutions.

Deep Convolutional Neural Network (CNN) has recently gotten a lot of interest for image pattern recognition and abnormality detection in medical imaging [9]. A CNN is a type of model design for deep learning algorithms that is primarily utilized for image classification and pixel data analysis applications. In medical scans, image segmentation methods are critical for detecting aberrant growth or malformed structures. The challenge of automated monitoring in diverse medical remote sensing applications relies heavily on scene interpretation of high-resolution aerial scans [10]. This is a difficult job because of the substantial within-class and little between-class variation in pixel values of items of interest. Deep CNN has been popular in remote sensing applications in recent years, demonstrating the state-of-the-art performance for object categorization at the pixel level [7]. Deep neural networks (DNNs) can train discriminative features autonomously, unlike standard methods that rely on hand-crafted features. Each level of the input data may be represented by the learnt features that include hierarchical information [11].

A neural network is one of the many approaches used for ML that has proven great success in image segmentation analysis and is composed of several layers. Images are processed using numerous types of filters in convolutional layers, which are known to be useful for pattern recognition [12]. Various segmentation approaches have been developed over the last 40 years, ranging from MATLAB picture segmentation and classic computer vision algorithms to cutting-edge deep learning methods. Image segmentation has come a long way, especially since the introduction of DNNs [13]. Unlike traditional machine learning methods, which need visual attributes to be retrieved prior to learning, convolutional layers enable the picture to be utilized throughout the learning process. Most image classification models employ an encoding-decoding network, as opposed to classifiers, which use a single encoder network. The encoder creates a hidden spatial representation of the data, which is used by the decoder to create segment maps, which reveal where each item in the picture is located [14]. As a result, deep learning using CNNs allows all of the data that is present in the pictures to be exploited, whereas standard ML limits this based on feature parameters. As a result, this approach has the ability to identify liver tumors without relying on the radiologist's experience.

This chapter will focus on utilizing a neural model with neural networks that can predict the presence of abnormal tumors present in the CT scans of liver. The liver lesions in contrast-enhanced abdominal CT images are segmented using automatic segmentation techniques. Hyper-parameters and epoch scores are utilized to determine the model's accuracy. Finally, the CT scans are used to train the proposed model to segment multiple liver tumors. This will serve as the foundation for developing an automated liver tumor diagnosis system for clinicians with increased accuracy, reducing the risk of manual mistakes during diagnosis.

8.2 PRIOR WORK

There has been a lot of work done on tumor classification, and many different forms of study for feature extraction and individual segmentation of tumors have been successfully implemented. Although individual disease studies and analyses are beneficial, a diagnostic and prognostic tool for multiple liver tumor detection is needed.

Yodit Abebe Ayalew and colleagues [15] employed a modified U-Net model that used a deep learning technique to distinguish the liver and tumor from abdominal CT scan pictures, which would cut down on the amount of labor and time needed to diagnose liver cancer. For the segmentation of liver, and segmentation of tumor using CT scan imaging of the abdomen, the approach received Dice scores of 0.96, 0.74, and 0.63, respectively. The model, on the contrary, failed to segment tiny and irregular tumors.

A FCN network with a localized area thresholding function is used in the suggested method by Omar Ibrahim Alirr [16]. The framework commences by utilizing a CT scan to segment the liver organ, then continues on to segmenting cancers inside the liver environment. The FCN is developed to evaluate rough tumor classification, while the localized area-based level tries to improve the anticipated segmentation in order to find the proper ultimate segmentation. The one-step model technique, on the other hand, was sensitive to misclassification, particularly when it came to tumor segmentation.

A unique convolution neural network approach was proposed by Shunyao Luan and company [17], in which an adaptive attention-based neural network (S-Net) is used for the segmentation of malignant tumors from CT scans from beginning to end, which is a novel convolution neural network technique. Researchers were using the doctors' manual outlines of a hospital data set to assess the network design. The results of the study indicated that this strategy increased tumor identification in CT images and might be used to aid doctors in diagnostic and treatment procedures. However, the model was quite slow compared to other works, which made it obsolete for real-time implementation.

A novel hybrid segmentation framework proposed by R.V. Manjunath and Karibasappa Kwadiki [18] approached to solve the issue by creating a binary segmented picture. To segment the liver and the tumors, the algorithm employed 2D modified ResUNet designs. These structures were created to partition the abdomen. When it came to liver extraction and tumor segmentation, the modified ResUNet beat other designs with a high classification score. The ResUNet model was adjusted in this study to allow for resolution automated liver and tumor segmentation using CT images.

A 3-D dual path multi-scale CNN (TDPCNN) was constructed by Lu Meng, Yaoyu Tian, and Sihang Bu [19]. A dual path was employed in the network to maximize segmentation performance and computational resource requirements, and the feature maps from both pathways were fused at the conclusion of the paths. Researchers used conditional random fields (CRF) to minimize the inaccurate segmentation areas in the results, which improved the accuracy of the segmentation findings. According to the results of the studies, the recommended technique worked well in both liver and liver tumor identification.

On a plain CT scan, Liping Liu and colleagues [20] demonstrated the use of K-means clustering (KMC) technique, which indicated that the liver tumors have low density. In the arterial phase of the CT scan, the study was unusual in that it employed the recommended approach to create mild enhancement, and in the portal venous phase (PVP), there is a low-density filling defect in the affected blood vessel. The CT scan was found to be more responsive to liver metastasis than to hepatocellular carcinoma, and the KMC algorithm's segmentation impact was found to be superior to that of standard methods.

Lu Meng and team [21] developed a two-stage liver and tumor segmentation approach wherein the network segments the liver region and utilizes the location information of shallow features to improve liver identification. A CNN model was built to consistently detect liver tumors based on the liver segmentation discoveries using the 2D image characteristics and 3D spatial information of the CT image segments during the tumor segmentation stage. The suggested algorithm's segmentation outputs generally possess one of the highest Dice score coefficients.

Another popular model of semantic segmentation is called SegNet, which was employed by numerous works. One such proposed model was by Sultan Almotairi and colleagues [22] who devised a modified SegNet model. The methodology for conceptual resolution categorization road scenes was adopted and adapted to suit hepatic CT classification and segmentation. The architecture of the deep convolving encoding-decoding is the hierarchical correspondence of encoder-decoder layers. The scheme was evaluated on a dataset consisting of liver CT images during the training phase, and tumor accuracy of up to 99.9% was achieved.

Nadja Gruber and her colleagues [23] examined a deep learning technique for segmenting the CT scans of the liver and lesions. The researchers suggested a network design that combines two hierarchical FCN with a combined minimization technique. First sub-network is in charge of segregating the liver, whereas the second layer is responsible for segmenting the actual tumor within the liver. Each pixel in the image is assigned to distinct classes as either liver or tissue and tumor, with a certain probability. The one-step network technique is efficient, but it is prone to errors, especially when it comes to tumor segmentation. In terms of several accuracy measurements, the layered technique outperforms the one-step network substantially.

The work of Lei Chen et al. [24] devised a cascaded adversarial training method for segmenting liver tumors from abdominal CT data. For liver tumor segmentation, a cascaded structure was employed, in which two protocols were used consecutively to segment the liver (MPNet) and liver tumor (ADCN). The deployed networks used a multi-plane convolution method to balance computation memory usage and receptive field. The results of the testing demonstrated that the recommended approach outperforms the competition, proving that an adversarial training-based technique on the liver tumor segmentation issue might produce more accurate and effective results.

The amount of research on liver and liver tumor segmentation has doubled in the previous decade. The majority of existing semi-automated liver and tumor segmentation techniques used traditional ML methodologies. In the development of studies, DNNs have been proven to perform better in segmenting medical images. A hybrid version of U-Net with the ResNet34 encoder is used in our suggested approach. ResNet34 is a CNN with 34 layers, exclusively used for image classification [25]. Modeled data is iterated multiple times to attain well-trained dataset, which can provide an accurate segmentation of liver and its tumor. The liver lesions in contrast-enhanced abdominal CT images are segmented using automatic segmentation techniques.

Upon successful liver tumor segmentation, Dice score is computed, exclusively quantifies the purposed method's performance of liver tumor segmentation. These performance evaluation matrices provide accuracy and efficiency of liver tumor segmentation. The resulting model matches the previous efforts and proves to be a viable option, which provides consistent results.

8.3 PROPOSED SOLUTION AND ARCHITECTURE

8.3.1 DATA SET USED

The LiTS data set is a publicly available data set that includes about 130 abdomen CT scans taken from a variety of medical sources such as hospital databases around the world. The CT scans include radiologists' annotations of the liver and tumors as a reference. The challenge includes reference annotations for both the outlines and lesions of the liver. To make training and testing easier, 760 images with data augmentation and 120 images with a slice thickness of 0.7–5 mm were meticulously segregated as training CT scans and testing CT scans, respectively. The data set contains 908 lesions, comprising 63%, with an axial diameter ≥10 mm [26].

8.3.2 FastAI LIBRARY

FastAI is a DL library that allows experts' access to complex neural network methods for fast and easily generating highly accurate results in common DL domains, as well as fundamental methods that may be combined and enhanced to create novel techniques. It aims to achieve both targets without compromising on the usability, flexibility, or performance. FastAI approaches give a suitable visualization of a model's input, target, and outcomes automatically. It reads an input image, generates a target segmentation mask, and displays results using a color-coded overlay for the mask. For the work discussed in this chapter, FastAI library was used to process the data and do visualizations appropriately [27].

8.3.3 U-NET ARCHITECTURE

The U-Net model is a popular choice for image segmentation. The notion that the inputs are not only the feature map from the previous layer but also the relevant module, which is a key component of the U-Net model. This ensures that no spatial information is lost as a result of image compression. U-Net is a biomedical image segmentation method that can be processed with few training samples and produces highly accurate segmentations as seen in Figure 8.1 [11]. A dwindling path collects contextual data from the medical scans, whereas an increasing path adds data related to the location for each pixel and responds where they are located. The two routes are roughly symmetrical to one another, resulting in a U-shaped design. The architecture of this model was modified and improved for tumor segmentation by expansion of the depth of the structure and incorporation of more skipping links and dropout surfaces [28].

The U-Net architecture is depicted in this diagram (Figure 8.1) [29]. The U-Net design is seen in the diagram, which has a large patch size of 96×96 voxels. U-Net is an encoding-decoding network design with a dwindling path (encoder portion, left-hand side) that shrinks the input images' length and breadth and an expanding path (decoder part, right-hand side) that restores the input images' initial dimensionality. A multi-channel feature map is represented by each box. The key distinction between the half U-Net and the full U-Net is that the half U-Net has half the number of channels.

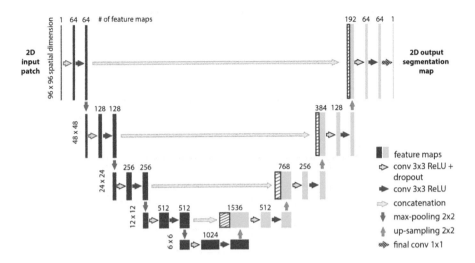

FIGURE 8.1   U-Net architecture diagram reference [29].

8.3.4 EMPLOYED DYNAMIC U-NET WITH RESNET34 ENCODER

ResNet34 is an intricate image segmentation model with 34 layers of CNNs. It is, however, unique from regular neural networks design due to the use of the residuals from each layer in the next connected layer and so on. ResNets come in a variety of sizes, depending on how big each of the model's layers is and how many layers there are. It comprises inserting shortcut connections into a simple network to transform it into its residual network counterpart convolutional networks with 33 filters. ResNets, on the other hand, have fewer filters and are less robust than VGGNets. The 34-layer ResNet reaches 3.6 billion FLOPs in comparison with 1.8 billion FLOPs for smaller 18-layer ResNets. This design follows two constraints, given the same output feature size of the feature map; each preceding layer has the equivalent filters; and the filters are doubled to ensure the same runtime complexity of each layer.

The identity shortcuts were used directly because the I/O dimensionalities were approximately equal. It was observed that with the increase in number of dimensionality, the first shortcut conducts identity mapping, while the other shortcut uses the projection shortcut to match dimensions [30].

As seen in Figure 8.2 [31], ResNet34 is utilized for the encoding or down-sampling part, a part of the U-Net as discussed earlier (left-hand side). Each block contains two interconnections from its input, and one passes through a sequence of convolution operations, batch-wise normalization, and linear functions, while the other skips those steps. Both connections' tensor outputs are combined together. When a ResBlock gives a tensor addition as an output, it can be transformed to tensor concatenation. The network grows increasingly dense with each cross/skip link. The ResBlock is subsequently upgraded to a DenseBlock, and the network is upgraded to a DenseNet. This enables the calculation to skip through larger portions of the

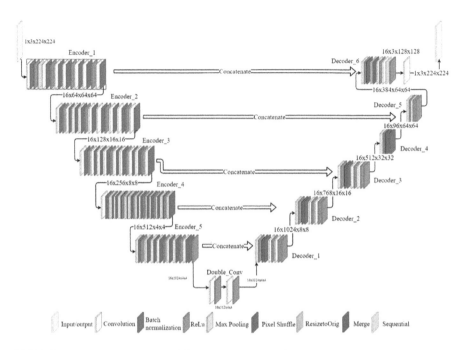

FIGURE 8.2   U-Net with ResNet34 encoder reference [31].

design. The FastAI U-Net learner module and an encoder architecture generate the decoding side of the U-Net layout instantly; in this instance, altering the encoder, this gets converted into a U-Net with cross-connections. We utilized ResNet34, a 34-layer architecture, in our model since FastAI researchers found it to be more effective, quicker to train than other ResNet designs, and requires less memory space [27].

8.3.5   DATA PREPROCESSING

Since images in the data set contained noise, they had to be processed before being used for evaluation and learning of the proposed model. LITS data is multi-dimensional and has no distinct mask for the liver part and the tumor.

Alternatively, masks are located in the data set's segmentation folder.

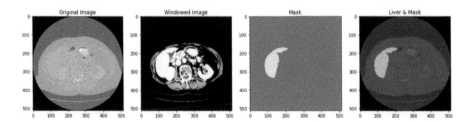

FIGURE 8.3   Data processing and masks constructions.

It was necessary to construct separate masks for the liver and the tumor. To minimize overfitting, address class unbalancing, and increase training accuracy, this data was prepared using Hounsfield windowing (to exclude irrelevant organs) [32], mask normalization, and augmentation to extend the training data set. After that, two-dimensional picture slices were recovered as shown in Figure 8.3. This is done to remove the liver pixels from a CT abdominal picture that generally includes other organs such as the stomach, kidney, spleen, and pancreas.

8.3.6 PROPOSED ARCHITECTURE AND METHODOLOGY

Figure 8.4 depicts a condensed pipeline of the proposed model as discussed for tumor segmentation process. The methodology deals with NII files, which consist of multi-dimensional neuroimaging data. First, Nii files are processed for the identification of liver segmentation and then for tumor segmentation. Upon successful identification, these Nii files are classified according to tumor volume as CT and segmentation as CT scan mask. Consequently, these are classified into sample_ct and sample_mask, as these variables undergo NumPy computation such as attaining minimum and maximum values of each sample. Fastai enables usages of Dicom Window, which enhances the CT scans by normalizing the images, by manipulating pixel values using computed lowest and highest values, making it facile for tumor segmentation. Using Windowed image, image tensors and CT scan tensor were generated using functions like freqhist_bins, hist_scaled, to_nchan, and save_jpg. Freqhist_bins function helps to split pixels values in the CT scan image; using the output of frenqhist_bins functions, generated tensors are scaled between the values of 0 and 1, thus producing output of scaled CT scan tensor. As the tensors are generated, to_nchan function is applied, resulting in multiple one-channel images. As these tensor images are generated, they are converted into JPG files. NII files are sliced into 2-dimensional file to generate JPG files, as these JPG files are used for U-Net training. The technique is based on the principle of U-Net model.

This technique is made up of two U-Net designs: one for the liver part and the other for the tumor. It is a fully convolutional encoder-decoder network with skip connections between encoder blocks and symmetric decoder blocks. For U-Net training, we utilized one-third of NII files, the corollary being that one-third of the NII files are sliced into 2-dimensional JPG files. Data Block API in FastAI is used for loading trained data set for data modeling. Data is later modeled using U-Net learning, which deploys RESNET34 architecture, and Data Block API of FastAI. Modeled data is iterated five times to attain well-trained data set, which can provide an accurate segmentation of liver and its tumor. We used a U-Net to segment the tumors in the liver but got poor results, so we sought to use the ResUNet to segment the tumors. Trained data is applied to the testing data set, to understand accuracy and efficiency of tumor segmentation in liver. Upon successful liver tumor segmentation, Dice score is computed, which exclusively quantifies the purposed method's performance of liver tumor segmentation. Moreover, Dice similarity coefficient (DSC) is calculated to understand the similarity between sample data sets used in liver segmentation. These performance evaluation matrices provide accuracy and efficiency of liver tumor segmentation.

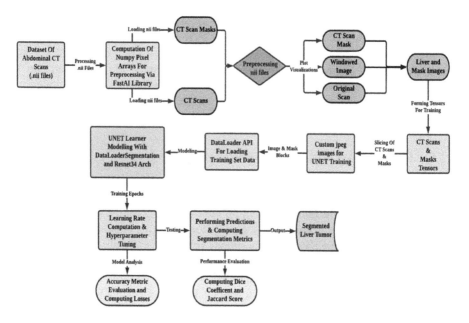

FIGURE 8.4   Proposed architecture.

Figure 8.5 illustrates the different contrast-enhanced CT scans. Most of the images are augmented, and the lesions are unclear in many of them. There is a large variation of shape, size, and location of the liver lesion. Each row pertains to the CT scan of an individual patient. The red region denotes the liver organ, whereas the pink highlights on the liver indicate the presence of lesions. The existence of liver tumor can be detected on a CT scan by a change in pixel intensity when compared to the healthy liver around it.

8.3.7   MODEL TRAINING METRICS

The dynamic U-Net Neural model with ResNet34 architecture was trained on the discussed data set at 100 epochs. An epoch is a unit of time that is employed to train a neural network for a single cycle utilizing all of the data sets. In an epoch, we use all of the data precisely once. A forward pass and a backward pass are combined to form a single pass. U-Net_learner module of FastAI was employed, and each epoch took on average 2 minutes of processing time. The metrics chosen were cross-entropy loss flat and foreground accuracies to pick the best model.

The dynamic U-Net model was trained for over about 100 epochs. Figure 8.6 depicts the loss and accuracy score of each model. Following the trend, more the number of epochs ran, a better model was found as the learning rate (LR) was adjusted with each epoch. The LR is an adjustable hyper-parameter that has a low positive value, and is used in the training phase of the neural networks. The LR, as seen in Figure 8.7, is a factor in controlling how fast the model adjusts to a specific guise. In our analysis, the most efficient LR for the model was around 0.7, which provided the most accurate results.

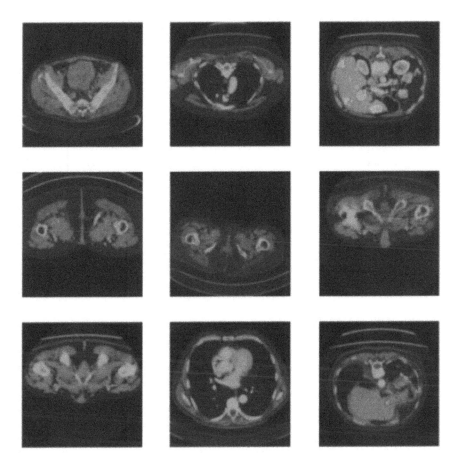

FIGURE 8.5 Segmentation of liver and lesions.

epoch	train_loss	valid_loss	foreground_acc	cust_foreground_acc	time
0	0.006865	0.007799	nan	0.997103	01:40
1	0.005162	0.005473	nan	0.998077	01:41
2	0.003919	0.003960	nan	0.998488	01:42
3	0.002844	0.003425	nan	0.998673	01:41
4	0.002714	0.003287	nan	0.998721	01:42

```
Better model found at epoch 0 with valid_loss value: 0.007798897568136454.
Better model found at epoch 1 with valid_loss value: 0.005472919438034296.
Better model found at epoch 2 with valid_loss value: 0.003959852270781994.
Better model found at epoch 3 with valid_loss value: 0.0034254654310643673.
Better model found at epoch 4 with valid_loss value: 0.003286961931735277.
```

FIGURE 8.6 Dynamic U-Net model training.

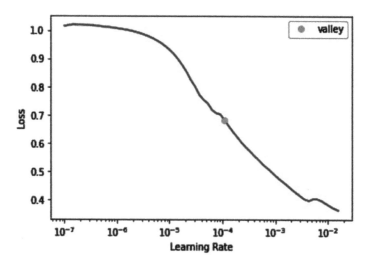

FIGURE 8.7 Dynamic U-Net learning rate.

8.4 MODEL ANALYSIS

As expected, the model was successful in segmenting the liver from the CT scans and the tumors were located on the basis of pixel densities as discussed in architecture section earlier. The crux of the working and computation of the segmented tumor is depicted in Figure 8.8. The input image is preprocessed, and slices are generated. The slices along with the masks are concatenated and are fed to the U-Net learner model. The liver is segmented, and following a second cycle, the tumors are identified within the segmented liver.

The predictions were interpreted with the help of FastAI's segmentation class that computes the predicative loss of the model. It is defined as a helper base class for exploring predictions from trained models. The most often used loss function for visual classification is a pixel-dependent cross-entropy loss. The class predictions are compared to the encoded target vector in this loss, which checks each pixel separately. Figure 8.9 shows few of the results predicted by the proposed model, and the average loss was observed to be around 0.05.

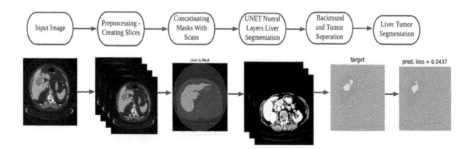

FIGURE 8.8 Model output for each phase.

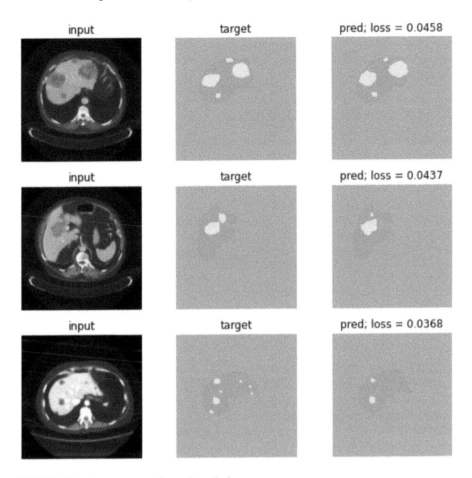

FIGURE 8.9   Loss computations of predictions.

8.5   MODEL SPECIFICATIONS AND RUNTIME ANALYSIS

Training and validation of the proposed model were performed on Google Collab and Kaggle notebooks whose hardware specifications are as shown in Table 8.1 [33].

TABLE 8.1
Hardware Specifications

Parameter	Kaggle	Google Collab
CPU family	Haswell	Haswell
CPU model name	Intel(R) Xeon(R)	Intel(R) Xeon(R)
No. CPU cores	4	2
GPU	Nvidia P100	Nvidia K80/T4
RAM & GPU memory	16GB	12GB

The model was trained on 16GB GPU with 13GB of RAM. The training of the model took about 45 minutes to be computed and was exported to perform the testing phase. Once the model was trained, the predictions were on par with prior work with accurate performance scores.

8.6   PERFORMANCE EVALUATION

Comparing images to assess segmentation results is an essential part of monitoring progress of the model. Different types of segmentation errors can be identified based on different performance characteristics in medical image segmentation. Depending on the data and the segmentation task, metrics should identify any or all of these issues. In medical imaging, the Dice score is extensively used metric for evaluating segmentation tasks. The (weighted) cross-entropy of CNNs trained for image segmentation tasks is frequently tuned. This results in a negative disparity between the learning optimization goal (loss) and the final target measure.

8.6.1   Dice Similarity Coefficient

$$Dice = \frac{2 \times TP}{(TP + FP) + (TP + FN)}$$

Equation 8.1. Dice similarity score.

The Dice score, also known as the Dice similarity coefficient (DSC), is a metric for determining how similar images are. The total size of the objects divided by the overlapping of the two segmentations equals the magnitude of the overlap. It may be represented as indicated in equation 8.1 using the same terminology as expressing accuracy by definition of true positive (TP), false positive (FP), and false negative (FN). The number of genuine positives is the number of positives identified by the model, the number of positives is the entire number of positives that can be found, and the number of false positives is the number of negative points classified as positive by the model. In a similar way to accuracy, the Dice score penalizes the algorithm for false positives. As a result, it resembles precision rather than accuracy.

DSC ranges between values 0 and 1. Whenever the tensor image and tensor mask have no similarities, DSC returns 0.0. While, on the other hand, if indeed the tensor image and tensor mask are identical, the DSC value is 1.0. In the proposed method, DSC value is 0.749, indicating that the image tensor set and mask tensor set overlap significantly. Dice score takes loss of data on a regional and global scale into consideration, which implies that DSC takes care of loss pixel data in between tensor image and mask in regional and global scales. DSC was achieved by combining the U-Net learner with the RESNET34 architecture, which indicates that per epoch iteration, training inputs are passed through 34 layers of CNN. Figure 8.10 depicts the Dice coefficient throughput the testing phase against the shift of pixels. From the plot, it is evident that as more number of samples are being tested, the better are the Dice score results. With the shift in pixels having a steady improvement of the score, it nears to become constant at around 400 shifts in pixels. From the analysis, it was found that the methodology attained an average overall Dice score of 0.749 in our proposed work.

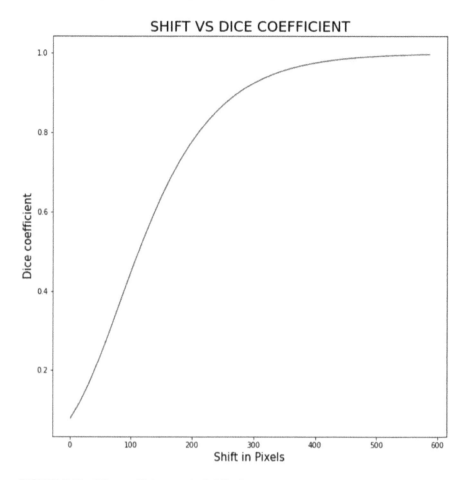

FIGURE 8.10   Dice coefficient vs pixel shift plot.

8.6.2 COMPARATIVE ANALYSIS

TABLE 8.2
Comparative Analysis

Prior Work	Model	Dice Similarity Coefficient
Reference [17]	Modified U-Net	0.630
Reference [18]	MPNet+ ACDN	0.685
Reference [21]	Adaptive attention CNN	0.755
Reference [22]	Semantic segmentation CNN	0.892
Reference [23]	3-D Dual path multi-scale CNN	0.689
Reference [24]	CNN + DCUNet	0.725
Proposed Work	**U-Net With ResNET34**	**0.749**

Table 8.2. comprises various deep learning algorithms developed for the segmentation of liver tumor; in each work, a variety of neutral network architectures are deployed. The DSC was used to evaluate each algorithm, with coefficient ranging from 0 to 1. Using this range of values as benchmark, the proposed method DSC resulted in the evaluated range. DSC indicates that overlap of the similarities in tensor image and tensor mask, which implies tumor segmentation, is achieved efficiently. As observed, all of the previous works had a DSC of above 0.6 with the best-performing model of semantic segmentation of CNN [22].

The proposed work proved to be on par with the prior work. Initially, the proposed model had an average DSC score of 0.4; however with hyper-parameter tuning and adjustment of the LRs, the DSC score increased to 0.749 on tumor segmentation and had an average focal loss of about 0.05 while performing predictions. Even though the model improved considerably in terms of tumor identification, it is unable to compute slices accurately. The proposed approach is involved in almost accurate identification of the liver in certain slices, but fails in others when the entire liver is not caught or where the liver is obscured by additional organs that overlap and appear to be divided into sections. When it comes to tumor segmentation, the algorithm has a hard time in segmenting small, irregularly shaped tumors. However, the model requires more fine tuning of hyper-parameters and hardware upgrades to improve the performance metric scores and runtime.

8.7 CONCLUSION

To summarize the proposed work, a neural network-based deep model to identify malignant tumors in liver CT scans was discussed. The U-Net architectural model was used as a baseline for tumor segmentation, and a hybrid version of U-Net with the ResNet34 encoder was employed and developed in this work. The model was trained and tested on the LiTS dataset, which is available publicly and includes about 130 contrast-enhanced abdomen CT scans from a variety of medical sites around the world. The liver lesions in abdominal CT images are segmented using automatic segmentation techniques and were preprocessed by the discussed windowing

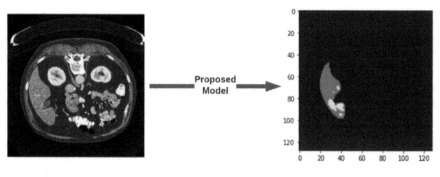

Input CT Scan   **Predicted Tumour**

FIGURE 8.11   Model input and predicted output.

methodology for the identification of the liver organ. The existence of a tumor is detected in the CT scans by observing the changes in the intensity of the pixels when compared to a healthy liver in the surrounding area. Hyper-parameters and epoch scores are utilized to determine the model's accuracy. Finally, the CT images are used to train the model to segment multiple liver tumors. The performance metrics revealed that the work had a DSC of 0.749, which performed better than most of the prior approaches discussed earlier. The results indicate that the proposed methodology can consistently segment liver tumors from abdominal CT scans as shown in Figure 8.11. However, the model fails when the entire liver is not captured or when the liver is obscured by organs that overlap, and moreover, the algorithm fails when dealing with minor and irregularly shaped tumors.

REFERENCES

1. Dhanasekaran R, et al. Hepatocellular carcinoma: Current trends in worldwide epidemiology, risk factors, diagnosis, and therapeutics. *Hepatic Medicine: Evidence and Research* 4: 19–37, 2012, https://doi.org/10.2147/HMER.S16316.
2. Ferlay J, Ervik M, Lam F, Colombet M, Mery L, Piñeros M, et al. *Global Cancer Observatory: Cancer Today*. Lyon: International Agency for Research on Cancer; 2020. Accessed February 2021, https://gco.iarc.fr/today.
3. Sung H, Ferlay J, Siegel RL, Laversanne M, Soerjomataram I, Jemal A, Bray F. Global cancer statistics 2020: GLOBOCAN estimates of incidence and mortality worldwide for 36 cancers in 185 countries. *CA: A Cancer Journal Clinicians* 71: 209–249, 2021, https://doi.org/10.3322/caac.21660.
4. Sherman M, Bruix J. Biopsy for liver cancer: How to balance research needs with evidence-based clinical practice. *Hepatology* 61: 433–436, 2015, https://doi.org/10.1002/hep.27563.
5. Jacques S, Christe B. Chapter 2 - Healthcare technology basics, Samantha Jacques, Barbara Christe (Eds.), *Introduction to Clinical Engineering*, Academic Press, 2020, pp. 21–50, ISBN 9780128181034, https://doi.org/10.1016/B978-0-12-818103-4.00002-8.
6. Oliva, MR, Saini S. Liver cancer imaging: Role of CT, MRI, US and PET. *Cancer Imaging: The Official Publication of the International Cancer Imaging Society* 4, 2004, https://doi.org/10.1102/1470-7330.2004.0011.
7. Hennedige T, Venkatesh SK. Imaging of hepatocellular carcinoma: Diagnosis, staging and treatment monitoring. *Cancer Imaging* 12(3):530–547, 2013, https://doi.org/10.1102/1470-7330.2012.0044.
8. Sarker IH. Deep learning: A comprehensive overview on techniques, taxonomy, applications and research directions. *SN Computer Science* 2: 420, 2021, https://doi.org/10.1007/s42979-021-00815-1.
9. Lundervold AS, Lundervold A. An overview of deep learning in medical imaging focusing on MRI, *Zeitschrift für Medizinische Physik* 29(2): 102–127, 2019, ISSN 0939-3889, https://doi.org/10.1016/j.zemedi.2018.11.002.
10. Sharma N, Aggarwal LM. Automated medical image segmentation techniques. *Journal of Medical Physics* 35(1): 3–14, 2010, https://doi.org/10.4103/0971-6203.58777.
11. Alzubaidi L, Zhang J, Humaidi AJ, et al. Review of deep learning: Concepts, CNN architectures, challenges, applications, future directions. *Journal of Big Data* 8: 53, 2021, https://doi.org/10.1186/s40537-021-00444-8.
12. Yamashita R, Nishio M, Do RKG, et al. Convolutional neural networks: An overview and application in radiology. *Insights Imaging* 9: 611–629, 2018, https://doi.org/10.1007/s13244-018-0639-9.

13. Abd A, Varol S. A review of image segmentation using MATLAB environment, 1–5, 2020, https://doi.org/10.1109/ISDFS49300.2020.9116191.
14. Rogowska, J. Chapter 5 - Overview and fundamentals of medical image segmentation, ISAAC N. Bankman (Ed.), *Handbook of Medical Image Processing and Analysis* (Second Edition), Academic Press, 2009, pp. 73–90, ISBN 9780123739049, https://doi.org/10.1016/B978-012373904-9.50013-1.
15. Alirr OI. Deep learning and level set approach for liver and tumor segmentation from CT scans. *Journal of Applied Clinical Medical Physics* 21(10): 200–209, 2020, https://doi.org/10.1002/acm2.13003.
16. Almotairi S, et al. Liver tumor segmentation in CT scans using modified segnet. *Sensors* 20(5): 1516, 2020, https://doi.org/10.3390/s20051516.
17. Ayalew YA, et al. Modified U-Net for liver cancer segmentation from computed tomography images with a new class balancing method. *BMC Biomedical Engineering* 3(1), 2021, https://doi.org/10.1186/s42490-021-00050-y.
18. Chen L, et al. Liver tumor segmentation in CT volumes using an adversarial densely connected network. *BMC Bioinformatics* 20(S16), 2019, https://doi.org/10.1186/s12859-019-3069-x.
19. Gruber N, et al. A joint deep learning approach for automated liver and tumor segmentation. *2019 13th International Conference on Sampling Theory and Applications (SampTA)*, 2019, https://doi.org/10.1109/sampta45681.2019.9030909.
20. Liu L, et al. CT image segmentation method of liver tumor based on artificial intelligence enabled medical imaging. *Mathematical Problems in Engineering* 2021: 1–8, 2021, https://doi.org/10.1155/2021/9919507.
21. Luan S, et al. Adaptive attention convolutional neural network for liver tumor segmentation. *Frontiers in Oncology* 11, 2021, https://doi.org/10.3389/fonc.2021.680807.
22. Manjunath RV, Kwadiki K. Automatic liver and tumor segmentation from CT images using deep learning algorithm. *Results in Control and Optimization* 6: 100087, 2021, https://doi.org/10.1016/j.rico.2021.100087.
23. Meng L, et al. Liver tumor segmentation based on 3D convolutional neural network with dual scale. *Journal of Applied Clinical Medical Physics* 21(1): 144–157, 2019, https://doi.org/10.1002/acm2.12784.
24. Meng L, et al. Two-stage liver and tumor segmentation algorithm based on convolutional neural network. *Diagnostics* 11(10): 1806, 2021, https://doi.org/10.3390/diagnostics11101806.
25. Wang W, Su C. Semi-supervised semantic segmentation network for surface crack detection. *Automation in Construction* 128, 2021, ISSN 0926-5805, https://doi.org/10.1016/j.autcon.2021.103786.
26. Bilic P, Christ P, Vorontsov E, Chlebus G, Chen H, Dou Q, Fu C-W, Han X, Heng P-A, Hesser J, Kadoury S, Konopczyński T, Le M, li F, Li X, Lipková J, Lowengrub J, Meine H, Moltz J, Wu J. The Liver Tumor Segmentation Benchmark (LiTS), arXiv:1901.04056, Computer Vision and Pattern Recognition (cs.CV), FD 2019/01/1, 2019
27. Howard J, Fastai GS. A layered API for deep learning. *Information* 11(2): 108, 2020, https://doi.org/10.3390/info11020108.
28. Alom Md Z, Hasan M, Yakopcic C, Taha T, Asari V. Recurrent residual convolutional neural network based on U-Net (R2U-Net) for medical image segmentation, arXiv:1802.06955, Computer Vision and Pattern Recognition (cs.CV), 2018.
29. Livne M, Rieger J, Aydin O, Taha AA, Akay E, Kossen T, Sobesky J, Kelleher J, Hildebrand K, Frey D, Madai V. A U-Net deep learning framework for high performance vessel segmentation in patients with cerebrovascular disease. *Frontiers in Neuroscience* 13, 2019, https://doi.org/10.3389/fnins.2019.00097.

30. Pashaei M, Kamangir H, Starek M, Tissot P. Review and evaluation of deep learning architectures for efficient land cover mapping with UAS hyper-spatial imagery: A case study over a Wetland. *Remote Sensing* 12: 959, 2020, https://doi.org/10.3390/rs12060959.

31. Howard J and others. *U-Net with Resnet: Fastai*, GitHub; 2018. https://github.com/fastai/fastai.

32. Alirr OI. Deep learning and level set approach for liver and tumor segmentation from CT scans. *The Journal of Applied Clinical Medical Physics* 21: 200–209, 2020, https://doi.org/10.1002/acm2.13003.

33. Kazemnejad A. How to do deep learning research with absolutely no GPUs' blog, 2021. Accessed January 29, 2022, https://kazemnejad.com/bloghow_to_do_deep_learning_research_with_absolutely_no_gpus_part_2/#summary.

9 Deep Learning Algorithms for Classification and Prediction of Acute Lymphoblastic Leukemia

I. Amrita and Snigdha Sen
Global Academy of Technology

CONTENTS

9.1 INTRODUCTION

Acute lymphoblastic leukemia (ALL) is also known as blood cancer, a type of cancer of blood and bone marrow in children, which is responsible for 25% of pediatric cancers. The symptoms of this disease are pain in the bone, bleeding gums, fever, high frequency of infections, severe or frequent bleeding in the nose, shortness of breath, weakness, or fatigue. This is examined by an expert by collecting the blood samples, and a decision based on classification is done. To automate the process of classification and detection of ALL cells, the use of deep learning is important. The image of normal cells and infected leukemia cells can be referred from the dataset link present in the dataset description section, and the images are separated by folders.

The disease can be fatal when untreated, and hence, proper detection and diagnosis along with timely treatment are essential. The survival rate in ALL is 68.8%. The risk of ALL is increased by a previous history of cancer treatments, exposure to radiation, and some genetic disorders. Artificial neural network (ANN) is caused by the

DOI: 10.1201/9781003277002-9

mutations that are taking place in the DNA of bone marrow cells, which are continuously growing and dividing at a faster rate. In this process, the immature cells that are produced are called a lymphoblast. The treatments for this condition include radiation therapy, chemotherapy, bone marrow transplant, and many other techniques.

Deep learning finds its applications in determining the current solutions to problems that are time-consuming to solve by any expert. Machine learning techniques are also employed in determining various infections that are spreading across the world in the current times [1–3]. There are different classical machine learning and deep learning algorithms that are used in different medical diagnoses such as sepsis [4], lung infections [5], and much more. The Deep learning (DL) techniques are extended to the field of astronomy for the detection of celestial objects [6].

This chapter is organized as follows: Abstract contains the brief overview of the work. Section 1 (Introduction) gives an information of the chapter that is implemented. Section 2 (Related works) has information about the related literatures referred in this chapter. Section 3 (Dataset description) gives an insight of the data that is used in this chapter. Section 4 (Methodology) describes the workflow of the current textbook chapter. Section 5 (Results and discussions) is concerned with the obtained results in this chapter. Section 6 is the conclusion. Section 7 (Author Description) is provided, and references are given at the end of this chapter.

9.2   RELATED WORKS

There are many related publications, which are seen in this chapter. Genovese et al. [7] used shallow convolutional neural network (CNN) for tuning the adaptive image and deep CNN for classification on ALL-IDB2 and obtained an accuracy of 96.8% for unsharp images using VGG16 and 96.76% accuracy for the original images. The use of innovative and adaptive image processing techniques can be identified in this work. Arjun Abhishek et al. [8] used the ALL-IDB2 dataset along with some data, making it a heterogeneous dataset, which consists of 1,700 cancerous blood cell images. Different variants of CNN along with the support vector machine are used for pretraining the data. The best accuracy of 98% was able to achieve with the help of DenseNet121. In the future, the focus is to improve test performance. Priyanka et al. achieved 96% accuracy by using the ALL-IDB2 dataset by proposing the LeuFeatx model. Pradeep et al. [9] proposed a hybrid model, which gave the properties of Mobilenet v2 and resnet 18 to achieve the highest accuracy of 99.39%. They found that the accuracy is getting decreased with an increase in the testing set and a decrease in the training set—hence being the scope for future implementation.

Pradeep et al. [10] suggested a deep learning, lightweight-based feature extraction for the detection of leukemia automatically. To achieve this purpose, ALLDB1, ALLDB2, and ASH databases are used, and nearly 100% accuracy is obtained. Such models that are equally efficient are a motivation for the researchers to deploy many such models on different databases and diseases. Astha et al. [11] reviewed different kinds of literature which used different databases that used transfer learning methods to classify ALL. It was found that most of the pieces of literature extracted 75%–95% accuracies. Saba et al. [12] made use of the ALL-IDB and LISC datasets for experimentation. The accuracies came out to be 100% for the ALL-IDB dataset and 98.6% accuracies for the LISC dataset using the cosine function of SVM.

Tusneem et al. [13] divided the dataset into two: primary dataset, which is AML_ Cytomorphology_LMU having 18,365 blood samples of 100 patients between 2014 and 2017 at Munich Hospital, and secondary dataset having 17,092 normal peripheral images. RF, XGBoost, SVM, and FCL methods are used. 97.57% accuracy using XGBoost on the primary dataset and 96.41% accuracy by using SVM on the secondary dataset were achieved. Rohan et al. [14] applied YOLOv4 for cancerous cell detection and classification on ALL-IDB1 and CNMC_2019 datasets. The mean average precision was 96.06% on ALL-IDB1 and 98.7% for CNMC_2019 datasets. Anilkumar et al. [15] pre-trained CNN for classification and image detection without feature extraction, and image segmentation is done. This gave the results of 100% accuracy except for Alexnet and VGG16. Classification into various types and subtypes of leukemia can be done.

Minh et al. [16] performed the feature extraction and cleaning of data by the Cytominer to remove the additional features with high correlation. Machine learning algorithms like GNB, RF, and SVM were tested, and their hyperparameters were tuned by hyperopt. Resnet architecture was implemented as a deep learning technique in the work, achieving 90% accuracy. Shakir et al. [17] used CNN for leukemia classification and YOLOv2 for detection. Ninety-eight percent average precision was achieved with the help of the YOLO and BCCD datasets. Malia et al. [18] performed experiments with 16 datasets consisting of 2,415 images with ALL, AML, and healthy blood cell (HBS) images. AlertNet-RWD is the model that gave the highest accuracy of 97.15% in this work.

Animesh et al. [19] reviewed traditional machine learning techniques and deep learning techniques for the classification of blood smear images and found that both these methods perform equally well. Snehanshu Saha [20] analyzed the performance of different activation functions on deep learning architectures. The comparison was done for three different datasets, i.e., CIFAR 100, MNIST, and MNIST fashion datasets. ReLU, AReLU, ELU, Mish, Swish, and other activation functions were examined. Fredric Samson [21] used the HCNN-IAS algorithm that performs classification, feature extraction, and fusing operations. Accuracy of 99.87% is achieved. Anilkumar et al. [22] surveyed various works of literature on automated detection of leukemia. It was found that the majority of the works were based on the detection of acute leukemia; however, there are limited works to find chronic leukemia.

These are the works of literature that are referred to for the study and implementation of the current chapter, and the majority of the works are based on ALL-IDB databases and could achieve accuracies greater than 95%.

9.3 DATASET DESCRIPTION

The blood smear images of 118 patients are considered. This is available in Kaggle (https://www.kaggle.com/andrewmvd/leukemia-classification). The data consists of 15,135 images having two labels (normal and leukemia blast). There are a total of 10,661 training images and 4,474 testing images, out of which 7,272 are leukemic blast and 3,389 normal images.

9.4 METHODOLOGY

In this chapter, the variants of CNN are demonstrated along with Rectified Linear Unit (ReLU), Attention-Based Rectified Linear Unit (AReLU), and Exponential Linear Unit (ELU) activation functions. The methodology diagram is shown in Figure 9.1, which illustrates the workflow of the current chapter. The steps followed in the current chapter are described below.

- **Data preprocessing and augmentation** are done with the help of ImageDataGenerator[1].

  The ImageDataGenerator is used for shear rotation of the images from 0 to 360 degrees for producing multiple images per epoch and hence increasing the training data.
- **Split the dataset into training and testing sets** is done in the dataset folder, which contains a differentiation of training and testing sets.
- **The development of deep learning models** includes the development of CNN, Residual Network of 50 depth (ResNet50), very deep convolutional network with 16 depth (VGG16), with 19 depth (VGG19), Lenet, Alexnet,

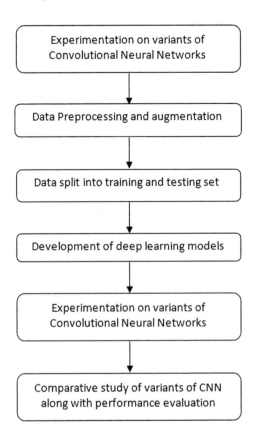

FIGURE 9.1   Workflow diagram.

Inceptionv3, and Xception models for the classification of leukemia images. These models are demonstrated with different activation functions.

- **Experimentation on variants of convolutional neural networks** is done by considering ReLU, AReLU, and ELU activation functions.
- **A comparative study** for the best model with the best activation function used in this chapter is done, which gives inspiration to the readers of this chapter to implement the models with different activation functions. The evaluation metrics used for this purpose is the loss and the accuracy. Higher is the loss, lesser is the accuracy and lower is the model performance.

9.5 RESULTS AND DISCUSSION

The goal of this chapter is to apply deep learning image classification on ALL images and obtain the best model to train and validate. This experiment is done in Keras, which makes use of TensorFlow in the backend. The evaluation is based on the accuracy of the models (Table 9.1). Clearly, it can be stated that ResNet50 with ELU activation function is outperforming any other models.

The time taken to execute these deep learning algorithms is very high: On an average, the classification takes place in 120 minutes. This is because of the complexity of the images and the complexity of architectures of each model. Activation

TABLE 9.1

Comparison of Accuracies and Loss of Different Models Along with Different Activation Functions[a]

Model	Evaluation Metrics	ReLU	AReLU	ELU
CNN	Accuracy score	63.00%	63.64%	63.93%
	Loss	0.8600	0.8632	0.8648
ResNet50	Accuracy score	79.99%	79.98%	**81.04%**
	Loss	0.4573	0.4575	**0.4362**
VGG16	Accuracy score	78.05%	76.35%	78.41%
	Loss	0.4623	0.4715	0.4596
VGG19	Accuracy score	78.15%	77.65%	78.10%
	Loss	0.4843	0.4735	0.4849
Lenet	Accuracy score	76.49%	75.20%	77.05%
	Loss	0.5943	0.6300	0.4986
Alexnet	Accuracy score	77.95%	78.01%	76.98%
	Loss	0.4747	0.4659	0.5956
Inceptionv3	Accuracy score	78.05%	79.94%	78.23%
	Loss	0.4365	0.4198	0.4316
Xception	Accuracy score	76.49%	77.01%	76.59%
	Loss	0.4736	0.4696	0.4701

[a] The numbers in the table indicate best accuracies and loss values captured after every epoch.

functions are also an important factor for time complexity. It is observed that ELU activation executed at a faster rate compared to that of the other activation functions. Generally, ReLU training happens at a faster rate but in this case, this function took longer time to execute.

Accuracy is the metric used in this chapter to evaluate our model. Accuracy is used for classifiers to check the number of correct predictions over the total number of predictions made. The model efficacy increases with an increase in the accuracy, and hence in comparing various models, the one with the highest accuracy is considered the best model (ResNet50) in this case. The formula to calculate the accuracy is given below:

$$\text{Accuracy} = \frac{\text{Number of correct predictions}}{\text{Number of predictions}}$$

Let us move on to the discussion part of this chapter, which includes the brief of working on a few of the algorithms and activation functions used. The image cannot be directly considered for input to the deep learning models. Hence, the preprocessing and data augmentation have to be done along with the resizing of images to (128,128) pixel values. The introduction to pooling layer, flatten layer, and finally the compilation with adam optimizer, binary cross-entropy as loss, and accuracy metrics are used to evaluate the model. For faster computation and avoiding unnecessary steps in computation, early stopping with patience 15 is used.

The plain CNN model gave computationally lesser accuracy compared to the other models used in this chapter because of the data entanglement. VGG 16 and VGG 19 are designed for the classification of images with 16 and 19 layers of weight, respectively. VGG 19 is computationally better than VGG16 because of its increased layers. Vanishing or exploding gradient problems are seen in these architectures. Alexnet has five convolutional layers, three fully connected layers, and 60M hyperparameters, which are too much for training—hence being computationally slower [23,24]. Lenet faced a similar issue. There are different filters at each layer in the architecture of inception, which makes it flexible for the network to train the data with different weights.

Since the best performance in this chapter is achieved by ResNet50, let us look into briefly about ResNet50 architecture. Residual networks are a solution to the problem of vanishing gradient and exploding gradient descent. The concept of skip connections is introduced, which helps in skipping the training from layers that yields poor results and connecting directly to the output layer increasing the performance of the model. The diagram of ResNet 50 model is shown in Figure 9.2.

There are five stages in the ResNet50 model—each stage having a convolutional and an identity block and over 23 million tunable hyperparameters. The entire architecture is complex, hence making it difficult for the developers to code from scratch. ResNet50 can be directly used by using the below snippet of code:

```
model = applications.resnet50.ResNet50(weights= None,
        include_top=False,
    input_shape= (img_height,img_width,3))
```

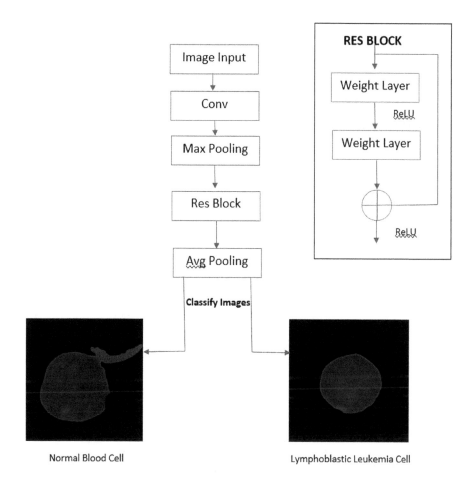

FIGURE 9.2   Diagram of ResNet50 model.

The activation functions used are ReLU, AReLU, and ELU. Let us glance at the differences between each of these activation functions.

- ReLU: A linear function that outputs the input values directly if it is positive and returns 0 if the input is something else. It is the most common activation function in neural networks. It is easy to train. ReLU activation function plot is represented in Figure 9.3.
- AReLU: Performs well when the learning rates are less. Attention modules are present in addition to ReLU, which helps in faster learning even at smaller learning rates, making it more efficient than ReLU.

$Y = x^\wedge n$ is the equation for AReLU.

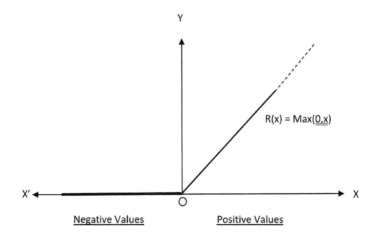

FIGURE 9.3   ReLU activation function.

$$\text{ELU (a)} = a, \text{ if a>0.}$$
$$\text{ELU (a)} = \alpha\,(e^a - 1), \text{ if a<0.}$$

FIGURE 9.4   Representation of ELU activation function.

- ELU: Uninterrupted and distinguishable activation function at all the places is ELU. It is computationally faster and gives good results. The representation of the ELU activation function is shown in Figure 9.4.

9.6   CONCLUSION

Deep learning is an area where most medical diagnosis finds the most accurate solution, and one such proven example is in the diagnosis of ALL. Using ResNet50, 81.04% accuracy is obtained. The demonstration of three different activation functions is done and found that ELU is faster and more efficient compared to other activation functions in this study. The reasons for the lesser accuracy of architectures of CNN are explained along with the detailed information of the ResNet50 model. In the future, the accuracies can be enhanced with the help of different kinds of learning and activation functions. Other models for image classification can be used. The time complexity functions can be reduced by the use of GPU systems, and other methods can be executed.

DETAILS OF AUTHORS

Amrita I is currently pursuing Master of Technology in Computer Science and Engineering, Global Academy of Technology, Bangalore, India. She is also in the course of internship in Bosch Global Software Technologies, Bangalore. She completed her bachelors of technology in Computer Science and Engineering Global

Academy of Technology, Bangalore. She has published several papers in international conferences. Her area of interest lies in Machine Learning, Bigdata, Automation and Deep Learning.

Snigdha Sen is currently working as an Assistant Professor in Department of Computer Science and Engineering, Global Academy of Technology, Bangalore, India. She is having around 12 years of teaching experience. She is pursuing PhD in Machine Learning and big data analytics from IIIT, Allahabad. She completed her master's in Information technology from Jadavpur University, Kolkata. She has published several 18 papers in international journal and conferences. She has also contributed to CSI communication with 10 articles publications. Her area of interest lies in Machine Learning, Bigdata, Internet of Things and Cloud Computing.

REFERENCES

1. Sen, Snigdha, B. K. Thejas, B. L. Pranitha, and I. Amrita. "Analysis, visualization and prediction of COVID-19 pandemic spread using machine learning." In *Innovations in Computer Science and Engineering*, Saini, H.S., Sayal, R., Govardhan, A., Buyya, R. (Ed.), pp. 597–603. Springer, Singapore, 2021.
2. Sen, Snigha, et al. "Astronomical big data processing using machine learning: A comprehensive review." *Experimental Astronomy* 53 (2022): 1–43.
3. Khasnis, Namratha S., Snigdha Sen, and Shubhangi S. Khasnis. "A machine learning approach for sentiment analysis to nurture mental health amidst COVID-19." In *Proceedings of the International Conference on Data Science, Machine Learning and Artificial Intelligence*, pp. 284–289, 2021, Namibia.
4. Amrita, I., Roshan Joy Martis, and K. Ashwini. "Modelling and classification of sepsis using machine learning." In *2021 5th International Conference on Electrical, Electronics, Communication, Computer Technologies and Optimization Techniques (ICEECCOT)*, pp. 262–266. IEEE, 2021, India.
5. Sen, Snigdha, and I. Amrita. "A transfer learning based approach for lung inflammation detection." In *International Conference on Emerging Applications of Information Technology*, pp. 29–36. Springer, Singapore, 2021.
6. VY, S., S. Sen and K. Santosh, "Analyzing and processing of astronomical images using deep learning techniques." *2021 IEEE International Conference on Electronics, Computing and Communication Technologies (CONECCT)*, pp. 1–6, 2021, doi: 10.1109/CONECCT52877.2021.9622583.
7. Genovese, Angelo, Mahdi S. Hosseini, Vincenzo Piuri, Konstantinos N. Plataniotis, and Fabio Scotti. "Acute lymphoblastic leukemia detection based on adaptive unsharpening and deep learning." In *ICASSP 2021-2021 IEEE International Conference on Acoustics, Speech and Signal Processing (ICASSP)*, pp. 1205–1209. IEEE, 2021, Toronto.
8. Abhishek, Arjun, Rajib Kumar Jha, Ruchi Sinha, and Kamlesh Jha. "Automated classification of acute leukemia on a heterogeneous dataset using machine learning and deep learning techniques." *Biomedical Signal Processing and Control* 72 (2022): 103341.
9. Das, Pradeep Kumar, and Sukadev Meher. "An efficient deep convolutional neural network based detection and classification of acute lymphoblastic leukemia." *Expert Systems with Applications* 183 (2021): 115311.
10. Das, Pradeep Kumar, Biswajit Nayak, and Sukadev Meher. "A lightweight deep learning system for automatic detection of blood cancer." *Measurement* 191 (2022): 110762.
11. Ratley, Astha, Jasmine Minj, and Pooja Patre. "Leukemia disease detection and classification using machine learning approaches: A review." In *2020 First International Conference on Power, Control and Computing Technologies (ICPC2T)*, pp. 161–165. IEEE, 2020, India.

12. Saleem, Saba, Javeria Amin, Muhammad Sharif, Muhammad Almas Anjum, Muhammad Iqbal, and Shui-Hua Wang. "A deep network designed for segmentation and classification of leukemia using fusion of the transfer learning models." *Complex & Intelligent Systems* 8 (2021): 1–16.
13. Elhassan, Tusneem A., Mohd Shafry Mohd Rahim, Tan Tian Swee, Siti Z. Mohd Hashim, and Mahmoud Aljurf. "Feature extraction of white blood cells using CMYK-moment localization and deep learning in acute myeloid leukemia blood smear microscopic images." *IEEE Access* 10 (2022): 16577–16591.
14. Khandekar, Rohan, Prakhya Shastry, Smruthi Jaishankar, Oliver Faust, and Niranjana Sampathila. "Automated blast cell detection for acute lymphoblastic leukemia diagnosis." *Biomedical Signal Processing and Control* 68 (2021): 102690.
15. Anilkumar, K. K., V. J. Manoj, and T. M. Sagi. "Automated detection of leukemia by pretrained deep neural networks and transfer learning: A comparison." *Medical Engineering & Physics* 98 (2021): 8–19.
16. Doan, Minh, Marian Case, Dino Masic, Holger Hennig, Claire McQuin, Juan Caicedo, Shantanu Singh, et al. "Label-free leukemia monitoring by computer vision." *Cytometry Part A* 97, no. 4 (2020): 407–414.
17. Abas, Shakir Mahmood, Adnan Mohsin Abdulazeez, and Diyar Qader Zeebaree. "A YOLO and convolutional neural network for the detection and classification of leukocytes in leukemia." *Indonesian Journal of Electrical Engineering and Computer Science* 25, no. 1 (2022): 200–213.
18. Claro, Maíla, Luis Vogado, Rodrigo Veras, André Santana, João Tavares, Justino Santos, and Vinicius Machado. "Convolution neural network models for acute leukemia diagnosis." In *2020 International Conference on Systems, Signals and Image Processing (IWSSIP)*, pp. 63–68. IEEE, 2020, Niteroi.
19. Khan, Siraj, Muhammad Sajjad, Tanveer Hussain, Amin Ullah, and Ali Shariq Imran. "A review on traditional machine learning and deep learning models for WBCs classification in blood smear images." *IEEE Access* 9 (2020): 10657–10673.
20. Chaturvedi, Animesh, N. Apoorva, Mayank Sharan Awasthi, and Shubhra Jyoti. "Analysing the performance of novel activation functions on deep learning architectures."
21. Sakthiraj, Fredric Samson Kirubakaran. "Autonomous leukemia detection scheme based on hybrid convolutional neural network model using learning algorithm." *Wireless Personal Communications* 126 (2021): 1–16.
22. Anilkumar, K. K., V. J. Manoj, and T. M. Sagi. "A survey on image segmentation of blood and bone marrow smear images with emphasis to automated detection of Leukemia." *Biocybernetics and Biomedical Engineering* 40, no. 4 (2020): 1406–1420.
23. https://medium.com/analytics-vidhya/types-of-convolutional-neural-networks-lenet-alexnet-vgg-16-net-resnet-and-inception-net-759e5f197580.
24. https://towardsdatascience.com/.

NOTE

1. ImageDataGenerator(horizontal_flip=True, vertical_flip=True, zoom_range = 0.2, preprocessing_function=preprocess_input) [24].

10 Cervical Pap Smear Screening and Cancer Detection Using Deep Neural Network

Munakala Lohith, Soumi Bardhan,
and Oishila Bandyopadhyay
Indian Institute of Information Technology

CONTENTS

10.1 INTRODUCTION

Cervical cancer is the second most common cancer among women in the Indian population. As per international data, it is the fourth common cancer among women worldwide [1]. More than 77,000 new cases of cervical cancer are reported annually. As per medical practitioners, preventive measures and early-stage diagnosis are the two major steps to fight cervical cancer. Pap smear screening is a well-proven technique for the detection and prevention of cervical cancer. Unfortunately, many developing and underdeveloped countries are struggling with this disease due to the unavailability of skilled manpower, specialized equipment, and lack of automation in the screening process. Hence, development of an automated tool for the analysis of pap smear images can expedite the screening process and help doctors to start the treatment at the initial stage of the disease. The proposed work is intended to develop a deep learning-based pap smear image assessment system for point-of-care screening. A convolutional neural network (CNN)-based classifier model is proposed to classify the multi-cell pap smear images based on Bethesda

DOI: 10.1201/9781003277002-10

classification [2]. The objective of this work also includes localization of the cells belonging to different classes in the multi-cell image. The main contribution of this work includes the design of YOLOv5-based classifier for pap smear image classification; analysis of the performance of small, medium, and large variants of YOLOv5 architecture; and selection of the best one suitable for automated classification of pap smear images. The rest of this chapter is organized as follows. Detailed discussion on existing research works related to pap smear image analysis has been performed in Section 2. Section 3 describes the methodology of the proposed approach. The data source and the detailed categories are discussed in Section 4. Section 5 focuses on the experimental observations and result analysis. The overall conclusion and future scope of work are covered in Section 6.

10.2   RELATED WORK

Pap smear screening is used for the detection and prevention of cervical cancer. The efficient adoption of this screening process in developed countries results in a significant decrease in cervical cancer-related mortality rate [3]. Unfortunately, many developing and underdeveloped countries are struggling with this disease due to the unavailability of skilled manpower, specialized equipment, and lack of automation in the screening process. Hence, in past few years, several research groups have started extensive research on artificial intelligence and machine learning-based pap smear analysis to automate the screening technique [4–7]. Conventional pap smears and liquid-based cytology (LBC) are the two major pap smear techniques used for cervical cancer screening [8, 9]. LBC is relatively new (introduced in the 1990s) and expensive technique. This process also requires pre-processing and debris removal from smear as the samples appear with background debris. This may result in the removal of inflammatory cells in the processed smear image and reduces the efficiency of the classification model. Although the number of unsatisfactory smears found in conventional pap smear technique is relatively high, the technique is widely used in developing countries due to its economic feasibility.

Research on computer-based pap smear analysis can be grouped in four categories: (i) single-cell or smear-level analysis, (ii) segmentation of individual cells, (iii) extracted features, and (iv) classification approach. The single-cell-level analysis involves the shape, texture, and cytoplasm/nucleus ratio analysis of normal and abnormal cervical cell images [10,11]. Smear-level analysis uses smear images, which consist of multiple cervical cells along with red blood cells (RBCs), debris, and inflammatory cells. Many research groups have applied pre-processing techniques such as filters based on discrete wavelet transform (DWT), morphological operations, bit-place-slicing, etc. to remove the background debris from smear image before using that image for the classification model [5,12]. Su et al. developed a two-level cascaded classification method to detect cervical cancer cells. They have used the thin LBC slides [4]. Segmentation and classification of single-cell pap smear image using Fuzzy C-means (FCM) clustering-based technique is proposed by Changkong et al. [10]. They have segmented nucleus, cytoplasm, and background from single-cell pap smear image. William et al. [11] have developed a pap smear

TABLE 10.1

Recent Approaches of Automated Pap Smear Analysis

Research Group	Dataset	Technique/ Architecture Used	Comments
Plissiti et al. [19]	SIPaKMed	SVM, multilayer perceptron, CNN	Prepared a new dataset with 4,049 annotated cell images. Utilized intensity-, shape-, and texture-based features to classify images using SVM. CNN-based classification used VGG19 architecture. Cytoplasm and nucleus regions of each image are marked manually in the dataset.
Sompawong et al. [13]	LBC slides obtained from Thammasat University Hospital	Mask RCNN	Identified normal and abnormal nuclear features from liquid-based histological slides (pap smear images). LBC is relatively new and expensive technique compared to traditional pap smear collection method. With Mask RCNN, they have achieved a mean average precision (mAP) of 57.8%.
GV et. al. [18]	SIPaKMeD and Herlev datasets	PCA-based interpretation method, RestNet34 for classification	Performed classification of whole-slide image cervical cell cluster. Used SIPaKMeD dataset for classification without localization of cells.
Yao Xiang et al. [23]	Own dataset	YOLOv3, Faster RCNN	Classification based on Bethesda model. Applied YOLOv3 and achieved MAP of 63.7% on cervical cell-level classification of their own dataset. An additional task-specific classifier is added with CNN to improve classification performance. Unbalanced distribution of classes in the dataset.
Matias [24]	UFSC OCPap (v3) dataset	RetinaNet, Faster RCNN, Mask RCNN	Segmentation and classification of nuclei using three CNN models. Achieved 0.51 intersection over union (IoU) using Mask R-CNN. Samples are collected in LBC technique, and total number of samples is relatively small. The results from automated testing featured in the paper do not show good results for abnormal nuclei.
Orhan Yaman et al. [25]	SIPaKMeD and Mendeley LBC datasets	DarkNet19, DarkNet53, cubic SVM	Used transfer learning-based DarkNet architecture for feature extraction and support vector machine (SVM) for classification. Reported more than 98% accuracy in both SIPaKMeD and Mendeley LBC. Proposed architecture is relatively complex.

screening tool based on enhanced FCM algorithm. Their approach exhibits good results on both single-cell and multi-cell images. Win et al. [12] have proposed watershed transform-based segmentation followed by machine learning-based classification model for the classification of pap smear images. Jantzen et al. [14] have prepared a benchmark dataset (Herlev dataset) for pattern classification of pap smear images. This dataset has 917 single-cell images. With the advent of deep neural network, different research groups have proposed CNN-based models to classify the smear images [13–17] in past few years. Principal component analysis (PCA)-based interpretation method has been used by GV et al. [18] for the segmentation of multi-cell into single-cell images. They have performed classification of each single-cell path using RestNet34. Transfer learning technique has been applied in that work to develop the trained model. Sompawong et al. [13] have proposed a Mask RCNN architecture to analyze the nucleus of cervical cells and detect abnormality in nuclear features from pap smear images. They have used a data set containing LBC slides of 460 patients. The dataset was collected from Thammasat University (TU) Hospital. Plissiti et al. [19] have prepared another dataset (SIPaKMed) with 4049 annotated cervical cell images. Those cells have been classified into five different classes under normal (superficial-intermediate, parabasal), benign (metaplastic), and abnormal category (koilocytes and dyskeratotic). Different research groups are working on this dataset [20,21]. Intensity-, texture-, and shape-based features (26 features) have been extracted and feed to different machine learning and AI-based classifiers. Support vector machine (SVM), multilayer perceptron, and CNN-based model are used to classify SIPakMed dataset. Table 10.1 shows the few recent works on the classification of pap smear images using different conventional and CNN-based classifiers.

As per literature [22], YOLOv5 model works efficiently for small object detection compared to other RCNN-based models. The bounding boxes generated by the model during classification can be used for the extraction of respective cells from multi-cell image and detailed study of the presence of abnormality in those cells. For this reason, the proposed approach has used YOLOv5 model for the classification and localization of cells.

10.3 METHODOLOGY

In the proposed approach, YOLOv5 [21,26,22]-based architecture is used to classify pap smear images into five classes: parabasal, metaplastic, dyskeratotic, koilocytotic, and superficial intermediate. The model takes the pap smear images as input and applied contrast enhancement techniques to prepare the data for the CNN model. The multi-cell images are then fed to a trained YOLOv5 model for the classification of cells.

Detection of objects on different scales is a challenging task, especially for small objects. YOLO object detection model first creates bounding boxes around objects and then classifies the cropped image into one of the classes the model is trained on. YOLO model has three major components: backbones, neck, and head. In YOLOv5 [22], CSP DarkNet53 is used as a backbone to overcome the repetitive gradient problem. The architecture has used Path Aggregation Network (PANet) as a neck to improve the flow of information. PANet allows the propagation of low-level features by using the feature pyramid network (FPN) in the backbone. FPN generates a bottom-up and a top-down feature hierarchy with lateral connections among the features generated at different scales. The model head performs the final object detection part. The final single output is generated by concatenating three different outputs of feature maps.

Figure 10.1 shows the phases of the proposed method, and Figure 10.2 shows the detail architecture of YOLOv5 model. Here, the backbone performs feature extraction from input image, PANet is used for feature fusion, and the head generates the result. YOLO generates the bounding boxes across the object and applies intersection over union (IOU) to select the best bounding box that covers the object. After this, non-maxima suppression is applied to remove other bounding boxes with low confidence scores. The input image is fed to the focus layer. Conv represents convolution. Three convolution layers are used in C3 along with a module cascaded by

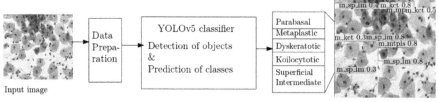

FIGURE 10.1 Phases of the proposed method.

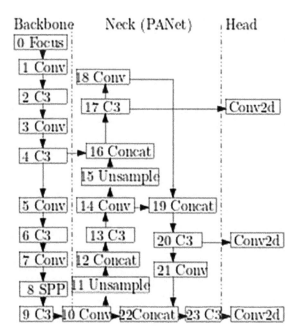

FIGURE 10.2 YOLOv5 architecture.

bottlenecks. Spatial pyramid pooling is used in pooling layer to remove fixed size constraints present in the network. The head section uses three Conv2d detection modules for final classification.

Thus, the classification operation is performed in two phases: (i) detection of the cell object and (ii) classification of the object with probability of being a known labeled class. During classification, bounding box is generated for each cell object with probability of the class.

10.4 DATASET

The SIPaKMeD dataset [19] is used for this work. This dataset consists of 4,049 isolated cell images. These isolated cell images are extracted from 967 cluster cell images of pap smear slides. A CCD camera with an optical microscope is used for pap smear image acquisition. The cell images can be broadly classified into normal, abnormal, and benign categories. Both normal and abnormal categories have two subcategories, and a benign group of cells have one subcategory, respectively.

10.4.1 NORMAL

Squamous epithelial cells are considered as normal cells. Subclasses under the normal category are detected based on the maturity of the cells and their positions at epithelium layers. Parabasal and Superficial Intermediate (Figure 10.3a) are the subclasses under the normal category.

- Parabasal – Parabasal cells consist of immature squamous cells. In a vaginal smear, these cells appear as the smallest epithelial cells. A large vesicular nucleus appears in cyanophilic cytoplasm of these parabasal cells. As meta-plastic cells and parabasal cells have similarities in morphological proper-ties, the separation of these two cells is quite challenging.
- Superficial Intermediate – A large number of superficial intermediate cells appear in pap smear. They appear with large polygonal cytoplasm and pyc-notic nucleus.

10.4.2 ABNORMAL

These cells exhibit morphological changes in the structural part. Koilocytotic cells and Dyskeratotic cells are the subclasses in this category.

- Dyskeratotic – These cells show the presence of three-dimensional clus-ters, and individual cells may appear with premature abnormal keratiniza-tion. Dyskeratotic (Figure 10.3b and c) and koilocytotic cells have a similar type of vesicular nuclei. Sometimes, such cells may be binuclear and/or multinuclear.
- Koilocytotic – Intermediate and superficial matured squamous cells and metaplastic type of koilocytotic cells are considered in this category. They are very lightly stained and have a large perinuclear cavity. Densely stained

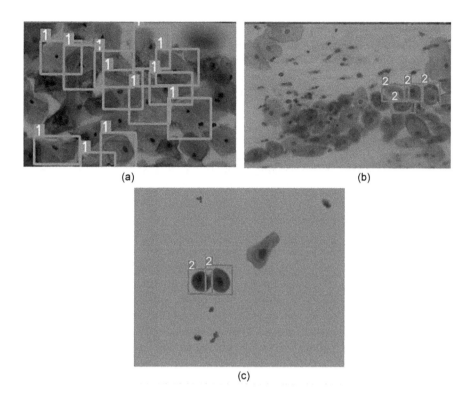

(a)   (b)

(c)

FIGURE 10.3 Sample training data (classes labeled). (a) Superficial intermediate cells (normal). (b–c) Dyskeratotic cells (abnormal).

cytoplasmic peripheral regions appear in these cells. The enlarged nuclei of koilocytes have irregular nuclear membrane contours.

10.4.3 BENIGN

These cells appear in the transformation zone where precancerous and cancerous cells develop.

- Metaplastic – These cells are parabasal-type cells. Metaplastic cells appear with distinct cellular borders and eccentric nuclei. They may contain large intracellular vacuoles. In comparison with parabasal cells, these cells have relatively uniform shape and size.

10.5 EXPERIMENTAL RESULTS

Experiments are done with small, medium, and large variants of YOLOv5. The models are trained with the augmented dataset prepared using SIPaKMeD. All the experiments are performed in a system with a Tesla T4 GPU with 15GB RAM.

Training

The training dataset is prepared by labeling five categories of cells among 967 multi-celled images. Eight hundred and thirteen dyskeratotic cells, 831 superficial intermediate cells, 793 metaplastic cells, 825 koilocytotic cells, and 787 parabasal cells are labeled and used to train the model.

Model parameters

Images of size 2,048 × 1,536 are used for the experiments. The batch sizes for each of the YOLOv5 variants are set to 2. The epochs for YOLOv5 Large are used as 25. For medium and small variants, it is 50 epochs.

The performances of the models are shown in Table 10.2. YOLO model generates the bounding box covering the object, and the mean average precision (mAP) can represent the proper coverage of the region of interest (ROI) by the bounding box. So mAP@0.5 score is computed for each model.

The highest mAP@0.5 score of 0.592 and recall of 0.679 are achieved by the medium variant of YOLOv5, and the highest precision of 0.58 is achieved by the larger version of YOLOv5. Although the medium variant is performing better, it has been observed that the cell detection in the validation set of images is more generalized in large variant of YOLOv5 compared to that of the small and the medium variants. Figure 10.4 shows the test bench prediction of respective cells by the proposed model in multi-cell pap smear images. After being trained with labeled single-cell augmented images, the model efficiently localizes and predicts respective classes of different cells present in input test images.

F1 score (F1) is represented by the precision and sensitivity of the system. True-positive (TP), false-positive (FP), false-negative (FN), and true-negative (TN) cases of the confusion matrix are used to compute precision (P) and sensitivity (S).

$$K \in N^{H \times W \times R}, \quad K = \{K_1, K_2, ..., K_R\},$$

TABLE 10.2

Train Different Models of YOLOv5

YOLOV5 Model	Epochs	Precision	Recall	mAP@0.5
YOLOv5 small	50	0.57	0.643	0.584
YOLOv5 medium	50	0.555	**0.679**	**0.592**
YOLOv5 large	25	0.572	0.641	0.589
YOLOv5 large	50	**0.58**	0.66	0.591

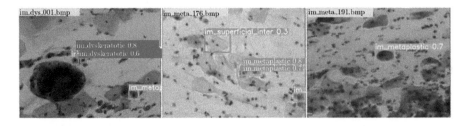

FIGURE 10.4　Test bench prediction of respective classes in multi-cell images.

Figure 10.5a shows the F1 score over the confidence of the predictions that has been made. It can be inferred that the maximum F1 score is reached by dyskeratotic cells at a score of 0.7 and the best F1 score is 0.57 at 0.405. Figure 10.6a and b show the

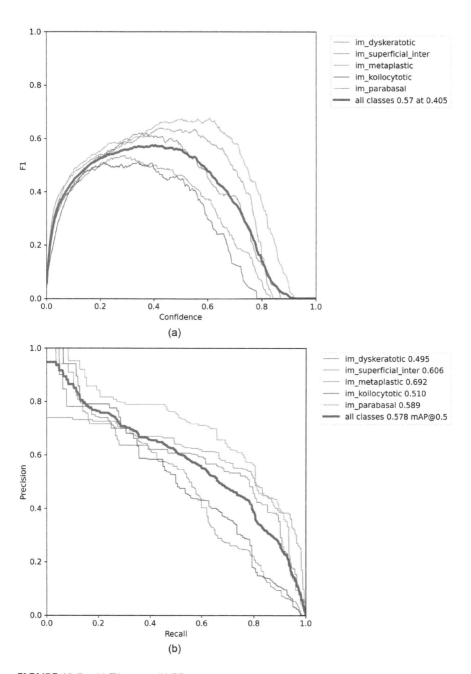

FIGURE 10.5   (a) F1 curve. (b) PR curve.

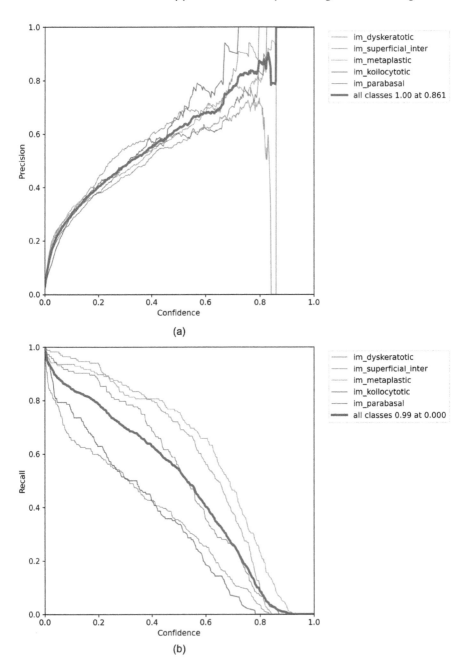

FIGURE 10.6   (a) Precision curve. (b) Recall curve.

precision and recall score over time, respectively. The best recall score that can be observed here is 0.7 for dyskeratotic. Figure 10.5b shows the precision over the recall curve. It has been observed that the best PR score is for metaplastic cells with a score

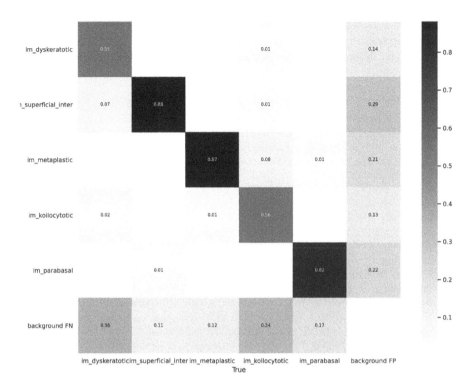

FIGURE 10.7 Confusion matrix.

of 0.69 and the mean average precision at 0.5 is 0.578. Figure 10.7 shows the confusion matrix over all the classes. The score is highest for Superficial Intermediate Cells at 0.88, and the least score is for Koilocytotic cells, which is at 0.56. Koilocytotic cells mostly lose their accuracy to the background of the PAP smear slide.

It can be concluded that the medium variant of YOLOv5 with mAP@0.5 score of 0.592 and recall of 0.679 can be used as the classifier for the classification of five pap smear categories.

10.6 CONCLUSION

The state-of-the-art YOLOv5 variants are studied in this work to localize and classify pap smear images as per Bethesda classification. The mAP@0.5 value shows better result as compared to other approaches targeting both classification and localization of cancerous pap smear cells. Further, each image that was labeled in the test sample contained only one kind of cell. The model accurately predicted other kinds of cells present in each image belonging to a different class when appropriately trained. This highlights the extent to which the model generalized the situations where there were multiple kinds of cells in a single slide. The proposed system can perform the automated classification of pap smear images and localization of cells in an efficient manner. As YOLOv5 generates bounding box for each object; each cell can be localized after classification. Hence, segmentation of localized cell from multi-cell pap smear image can be performed efficiently. This work may be extended in the future for the study of individual features of extracted abnormal cells also.

REFERENCES

1. F. Bray, J. Ferlay, I. Soerjomataram, R. L. Siegel, L. A. Torre, and A. Jemal. Global cancer statistics 2018: Globocan estimates of incidence and mortality worldwide for 36 cancers in 185 countries. *CA: A Cancer Journal for Clinicians*, 68(6): 394–424, 2018.
2. Eric Lucas. The bethesda system, accessed on 26/02/2022. https://screening.iarc.fr/atlasclassifbethesda.php.
3. Y.-F. Chen, P.-C. Huang, K.-C. Lin, H.-H. Lin, L.-E. Wang, C.-C. Cheng, T.-P. Chen, Y.-K. Chan, and J. Y. Chiang. Semi-automatic segmentation and classification of pap smear cells. *IEEE Journal of Biomedical Health*, 18(1): 94–108, 2014.
4. Jie Su, Xuan Xu, Yongjun He, and Jinming Song. Automatic detection of cervical cancer cells by a two-level cascade classification system. *Analytical Cellular Pathology*, 2016. https://doi.org/10.1155/2016/9535027.
5. K. Bora, M. Chowdhury, L. B. Mahanta, M. K. Kundu, and A. K. Das. Automated classification of pap smear images to detect cervical dysplasia. *Computer Methods and Programs in Biomedicine*, 138, 2017. https://doi.org/10.1016/j.cmpb.2016.10.001.
6. K. Li, Z. Lu, W. Liu, and J. Yin. Cytoplasm and nucleus segmentation in cervical smear images using radiating GVF snake. *Pattern Recognition*, 45(4): 1255–1264, 2012.
7. Z. Lu, G. Carneiro, and A. P. Bardley. An improved joint optimization of multiple level set function for the segmentation of overlapping cervical cells. *IEEE Transaction on Image Processing*, 24(4): 1261–1272, 2015.
8. E. Hussain, L. B. Mahanta, H. Borah, and C. Ray Das. Liquid based-cytology pap smear dataset for automatedmulti-class diagnosis of pre-cancerous and cervical cancer lesions. *Data in Brief*, 30: 105589, 2020. https://doi.org/10.1016/j.dib.2020.105589.
9. Elima Hussain. Liquid based cytology pap smear images for multi-class diagnosis of cervical cancer. *Mendeley Data*, 4, 2019. https://doi.org/10.17632/zddtpgzv63.4.
10. T. Chankong, N. Theera-Umpon, and S. Auephanwiriyakul. Automatic cervical cell segmentation and classification in pap smears. *Computer Methods and Programs in Biomedicine*, 113(2): 539–556, 2014.
11. W. William, A. Ware, A. H. Basaza-Ejiri, and J. Obungoloch. A pap-smear analysis tool (pat) for detection of cervical cancer from pap-smear images. *Biomedical Engineering Online*, 18(1), 2019. https://doi.org/10.1186/s12938-019-0634-5.
12. K.P. Win, Y. Kitjaidure, K. Hamamoto, and T. Myo Aung. Computer-assisted screening for cervical cancer using digital image processing of pap smear images. *Applied Sciences*, 10, 2020. https://doi.org/10.3390/app10051800.
13. N. Sompawong, J. Mopan, P. Pooprasert, et al. Automated pap smear cervical cancer screening using deep learning. In *International Conference of the IEEE Engineering in Medicine and Biology Society (EMBC)*, pp. 7044–7048, 2019. https://doi.org/10.1109/EMBC.2019.8856369.
14. J. Jantzen, J. Norup, G. Dounias, and B. Bjerregaard. Pap-smear benchmark data for pattern classification. In *Nature inspired Smart Information Systems (NiSIS)*, pp. 1–9, Albufeira, Portugal, 2005.
15. H. Chen, J. Liu, and QM. Wen, et al. Cytobrain: Cervical cancer screening system based on deep learning technology. *Journal of Computer Science and Technology*, 36: 347–360, 2021. https://doi.org/10.1007/s11390-021-0849-3.

16. W. Mousser and S. Ouadfel. Deep feature extraction for pap-smear image classification: A comparative study. In *Proceedings of the 2019 5th International Conference on Computer and Technology Applications (ICCTA)*, 2019. https://doi.org/10.1145/3323933.3324060.

17. O. Yaman and T. Tuncer, Exemplar pyramid deep feature extraction based cervical cancer image classification model using pap-smear images. *Biomedical Signal Processing and Control*, 73: 103428, 2022. ISSN 1746-8094, https://doi.org/10.1016/j.bspc.2021.103428.

18. K. K. GV and G. M. Reddy. Automatic classification of whole slide pap smear images using cnn with pca based feature interpretation. In *IEEE/CVF Conference on Computer Vision and Pattern Recognition Workshops*, pp. 1074–1079, 2019. https://doi.org/10.1109/CVPRW.2019.00140.

19. M. E. Plissiti, P. Dimitrakopoulos, G. Sfikas, C. Nikou, O. Krikoni, and A. Charchanti. Sipakmed: A new dataset for feature and image based classification of normal and pathological cervical cells in pap smear images. In *IEEE International Conference on Image Processing (ICIP)*, pp. 3144–3148, 2018. https://doi.org/10.1109/ICIP.2018.8451588.

20. M. T. Rezende, R. Silva, and F. D. O. Bernardo, et al. Cric searchable image database as a public platform for conventional pap smear cytology data. *Scientific Data*, 8, 2021. https://doi.org/10.1038/s41597-021-00933-8.

21. J. Redmon, S. Divvala, R. Girshick, and A. Farhadi. You only look once: Unified, real-time object detection. *ArXiv:1506.02640[cs.cv]*, 2016. http://arxiv.org/abs/1506.02640.

22. U. Nepal and H. Eslamiat. Comparing YOLOv3, YOLOv4 and YOLOv5 for autonomous landing spot detection in faulty UAVs, *Sensors*, 22, 464. https://doi.org/10.3390/s22020464.

23. Yao Xiang, Wanxin Sun, Changli Pan, Meng Yan, Zhihua Yin, and Yixiong Liang. A novel automation-assisted cervical cancer reading method basedon convolutional neural network, *arXiv:1912.06649v1*, 2019.

24. A. V. Matias, A.Cerentini, L. A. B.Macarini, J. G. A.Amorim, F. P.Daltoé, and A. V. Wangenheim, Comparison of object detection approaches applied to field images of papanicolaou stained cytology slides, https://doi.org/10.1101/2021.08.25.21262605.

25. Orhan Yaman and Turker Tuncer, Exemplar pyramid deep feature extraction based cervical cancer image classification model using pap-smear images, *Biomedical Signal Processing and Control*, 73, 2022, https://doi.org/10.1016/j.bspc.2021.103428.

26. Joseph Redmon, et al. You only look once: Unified, real-time object detection. *ArXiv:1506.02640 [Cs], arXiv.org*, 2016. http://arxiv.org/abs/1506.02640.

11 Cancer Detection Using Deep Neural Network Differentiation of Squamous Carcinoma Cells in Oral Pathology

Jayanthi Ganapathy
Sri Ramachandra Institute of Higher Education and Research

CONTENTS

DOI: 10.1201/9781003277002-11

11.1   HISTOPATHOLOGY – A REVIEW

Pathology is the medical investigation of diagnosing the disease, its cause and effects, especially after the examination of biological samples of body tissues, the biopsies. The role of a histopathologist is remarkable when biopsy of body tissue needs to be examined for a closer and detailed investigation of a medical condition. Tissue collection, annotation, differentiation of cell types, and segmentation of nucleus are the requirements of computer-aided diagnosis to ease the laborious job of pathologist in a clinical investigation. The various approaches to the development of diagnostic tools in digital pathology have highly motivated the author to present the workflow of systematic computational steps involved in the diagnosis of oral cancer. The following section presents the recent research findings in differential diagnosis of oral squamous carcinoma (OSCC).

Oral pathology is a branch of study in dentistry, a specialization of pathology that deals with screening, detection, identification, and diagnosis of diseases affecting the oral regions of humans, such as mouth cavity and teeth. Squamous cells are formed on the surfaces of skins. These cells are formed on the outer portion, the upper part of epidermis. OSCC is a cancerous cell type that can occur anywhere in the oral cavity. It is a medical condition that causes malignant tumors. This kind of oral cancer is diagnosed using whole-slide image (WSI) acquired by imaging using hematoxylin, the purple blue color and eosin, the pinkish color-stained tissue slides, the samples of epithelial tissue of oral cavity as seen in Figure 11.1a and b and 11.2a and b. The WSI is used to differentiate the abnormal nuclei from the normal tissue (Anuranjeeta et al. 2017; Fandango, 2018; Komura, 2018). In a clinical study, the differentiation of normal and cancerous cell types is highly challenging for a pathologist. Hence, there is a need for a clinical validation tool to resolve the laborious activity of pathologist in the evaluation of parameters such as color, shape, size, texture, chromatin patters, asymmetric cell count, and overlapping cell count, which was done manually or using conventional clinical procedures. The early stages of clinical activity are the evaluation of microscopic images of tissue samples. Also, the diagnostic steps involve two-stage process: (i) first stage – automatic detection of OSCCs, and (ii) second stage – accurate delineation of nucleus for quantifying the characterization of cancerous cells (Brownlee, 2020a, b, c). The morphology of nucleus is the structural property such as shape, color, and size, while the texture denotes the intensity values of pixels. In the first-stage histopathology image, WSI samples are used to automate the differentiation of squamous cells from normal epithelial cells. The concept of computer vision is implemented as an image processing framework to perform image analytics such as pixel quantification, counting cell types, and counting cancerous cells. Figure 11.1 shows the histopathological image of OSCC-positive cells in different resolutions of 10× and 40×, respectively. Figure 11.2 shows the OSCC-positive cells with resolutions of 100× and 400×, respectively. The nucleus of the OSCC is

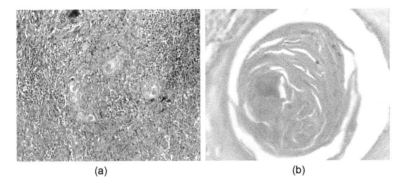

(a) (b)

FIGURE 11.1   Histopathological images of normal epithelial cells: (a) 10× (b) 40×.

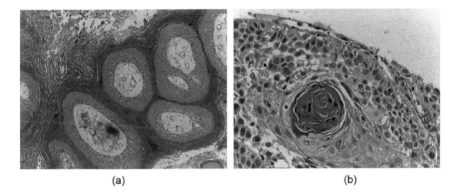

(a) (b)

FIGURE 11.2   Histopathological images of OSCC: (a) 10× (b) 40×.

the indigenous feature for the diagnosis of OSCC. Hence, it is essential to delineate the nucleus so as to quantify the properties of the detected feature nucleus such as morphological, texture, and intensity.

11.2   COMPUTER VISION IN FEATURE EXTRACTION

Computer vision is the concept of artificial intelligence (AI) used for developing image processing framework. This framework is used for the extraction of feature under study from image data. It is a collection of algorithms that use image statistics principles in automatic detection of edges, boundaries, and intensity of pixels. The different types of feature extraction algorithms that can be applied to extract the nucleus of OSCC WSIs are (i) adaptive threshold, (ii) OTSU, (iii) Sobel, (iv) Canny edge detection, and (v) watershed.

Threshold-based feature extraction algorithms are formulated by quantifying the intensity of pixels on region of images using fixed value as global parameter to extract the background and foreground images. However, these approaches are expensive in terms of execution time and memory utilizations. To overcome these issues, statistics based on neighboring pixels can be used as shown in equations 11.1–11.3.

$$I_{\text{intensity}} = \left\{ \begin{array}{ll} \mu & \text{The mean of the pixel intensity} \\ \sigma & \text{The median of pixel intensity} \\ \delta^+ & \text{The maximum pixel value} \\ \delta^- & \text{The minimum pixel value} \end{array} \right. \tag{11.1}$$

$$I_{\text{threshold}} = \frac{\delta^+ + \delta^-}{2} \tag{11.2}$$

$$\text{Adaptive thresholding } z(x,y) = \left\{ \begin{array}{l} 0\,, g(x,y) < I_{\text{threshold}} \\ 1\,, g(x,y) > I_{\text{threshold}} \end{array} \right. \tag{11.3}$$

The mean and median statistics of pixels are used for localizing the neighboring pixels. The statistical distribution of pixels based on intensity levels can be estimated using equation 11.1. The threshold is the mean of maximum and minimum pixel intensities. The computation involved in segmenting the features of image using

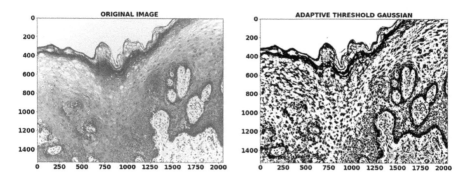

FIGURE 11.3   (a) Normal 100× resolution (b) Adaptive threshold Gaussian.

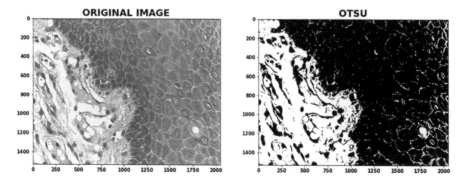

FIGURE 11.4   (a) Normal 400× resolution (b) OTSU.

dynamic threshold is the feature image. $z(x, y)$ is updated based on threshold as seen in equation 11.3. Algorithm 1 explains the steps used in adaptive threshold method of image segmentation (Figures 11.3–11.5).

An automated computation that returns a threshold on pixel intensity to separate the pixels into foreground and background classes is named after Nobuyuki Otsu. This algorithm is formulated to find *between-class* variance using equation 11.4:

$$\tau^2 = \gamma_{bg}(t)\tau_{bg}^2(t) + \gamma_{fg}(t)\tau_{fg}^2(t) \tag{11.4}$$

where τ^2 denotes the color variance, and $\gamma_{bg}(t)$ and $\gamma_{fg}(t)$ denote the number of pixels belonging to a class at t threshold based on probability of pixels.

The filtering operation performed on image using horizontal δ_x and vertical derivate approximations δ_y is given by equation 11.5. The image analytics on filter is denoted in equation 11.6 with image I.

$$\delta_x = \begin{bmatrix} 1 & -1 \\ 1 & -1 \end{bmatrix}, \delta_y = \begin{bmatrix} -1 & -1 \\ 1 & 1 \end{bmatrix} \tag{11.5}$$

$$\delta_x \times I, \ \delta_y \times I \tag{11.6}$$

OpenCV is the computer vision module library in Python for image processing analytics. Histopathologic images of normal epithelial tissues and OSCC-positive tissues are examined in openCV for image segmentation to extract the nucleus of

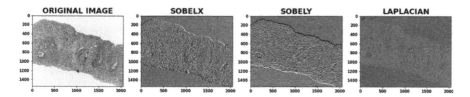

FIGURE 11.5   Sobel threshold OSCC 100×.

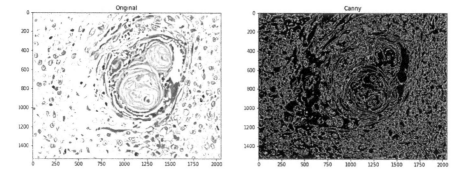

FIGURE 11.6   Canny edge detection (a) Normal (b) OSCC 400×.

normal epithelial and squamous cells of the oral cavity. The methods applied using openCV are adaptive threshold, Sobel filter, Otsu method, Canny edge detection, and watershed. These image segmentation algorithms are parametric method and are programed in openCV. These conventional feature extraction methods are applied on histopathological images to detect the regions of interest on the image under investigation. However, accurate delineation of cell nuclei is the interest of the clinician in the diagnosis of OSCC medical condition. Hence, data-intensive computational framework is necessary to segment the feature and delineate the cells based on structural properties such as size, shape, color, texture, and intensity. Of note, computational pathology is made reliable when using deep neural nets in the investigation of OSCC. The acute severity of OSCC is confirmed with the formation of horns and keratin pearls when examined on the WSI. The abnormal nucleus forms concentric layers also known as epithelial pearls. The concentric layers seen in Figures 11.2b and 11.6b are keratin pearls. The island of cells or group of overlapping cells as seen in Figure 11.2a are horn formations. The following section describes the significance of deep neural nets with a case study on automated detection and grading of OSCC.

The sequence of steps involved in image segmentation algorithm for Otsu threshold method is explained in Section 11.2. The different algorithmic approaches to image segmentation depend on computation of threshold value. This is a feature extraction technique using threshold value. The Otsu's method is significant in computing between-class variance as defined in equation 11.4. However, the threshold value in adaptive threshold method is based on intensity of pixel distributions. The feature extraction using Sobel's image segmentation method is based on convolution of two kernels using filter operators as shown in equations 11.5 and 11.6. Threshold computation with Canny edge detection algorithm is based on distance transformation. The result of Canny edge detection in shown in Figure 11.6b.

The most intensive computation required in image analytics is segmenting an image based on features. The importance of feature extraction can be well understood from the results obtained using OpenCV packages as shown in Figures 11.7–11.10.

However, these image segmentation algorithms are limited to access memory reads and writes. To overcome these inherent algorithmic complexities, most of the recent researches have focused on the development of deep neural net architectures

---

Adaptive Threshold (*I*)

Input: Image I.

Output: intensity

    1. For each pixel in the image *I*:

        1.1 Compute threshold value *T*.

$$T = (\text{mean}) \; OR(\text{median}) OR\left(\frac{\max + \min}{2}\right)$$

    2. If pixel value is less than threshold T, return background value. Otherwise, return foreground value.

Algorithm 1: Adaptive threshold

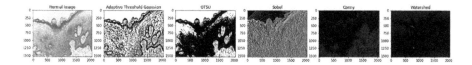

FIGURE 11.7 Feature extraction: (a) Normal oral cavity image 100× resolution (b) Adaptive threshold (c) OTSU (d) Sobel (e) Canny (f) Watershed.

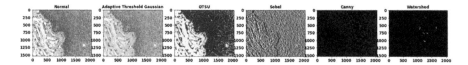

FIGURE 11.8 Feature extraction: (a) OSCC 100× resolution (b) Adaptive threshold (c) OTSU (d) Sobel (e) Canny (f) Watershed.

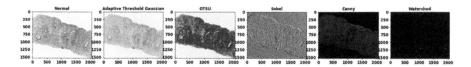

FIGURE 11.9 Feature extraction: (a) Normal oral cavity image 400× resolution (b) Adaptive threshold (c) OTSU (d) Sobel (e) Canny (f) Watershed.

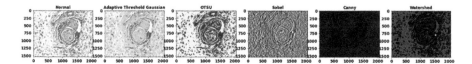

FIGURE 11.10 Feature extraction: (a) OSCC_400× resolution (b) Adaptive threshold (c) OTSU (d) Sobel (e) Canny (d) Watershed.

to shed light on AI concept applied to automated feature extraction using convolutional neural network (CNN). The following section explains the systematic computation of deep neural nets for cancer diagnosis.

11.3 DEEP NEURAL NETS FOR CANCER DIAGNOSIS

Anomalies with conventional feature extraction methods are error due to noisy data. Pixel-level quantification may lead to misinterpretation of boundaries of the region on the image. These practical issues can be eliminated by exploiting the learning ability of deep convolutional neural nets. The capacity of CNN is its ability to learn from representation, which is the primary significance of deep learners. Unlike shallow nets, deep architectures have their advantage in solving the problem of learning features from nonlinear inputs. The delineation of features using OpenCV has issues with pixel quantization, pixel count, and region-based boundaries. These feature extraction processes without using machine learning (ML) technique lead to anomalous detection. In turn, the deep nets can be devised to exploit the feature representation technique. Also, the levels of different features can be transferred by influencing the transfer learning concept of AI. Recent researches have reported the innovation in convolutional nets (CNN) by modifying the parameters, optimization by hyperparameter tuning. The exemplary performance of CNN in classification and segmentation has made deep CNN the benchmark architecture for differential diagnosis of OSCC (Salvi et al. 2021; Shavlokhova et al. 2021).

The modalities used by the physicians in diagnosing cancer using various biological samples are listed in Table 11.1. The accuracies reported by deep neural nets on these datasets are shown in Figure 11.11.

TABLE 11.1
Types of Data

Data	Modality
Clinical	Pathology report on tissue biopsy
Molecular	Cancer specific alterations in deoxyribonucleic acid (DNA) and ribonucleic acid (RNA)
Genomic	Sequencing DNA for predicting the growth of tumor.
Imaging	Whole-slide histopathological images – staining of nuclei using dyes.
Tissue genomic	Tumor profiling and biomarkers
Blood genomic	Blood pathology report to identify and predict the growth of cancer
Hyperspectral imaging	Detection of brain tumors by the identification of chemical composition of tissues
Gene expression	Gene expression and sequence are analyzed for the development of tumor
Mass spectrometry	To delineate the areas of cancerous tissue

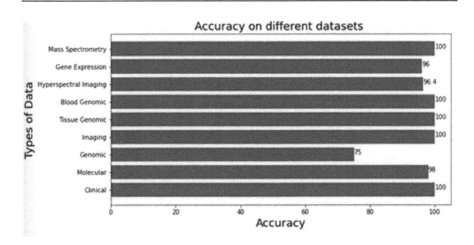

FIGURE 11.11   Accuracy on dataset.

11.4 DIFFERENTIAL DIAGNOSIS IN ORAL PATHOLOGY

The role of computational pathology is to exploit the potential of deep neural nets in the diagnosis of tumorous cell and differentiation of cancerous and non-cancerous tissues. The accurate delineation of nucleus cells is the fundamental task of automated diagnosis. In event of characterization of nucleus, the following techniques are in focus in literature by various researchers.

1. **Nucleus segmentation**
2. **Semantic segmentation**

The core operation in investigating a histopathologic WSI is nucleus segmentation, the process of detecting group of pixels representing cell nuclei. This laborious process of investigating a biopsy tissue can be replaced by a computer-assisted tool. Clinical difficulties vary among tissue types, type of cells, staining, and marking of cells leading to various interpretation of WSI. In effect, the level of difficulties faced by clinicians will vary in handling WSI of several patients collected at different health centers. Moreover, the conventional segmentation algorithm as part of image processing methods may fail to achieve results in such scenarios. Hence, a data-intensive computation is essential. In turn, computer vision encourages researchers to build image segmentation frameworks using convolutional deep neural nets. The maturity of deep nets lies in differentiating the cancerous cell nucleus from normal epithelial cells. Artificial intelligence and machine learning (AIML) in digital pathological tissue examination is recently established in oral carcinoma detection. Automated ML framework has assisted the physicians to overcome difficulties in conventional diagnostic methods that are based on skills of histopathologists.

11.4.1 Convolutional Neural Network

11.4.1.1 Convolution Operation

Let g_l^k be the convolution operation such that

$$g_l^k(u, v) = \sum_e \sum_{i, j} h_c(i, j) . e_l^k(p, q) \tag{11.7}$$

where $h_c(i, j)$ is an instance of the input tensor image H_C, which is instance-based product with $e_l^k(p, q)$ index of the kth convolutional kernel k_l of the lth layer. The output feature map of the kth convolutional operation can be represented as $\mathbb{G}_l^k = \left[g_l^k(1,1), \dots, g_l^k(u, v), \dots, g_l^k(U, V) \right]$. The convolution operation is shown in equation 11.7.

11.4.1.2 Pooling Operation

Let the feature map be $\mathbb{Z}_l^k$ for l^{th} layer such that the pooled feature is given as follows:

$$\mathbb{Z}_l^k = f_p\left(\mathbb{G}_l^k\right) \tag{11.8}$$

The pooled feature map is represented as $\mathbb{Z}_l^k$, which represents the pooled feature map of the lth layer for the kth input feature map $\mathbb{G}_l^k$, where f_p defines the type of pooling operation. The use of pooling formulation in CNN is acknowledged by various researchers. The pooling operation is shown in equation 11.8.

11.4.1.3 Decision Function

The intrinsic feature maps are learned by the decision function, also known as activation mechanism. The learning process is accelerated based on the selection of appropriate activation function. The convoluted feature is activated by mapping the feature convolution using the activation function defined in equation 11.9.

$$\mathbb{D}_l^k = f_a\left(\mathbb{G}_l^k\right) \tag{11.9}$$

The output of a convolution is given by $\mathbb{G}_l^k$ that is passed to decision function f_a, which is nonlinear and returns $\mathbb{D}_l^k$, the transformed l^{th} layer output. The most common activation function used to overcome vanishing gradient is ReLU shown in equation 11.10. The sigmoid activation is shown in equation 11.11.

$$ReLU = \begin{cases} 0 \ if \ x \le 0 \\ x \ if \ x > 0 \end{cases} \tag{11.10}$$

$$Sigmoid = \frac{x}{1+e^{-x}} \tag{11.11}$$

11.4.1.4 Normalization

The feature maps are corrected from internal covariance using equation 11.12.

$$\mathbb{N}_l^k = \frac{\mathbb{G}_l^k - \mu_B}{\sqrt{\sigma_B^2 + \varepsilon}} \tag{11.12}$$

where for a batch process, the normalized feature map is $\mathbb{N}_l^k$, input $\mathbb{G}_l^k$ the feature map, the mean μ_B, and the variance σ_B^2. The use of ε is to nullify division by zero.

11.4.1.5 Dropout

Dropout is required to improve the generalization by randomly skipping connections based on probability. This mechanism helps in augmenting the network topology by randomly dropping the connections to result in thin-layered network architecture.

11.4.1.6 Fully Connected Layer

The input from feature extraction stages and output of all preceding layers are analyzed globally. Thus, a nonlinear combination of feature set is selected and used for the classification process. A model CNN architecture describing convolutional operation, pooling, and activation functions is shown in Figure 11.12.

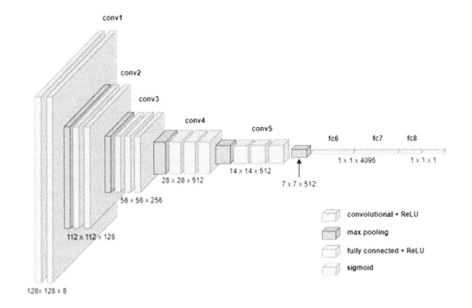

FIGURE 11.12 Basic CNN: Convolution, pooling and dropout.

TABLE 11.2
Dataset

Modality	Dataset-1	Dataset-2
Data collection	October 2016	November 2017
Tissue section	Buccal mucosa	
Acquisition	Punch biopsy acquires epithelial layer along with some connective tissue layers.	
Biopsy	4% buffered formalin solution	
Fixation	48 hours	
Modality	Whole-slide image	
Specification	100×	400×
Magnification	2048 × 1536 pixels	
Count	528	696
Histopathological normal epithelium	89	201
Oral squamous cell carcinoma	439	495
Size on disk	2 GB	
Data source	Hospital	
Data format	JPG	
Data type	Image	
Analysis	Cell and tissue level	
Repository link	https://data.mendeley.com/datasets/ftmp4cvtmb/1	

Rahman et al. (2020) have described the experimental design with materials and methods on the two set of data. The description of the dataset is as above. The link to the image dataset is given in Table 11.2. The significance of this dataset is that it is open to public for academic and research. This repository contains histopathological images of normal epithelium of oral cavity and OSCC. The gold standard dataset for extracting cytological as well as tissue-level features. This can further be used in establishing an automated diagnosis tool using AI approaches. The purpose of classifying the nucleus by grading the OSCC, classification applying deep learning/semantic segmentation tasks, can be implemented by adding/augmenting images in the dataset. This dataset can be used for comparative evaluation of one's experimental findings in the future when more datasets of such kind are available. Conventional image segmentation algorithms working on intensity levels using OpenCV are not capable of delineating the nucleus structures and its structural properties like color, shape, size, texture, and intensity. Hence, deep neural nets formulated to perform data-intensive computation at different layers are recommended. This computer-assisted diagnostic tool helps pathologist to speed up the clinical workflow by resolving the delay due to manual intervention in existing clinical settings. The following case study illustrates the ability of deep neural nets in differentiation and grading of OSCC.

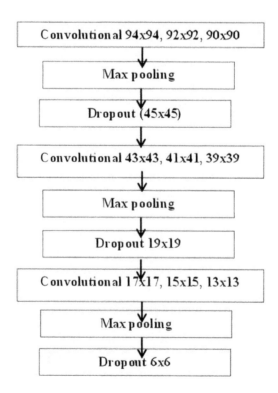

FIGURE 11.13   Workflow for differential diagnosis of OSCC.

TABLE 11.3
Deep Convolutional Neural Net Model Parameters

Layer	Output	Parameter
conv2d (Conv2D)	(94, 94, 32)	896
conv2d (Conv2D)	(92, 92, 32)	9,248
conv2d (Conv2D)	(90, 90, 32)	9,248
Max pooling	(45,45,32)	0
Dropout	(45,45,32)	0
conv2d (Conv2D)	43, 43, 64)	18,496
conv2d (Conv2D)	41, 41, 64)	36,928
conv2d (Conv2D)	39, 39, 64)	36,928
Max pooling	(19, 19, 64)	0
Dropout	(19, 19, 64)	0
conv2d (Conv2D)	(17, 17, 128	73,856
conv2d (Conv2D)	(15, 15, 128)	147,584
conv2d (Conv2D)	(13, 13, 128)	147,584
Max pooling	(6, 6, 128)	0
Dropout	(6, 6, 128)	0
Flatten	4608	0
Dense	256	1,179,904
Dropout	256	0
Dense	2	514

Table 11.3 explains the parametric inputs and outcome of the workflow defined by convolutional, max pooling, and dropout operations as shown in Figure 11.13.

11.5   AUTOMATED DETECTION AND GRADING OF SQUAMOUS CELL CARCINOMA FOR DIAGNOSIS OF ORAL CANCER

11.5.1   PROBLEM STATEMENT

Investigating squamous cell carcinoma in histopathologic images helps in differentiating the epithelial cells from cancerous cells. Several findings suggest the analysis of whole-slide histopathologic images for the detection of squamous cell carcinoma. This study conceptualizes the deep learning framework for accurate detection and grading of squamous cell for differential diagnosis.

11.5.2   OBJECTIVES

1. To collect the WSIs of epithelial tissues from biopsy images.
2. To investigate and analyze the morphological and textural features.
3. To develop a scalable deep learning framework for differentiating the epithelial cells.
4. To develop deep learning framework for grading squamous cells based on morphology of cell nuclei.

11.5.3 Methodology/Experimental Design and Sampling Strategy

Objective – 1:

1. Collection of indigenous cell from OSCC biopsy images.
2. Tissue processing, annotation, and preparation of data for statistical modeling.
3. Statistical inferences with correlation report on annotated image and WSI.

11.5.4 Methodology/Experimental Design and Sampling Strategy

Objective – 2:

1. Exploratory data analysis with correlation plots, and statistical estimate on various morphological delineations.
2. Hypothesis testing on the formation of various delineations like keratinizing horn formation, and clear cells of squamous cell carcinoma.

11.5.5 Methodology/Experimental Design

Objective – 3:

1. Feature extraction: Segmentation of cell nuclei based on size, shape, structure, color, and texture.
2. Assessment of morphological features and statistical inference with correlation measures.

11.5.6 Methodology/Experimental Design

Objective – 4:

1. Model formulation based on estimated statistics of the detected features.
2. Preparation of training samples and test samples.
3. Model formulation, fitting, and development using training and test sets.
4. Reporting of results with correlation of features and statistics.

The above-stated objectives are developed into computer-assisted tool for the pathologist to assist in differentiating the normal and squamous cell carcinoma in WSI and automated grading of OSCC. The performance of CNN is evaluated in training and validation loss. It is seen in Figure 11.14 that the validation loss of CNN follows the path of validation loss, which confirms that performance of model is up to acceptable standards both in training and in testing. Of note, the dataset has acceptable proportion of classes of normal and abnormal WSI in both training and test sets. Hence, the performance of CNN is found to be good fit for the dataset.

11.5.7 Performance Measures and Metrics

The metrics used for the evaluation of deep learning framework are (i) recall, (ii) Dice similarity coefficient (DSC), (iii) accuracy, and (iv) F1 score.

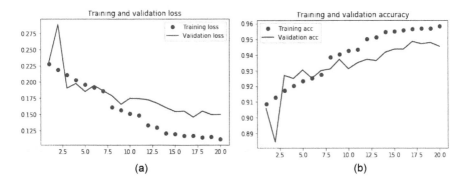

FIGURE 11.14   (a) Training and validation loss (b) training and validation.

11.5.7.1   Recall

The statistical measure tests the performance of the proposed nucleus detection method, based on Haar wavelet decomposed deep CNN model. In second stage, nucleus segmentation performances are evaluated using Dice coefficient and Jaccard index.

$$\text{Recall} = \frac{\text{Total number of cells detected}}{\text{Total number of cell present in the image}} \tag{11.13}$$

11.5.7.2   Dice Similarity Coefficient (DSC)

Let α and β be the two sets, the cardinality of sets are denoted by $|\alpha| \, and \, |\beta|$.
The segmentation similarity score is given by equation 11.14.

$$\text{DSC} = 2| \; |/(\|+\|) \tag{11.14}$$

11.5.7.3   Intersection over Union (IOU)

Jaccard index or IOU is the commonly used metric in semantic segmentation process. Let α and β be the two sets, the ratio of the area of overlap to the area of union represented in sets to measure similarity between two finite sets as shown in equation 11.15.

$$\text{IOU}(,) = \|/(\|+\|-\|) \tag{11.15}$$

11.5.7.4   Confusion Matrix (CM)

The tabular representation of actuals and predicted is confusion matrix. This matrix enables the amount of instances X classified accurately. Figure 11.15 shows the confusion matrix reported by the CNN model.

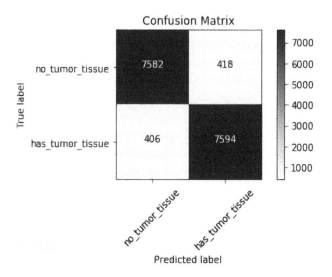

FIGURE 11.15 Confusion matrix.

11.5.7.5 Accuracy

It is the ratio of sum of instance X that are true positives (TP) and true negatives (TN) to the sum of all instances as in equation 11.16.

$$\text{Accuracy} = \frac{X_{TP} + X_{TN}}{X_{TP} + X_{TN} + X_{FP} + X_{FN}} \qquad (11.16)$$

11.5.7.6 F1 Score

F1 measures the accuracy of testing results by relating precision and recall as shown in equation 11.17.

$$F1 = 2\left(\frac{\text{Precision} \times \text{Recall}}{\text{Precision} + \text{Recall}}\right) \qquad (11.17)$$

11.6 RESEARCH CHALLENGES IN DIGITAL PATHOLOGY

Deep neural nets have high potential in differentiating the abnormal SCC from normal in a WSI (Tanriver et al. 2021). However, the accurate delineation of cell nuclei based on morphological features such as color, shape, size, texture, and intensity is still in premature levels. Thus, semantic segmentation considering the pixel-level computation is yet to be addressed in the literature to assist the pathologist not only in differential diagnosis, but also in grading the squamous cell cancers.

11.7   CONCLUSION

The role of AIML was recently established in computational pathology. This has highly motivated the author to present the significance of computer vision and deep learning concepts of AI in this study. This chapter presented the principle of pathology in medical sciences for the diagnosis of OSCC. The differentiation of normal and abnormal epithelial cells is illustrated with sketch. The severity and developmental stages of OSCC that leads to horn and keratin pearl formations are explained with datasets. The analysis of automated differentiation and grading of OSCC was explained with data dictionary. The samples collected from patient cohort on different datasets are explained. The workflow of deep CNN for the differential diagnosis of OSCC is illustrated with a case study on model formulation, fitting with performance evaluation measures and metrics. In addition, the interest of researchers in recent works reported the accurate delineation of nucleus considering the morphological features such as shape, size, color, texture, and intensity. The workflow needed to meet such demands of pathologist is left to work in the future.

REFERENCES

A. Anuranjeeta, K. K. Shukla, A. Tiwari, S. Sharma, "Classification of histopathological images of breast cancerous and non-cancerous cells based on morphological features", *Biomedical and Pharmacology Journal*, 2017;10:353–366.

Jason Brownlee, "Imbalanced classification with python better metrics, balance skewed classes, cost-sensitive learning", *Machine Learning Mastery*, 2020a;463.

Jason Brownlee, "Deep learning for time series forecasting predict the future with MLPs, CNNs and LSTMs in python", *Machine Learning Mastery*, 2020b; 575.

Jason Brownlee, "Data preparation for machine learning - Data cleaning, feature selection, and data", *Machine Learning Mastery*, 2020c;398.

Armando Fandango, "Mastering TensorFlow 1.x_ Advanced Machine Learning and Deep Learning Concepts using TensorFlow 1.x and Keras", Packt, 2018, UK.

Daisuke Komura, Shumpei Ishikawa, Machine learning methods for histopathological image analysis", *Computational and Structural Biotechnology Journal*, 2018;16:34–42. ISSN 2001-0370.

Massimo Salvi, U. Rajendra Acharya, Filippo Molinari, Kristen M. Meiburger, "The impact of pre- and post-image processing techniques on deep learning frameworks: A comprehensive review for digital pathology image analysis", *Computers in Biology and Medicine*, 2021;128:104129, ISSN 0010-4825.

Tabassum Yesmin Rahman, Lipi B. Mahanta, Anup K. Das, Jagannath D. Sarma. Histopathological imaging database for oral cancer analysis. *Data Brief*, 2020;29:105114.

G. Tanriver, M. Soluk Tekkesin, O. Ergen, Automated detection and classification of oral lesions using deep learning to detect oral potentially malignant disorders", *Cancers (Basel)*, 2021;13(11):2766, doi:10.3390/cancers13112766. PMID: 34199471; PMCID: PMC8199603.

Veronika Shavlokhova, et al. "Deep learning on oral squamous cell carcinoma ex vivo fluorescent confocal microscopy data: A feasibility study", *Journal of Clinical Medicine*, 2021;10(22):5326, doi:10.3390/jcm10225326.

12 Challenges and Future Scopes in Current Applications of Deep Learning in Human Cancer Diagnostics

C.S. Vidhya
National Institute of Food Technology,
Entrepreneurship and Management-Thanjavur,
Affiliated to Bharathidasan University

M. Loganathan and R. Meenatchi
National Institute of Food Technology,
Entrepreneurship and Management-Thanjavur

CONTENTS

DOI: 10.1201/9781003277002-12

12.1   INTRODUCTION

Cancer is the predominant cause of deaths worldwide. Fighting cancer is a challenge for both researchers and doctors. Deaths due to skin cancer, lung cancer, breast cancer, prostate cancer, and brain cancer have led to cancer diagnosis using visual examination and manual techniques. To improve the efficiency of medical image interpretation by computer-aided diagnosis, systems were brought to assist doctors in the early 1980s. The fundamental goals of cancer prediction and prognosis are distinct from the goals of cancer detection and diagnosis (Kourou et al., 2015).

In cancer prediction/prognosis, there are three predictive foci: the prediction of cancer susceptibility to risk assessment, the prediction of cancer recurrence, and the prediction of cancer survivability. In the first case, one is trying to predict the likelihood of developing a type of cancer prior to the occurrence of the disease. In the second case, one is trying to predict the likelihood of redeveloping cancer after the apparent resolution of the disease. In the third case, one is trying to predict an outcome (life expectancy, survivability, progression, tumor-drug sensitivity) after the diagnosis of the disease. In the latter two situations, the success of the prognostic prediction is obviously dependent, in part, on the success or quality of the diagnosis. However, a disease prognosis can only come after a medical diagnosis, and a prognostic prediction must take into account more than just a simple diagnosis (Sunny et al., 2020).

Deep learning is a broad term used for the Machine Learning (ML) and for the Artificial Intelligence (AI). Deep learning is a subset of ML that has grown in recent years due to the advances in computational power and the access to large datasets. It relies on the collection of ML algorithms, which models high-level abstractions in the data with multiple nonlinear transformations. In the deep learning methodology, the term "deep" enumerates the concept of numerous layers through which the data is transformed. This novel learning approach is widely used in the fields of adaptive testing, big data, cancer detection, data flow, document analysis and recognition, health care, object detection, speech recognition, image classification, pedestrian detection, natural language processing (NLP), and voice activity detection. There are three main categories of deep learning algorithms: supervised learning, unsupervised learning, and reinforcement learning. Supervised learning fits a nonlinear function using features as input data and labels as output data where the labels, or outputs, are known when training the algorithm. Common supervised deep learning algorithms are convolutional neural networks (CNNs) and recurrent neural networks (RNNs) (Saba, 2020).

Deep learning has the advantage of generating directly from raw images the high-level feature representation. Explainability attempts to mitigate the black box nature of these algorithms. There are legal and ethical requirements along with laws and regulations that are required for deep learning cancer detection systems to be implemented in a clinical setting. The inability to provide such explanations on demand may result in large penalties for the organizations involved. Beyond ethical and legal issues, clinicians and patients have to trust the classifications provided by these systems. The algorithm's performance was compared to multiple physician's detection abilities on the same images. These results demonstrate the potential for using deep learning to aid medical practitioners (Chauhan et al., 2021).

Six basic types of the deep learning architectures are:

- Auto-Encoder (AE)
- Convolutional Neural Network (CNN)
- Restricted Boltzmann Machine (RBM)
- Deep Stacking Network (DSN)
- Long Short-Term Memory (LSTM)/Gated Recurrent Unit (GRU) Network
- Recurrent Neural Network (RNN)

Out of these, LSTM and CNN are two of the fundamental and the most commonly used approaches.

12.1.1 CHALLENGES IN DEEP LEARNING

- Deep learning networks are black box networks, and their working is very difficult to understand because of hyper parameters and complex network design.
- The time requirement to train is much more.
- Transparency is not shown in the deep learning methods.
- Challenging and complex feature engineering phase is eliminated in the deep learning, which is present in the ML.
- Deep networks need high-end graphical processing units (GPUs), which are very expensive and are skilled in sufficient time with big data.

12.1.2 ADVANTAGES OF DEEP LEARNING

- From the raw sensor, deep learning methods can learn features and find the most suitable pattern for improving the recognition accuracy.
- Pre-processing of the data and normalization are not mandatory.
- To avoid overfitting, deep learning requires large amounts of sensor dataset. GPU is used to speed up the training.

Deep learning is a branch of ML based on structured data, fully connected neural networks (or simply NN), CNN, and RNN. It has mostly been used in the diagnosis and detection of cancer (Omondiagbe et al., 2019).

To calculate a cancer prognosis, several clinicians from several disciplines evaluate different subsets of biomarkers as well as multiple clinical parameters, such as the patient's age, general health, the tumor's grade and size, as well as the location and type of cancer. Cancer risk is influenced by factors like family history, age, diet, weight (obesity), high-risk behaviors (smoking, binge drinking), and environmental pollutants (UV radiation, radon, asbestos, PCBs) (Bertsimas & Wiberg, 2020). The rapid advancement of genomic (DNA sequencing, microarrays), proteomic (protein chips, tissue arrays, immunohistology), and imaging (fMRI, PET, micro-CT) technologies has made molecular-scale data on individual's malignancies possible. The existence or expression of various tumor proteins (MUC1, HER2, PSA), as well as the tumor's chemical environment (anoxic, hypoxic), has all been discovered to be critically important as prognostic or predictive indicators (Liu et al., 2021). When these molecular patterns are paired with macro-scale clinical data, cancer prognoses and predictions have become even more powerful and accurate (tumor type, hereditary traits, risk factors). As a result of the massive amount of data created by cancer detection, ML techniques are becoming more prominent. As part of a growing trend toward personalized, predictive medicine, computers (and ML) are increasingly being employed in disease diagnosis and prediction. This shift toward those who are sick in terms of lifestyle and quality-of-life decisions, clinicians in terms of treatment decisions, health economists, and policy makers all benefit from predictive medicine. Almost all predictions use only four sources of data: genetic-proteomic particular protein biomarkers, clinical protein biomarkers, 2D gel data, and mass spectral analysis (SNPs, mutations, microarrays, histology, tumor stage, tumor size, age, weight, risk behavior, and so on) (Bibault et al., 2021).

12.1.3 CURRENT APPLICATION OF DEEP LEARNING IN CANCER PROGNOSIS

Several deep learning approaches and feature selection algorithms have been widely used in cancer prognosis and prediction over the last two decades. The majority of these studies use deep learning approaches to simulate cancer growth and discover informative variables that may then be used in a categorization scheme. It includes gene expression profiles, clinical factors, and histological data, all of which are combined in a complementary way to feed into the prognostic method (Favorskaya, 2021). When forecasting cancer prognosis, factors such as (i) life expectancy, (ii) survival, (iii) progression, and (iv) therapeutic sensitivity are frequently examined. Simple NN models with 3–4 layers were constructed as well as studies that generated DNNs with more than 4 layers used for medical image comparison.

12.2 NEURAL NETWORKS AND THEIR TYPES

Based on the types of NN and feature extraction used, they are divided into 3 categories:

(i) non-feature-extracted NN models, (ii) CNN models using multi-omics data feature extraction, and (iii) fully connected NNs (Park & Han, 2018).

12.2.1 NON-FEATURE-EXTRACTED NN MODELS

The Cox-PH Cox proportional hazards model is a multivariate semi-parametric regression model that has been frequently used to evaluate health outcomes and survival features across two or more treatment groups in cancer studies. Simple NN models were shown to be equivalent to Cox-PH and/or Kaplan-Meier techniques. Cox regression was the output layer for creating the use of neural networks to predict cancer survival. Cox-nnet is a neural network created by Cox (NN) that uses TCGA genetic data as input and output. A sort of regression analysis known as Cox regression is a type of regression analysis (Akkus et al., 2017). Dropout and reducing NN complexity by deploying one hidden layer worked effectively in their cancer detection experiment to reduce overfitting. To perform survival analysis, a neural network model called Deep Sury was created. Another neural network model Rank Deep Survival employed Deep Sury's basic architecture for survival analysis in a range of datasets, including cancer datasets, to develop 3–4 hidden layers' DNN (Ribli et al., 2018). The Rank Deep Survival model outperforms Cox PH models and the Deep Sury. German Breast Cancer Study Group and Molecular Taxonomy of Breast Cancer International Consortium (METABRIC) datasets were used to create a model in breast cancer datasets (GBCSG) (GBSG) (Cruz-roa et al., 2017).

12.2.2 CREATION OF FULLY CONNECTED NNs BY EXTRACTING FEATURES FROM GENE EXPRESSION DATA

Dimension reduction of health data aids the integration of multi-omics data. The minimum redundancy maximum relevance (mRMR) technique was used to predict breast cancer prognosis in a study that reduced by removing 400 and 200 genes, respectively, gene expression dimensionality and copy number variation (CNA) data was increased (Amine et al., 2021). Subsequently, using weighted linear aggregation, the prediction outputs of these three NN models were combined to produce a final prediction score. Because their model included multidimensional data, they named it Multimodal Deep Neural Network (MDNNMD). When they used a threshold of 0.443–0.591, they determined that the specificity was excellent (0.95–0.99), while the sensitivity was low (0.2–0.45). MDNNMD, ROC (0.845), precision, and accuracy, as well as Matthew's correlation coefficient, all performed lower than SVM, random forest, and MDNNMD (MCC) (Miotto et al., 2017).

12.2.3 CNN-BASED MODELS

Deep learning has progressed thanks to cutting-edge networks that use CNN and RNN, which are two types of neural networks. CNN used deep learning for image recognition/classification and computer vision, whereas RNN used it for NLP and data sequencing inquiries. Deep Learning was in charge of classifying different types of skin cancer, identifying bad histology slides, identifying a plague zone in Alzheimer's patients, and separating cancer cells from normal cells—these are all things that researchers are working on. In cancer prognosis research, CNN has been used to characterize malignant tissue for survival prediction or feature extraction for downstream prognosis. Glioblastoma multiforme (GBM) is a type of glioblastoma that has spread across the brain. ResNet5, a 50-layer pre-trained CNN model, exhibited the highest accuracy of 95% when estimating the methylation state of the MGMT gene promoter and patient vulnerability to temozolomide when compared to ResNet18 and ResNet34. In the field of cancer prognosis, CNN has been used to classify malignant tissue for survival prediction and feature extraction for downstream prognosis (Litjens et al., 2016). The most prevalent and fatal type of ovarian cancer is high-grade serous ovarian carcinoma (HGSOC). Wang et al. built a Cox-PH survival prediction model using CT-based pictures and a CNN model to extract image attributes (Choy et al., 2018).

12.2.4 CANCER IMAGING WITH CONVOLUTIONAL NEURAL NETWORKS

The growth of AI driven by DL algorithms accelerated the creation of a specific DL architecture, the convolutional neural network. The discovery of a specific DL design, the convolutional neural network, sparked interest in image analysis (CNN). CNNs analyze picture data at the pixel level. In comparison with other DL arrangements, CNNs offer the advantage of accounting for the pixel's orientation in reference to one another. As a result, the CNN can now recognize lines, curves, and, eventually, objects in photographs (Kleppe et al., 2021). CNN was able to classify hazardous cancers with higher sensitivity and precision than a panel of 21 board-certified dermatologists after being trained on 130,000 skin photos. CNNs have also been used to automatically recognize digital photos and locate polyps during colonoscopies. After being trained on 1,290 colonoscopic pictures, CNN demonstrated a 94% sensitivity in detecting polyps (Coudray et al., 2018).

12.2.5 DIGITAL PATHOLOGY

The digitization of histopathologic tumor specimen slides is becoming more common, resulting in a stable 2D picture suited for DL evaluation. DL CNN algorithms have been found to diagnose lymph node metastases in breast cancer with at least the same accuracy as a panel of pathologists and in less time. CNN was used to predict six distinct genetic mutations from raw input data consisting of digitized formalin-fixed, paraffin-embedded tissue from lung cancer biopsies. STK11, EGFR, FAT1, SETBP1, KRAS, and TP53 are among of the genes that have been identified (Iqbal et al., 2021).

12.2.6 ELECTRONIC MEDICAL RECORDS (EMRs)

Deep learning has recently been used to manage data from cancer patients' EHRs, which include both structured (diagnosis, meds, laboratory tests) and unstructured (free-text clinical notes) data. Using a deep architecture, deep learning was used to process the EMRs of a health-care system for a specific, usually supervised, predictive clinical task. Deep learning beats typical ML models in various categories, containing the F-score, accuracy, and the area under the receiver-operating characteristic curve (Gulum & Trombley, 2021).

12.2.7 DEEP LEARNING AND ARTIFICIAL NEURAL NETWORKS (DL) IN HEALTHCARE

"Artificial intelligence" and "deep learning" are terms that are frequently used interchangeably. DL algorithms can find the best features for the data during the training phase, eliminating the requirement for pre-engineering and unstructured data. DL algorithms have outperformed typical ML methods in a range of AI challenges, such as image classification, NLP, and sequence prediction, because of their properties (Dargan et al., 2019).

12.3 CHALLENGES AND OPPORTUNITIES OF DEEP LEARNING IN CANCER DIAGNOSTICS

12.3.1 ENHANCEMENT OF FEATURES

Wearable devices, settings, surveys, online communities, genetic profiles, and omics data such as the proteome are all examples of data that can be collected and employ deep learning's hierarchical nature and process separation (e.g., deep Bayesian networks or layers of AEs) (Zhu et al., 2020).

12.3.1.1 Federated Inference

In this circumstance, it becomes possible to develop a deep learning model with patients from several sites without revealing their personal information, which is a major concern. Other mathematical fields, such as cryptography, will be able to interact with it (homomorphic encryption and safe multiparty computation) (Litjens et al., 2017).

12.3.1.2 Model Privacy

When it comes to scaling up deep learning, privacy is a major worry (e.g., through cloud computing services). "Differential privacy" is a framework for ensuring that individual samples in training data are indistinguishable based on their functional outputs (Chen et al., 2018).

12.3.1.3 Incorporating Expert Knowledge

Professional expertise must be added into the deep learning process to lead it in the right path due to the limited amount of medical data and its various quality issues. For example, credible content should be collected from online medical encyclopedias and PubMed abstracts to be integrated in the deep architecture to improve the systems' overall performance (Bejnordi et al., 2017).

12.3.1.4 Temporal Modeling

A time-sensitive deep learning model must be constructed to gain a better grasp of the patient's health and provide quick clinical decision assistance. To address these critical health-care issues, temporal deep learning is applied (Min et al., 2017).

12.3.1.5 Interpretable Modeling

The popularity of deep learning models stems from their high performance, dependability, and trustworthiness (i.e., what causes the networks' hidden units to turn on and off during the process, as well as approaches for assisting the networks with current tools that explain data-driven system predictions) (Sahiner et al., 2019).

12.4 CONCLUSION

In cancer research, deep learning is expected to yield encouraging outcomes. A detailed examination of deep learning applications in terms of input data, deep learning capabilities, multimodality, and deep learning acceleration is presented in this chapter. Deep learning has made significant progress in research and is now influencing our daily lives. Deep learning has been applied in a number of research in the medical field, with positive outcomes. One benefit of utilizing deep learning to construct a model is that it may continue to learn as fresh data becomes available. Furthermore, because health-care data is available in a number of formats, including genomics, expression, using many NN architectures to handle diverse data problems, such as clinical (structured) data, text, and picture (unstructured) data, is becoming more popular and helpful. This chapter discusses recent studies that employed deep learning to look at cancer prognosis. Deep learning models have been shown to perform as well as or better than other ML models in various tests. Future research should focus on testing and improving the algorithm, as well as developing the state-of-the-art models for better cancer prognostic prediction.

12.5 ACKNOWLEDGMENT

The authors would like to express sincere gratitude to the Director, National Institute of Food Technology, Entrepreneurship and Management—Thanjavur NIFTEM-T (formerly IIFPT), Thanjavur-613 005, Tamil Nadu, India, for providing all the support and technical facilities.

12.6 CONFLICT OF INTEREST

The authors declare no conflict of interest.

12.7 FUNDING STATEMENT

No funding was contributed for this chapter.

REFERENCES

Akkus, Z., Galimzianova, A., Hoogi, A., Rubin, D. L., & Erickson, B. J. (2017). Deep learning for brain MRI segmentation: State of the art and future directions. *Journal of Digital Imaging*, 30(4), 449–459. https://doi.org/10.1007/s10278-017-9983-4.

Bejnordi, B. E., Veta, M., Van Diest, P. J., Van Ginneken, B., Karssemeijer, N., Litjens, G., Van Der Laak, J. A. W. M., Hermsen, M., Manson, Q. F., Balkenhol, M., Geessink, O., Stathonikos, N., Van Dijk, M. C. R. F., Bult, P., Beca, F., Beck, A. H., Wang,

D., Khosla, A., Gargeya, R., ... Venâncio, R. (2017). Diagnostic assessment of deep learning algorithms for detection of lymph node metastases in women with breast cancer. *JAMA - Journal of the American Medical Association*, 318(22), 2199–2210. https://doi.org/10.1001/jama.2017.14585.

Bertsimas, D., & Wiberg, H. (2020). Machine learning in oncology: Methods, applications, and challenges. *JCO Clinical Cancer Informatics*, 4, 885–894. https://doi.org/10.1200/cci.20.00072.

Bibault, J.-E., Burgun, A., Fournier, L., Dekker, A., & Lambin, P. (2021). Artificial intelligence in oncology. *Artificial Intelligence in Medicine*, 361–381. https://doi.org/10.1016/b978-0-12-821259-2.00018-1.

Chauhan, A., Kharpate, H., Narekar, Y., Gulhane, S., Virulkar, T., & Hedau, Y. (2021). Breast cancer detection and prediction using machine learning. *Proceedings of the 3rd International Conference on Inventive Research in Computing Applications, ICIRCA 2021*, June, 1135–1143. https://doi.org/10.1109/ICIRCA51532.2021.9544687.

Chen, A. H., Engkvist, O., Wang, Y., Olivecrona, M., & Blaschke, T. (2018). The rise of deep learning in drug discovery. *Drug Discovery Today*, https://doi.org/10.1016/j.drudis.2018.01.039.

Choy, G., Khalilzadeh, O., Michalski, M., Do, S., Samir, A. E., Pianykh, O. S., Geis, J. R., Pandharipande, P. V., Brink, J. A., & Dreyer, K. J. (2018). Current applications and future impact of machine learning in radiology. *Radiology*, 288(2), 318–328. https://doi.org/10.1148/radiol.2018171820.

Coudray, N., Ocampo, P. S., Sakellaropoulos, T., Narula, N., Snuderl, M., Fenyö, D., Moreira, A. L., Razavian, N., & Tsirigos, A. (2018). Classification and mutation prediction from non–small cell lung cancer histopathology images using deep learning. *Nature Medicine*, 24(October). https://doi.org/10.1038/s41591-018-0177-5.

Cruz-roa, A., Gilmore, H., Basavanhally, A., Feldman, M., Ganesan, S., Shih, N. N. C., Tomaszewski, J., & González, F. A. (2017). Accurate and reproducible invasive breast cancer detection in whole- slide images: A deep learning approach for quantifying tumor extent. *Nature Publishing Group*, 1–14. https://doi.org/10.1038/srep46450.

Dargan, S., Kumar, M., Rohit, M., & Gulshan, A. (2019). A survey of deep learning and its applications: A new paradigm to machine learning. *Archives of Computational Methods in Engineering*, 0123456789. https://doi.org/10.1007/s11831-019-09344-w.

Favorskaya, M. N. (2021). Advances in machine learning approaches in cancer prognosis. *Intelligent Systems Reference Library*, 204, 3–11. https://doi.org/10.1007/978-3-030-71975-3_1.

Gulum, M. A., & Trombley, C. M. (2021). A review of explainable deep learning cancer detection models in medical imaging. *Applied Sciences*, 11(4573), 1–21. https://doi.org/10.3390/app11104573.

Iqbal, M. J., Javed, Z., Sadia, H., Qureshi, I. A., Irshad, A., & Ahmed, R. (2021). Clinical applications of artificial intelligence and machine learning in cancer diagnosis : Looking into the future. *Cancer Cell International*, 1–11. https://doi.org/10.1186/s12935-021-01981-1.

Kleppe, A., Skrede, O.-J., Kerr, D. J., & Danielsen, H. E. (2021). Designing deep learning studies in cancer diagnostics. *Nature Reviews Cancer*, 21(March). https://doi.org/10.1038/s41568-020-00327-9.

Kourou, K., Exarchos, T. P., Exarchos, K. P., Karamouzis, M. V., & Fotiadis, D. I. (2015). Machine learning applications in cancer prognosis and prediction. *Computational and Structural Biotechnology Journal*, 13, 8–17. https://doi.org/10.1016/j.csbj.2014.11.005.

Litjens, G., Kooi, T., Bejnordi, B. E., Setio, A. A. A., Ciompi, F., Ghafoorian, M., van der Laak, J. A. W. M., van Ginneken, B., & Sánchez, C. I. (2017). A survey on deep learning in medical image analysis. *Medical Image Analysis*, 42, 60–88. https://doi.org/10.1016/j.media.2017.07.005.

Litjens, G., Sánchez, C. I., Timofeeva, N., Hermsen, M., Nagtegaal, I., Kovacs, I., Kaa, C. H. Van De, Bult, P., & Ginneken, B. Van. (2016). Deep learning as a tool for increased accuracy and efficiency of histopathological diagnosis. *Nature Publishing Group*, 1–11. https://doi.org/10.1038/srep26286.

Liu, L., Chen, X., Petinrin, O. O., Zhang, W., Rahaman, S., Tang, Z. R., & Wong, K. C. (2021). Machine learning protocols in early cancer detection based on liquid biopsy: A survey. *Life*, 11(7), 1–39. https://doi.org/10.3390/life11070638.

Min, S., Lee, B., & Yoon, S. (2017). Deep learning in bioinformatics. *Briefings in Bioinformatics*, 18(5), 851–869. https://doi.org/10.1093/bib/bbw068.

Miotto, R., Wang, F., Wang, S., Jiang, X., & Dudley, J. T. (2017). Deep learning for healthcare: Review, opportunities and challenges. *Briefings in Bioinformatics*, 19(6), 1236–1246. https://doi.org/10.1093/bib/bbx044.

Omondiagbe, D. A., Veeramani, S., & Sidhu, A. S. (2019). Machine learning classification techniques for breast cancer diagnosis. *IOP Conference Series: Materials Science and Engineering*, 495(1). https://doi.org/10.1088/1757-899X/495/1/012033.

Park, S. H., & Han, K. (2018). Methodologic guide for evaluating clinical performance and effect of artificial intelligence technology for medical diagnosis and prediction. *Radiology*, 286(3), 800–809. https://doi.org/10.1148/radiol.2017171920.

Ribli, D., Horváth, A., Unger, Z., Pollner, P., & Csabai, I. (2018). Detecting and classifying lesions in mammograms with deep learning. *Scientific Reports*, 8(1), 1–7. https://doi.org/10.1038/s41598-018-22437-z.

Saba, T. (2020). Recent advancement in cancer detection using machine learning: Systematic survey of decades, comparisons and challenges. *Journal of Infection and Public Health*. https://doi.org/10.1016/j.jiph.2020.06.033.

Sahiner, B., Pezeshk, A., Hadjiiski, L. M., Wang, X., Drukker, K., Cha, K. H., Summers, R. M., & Giger, M. L. (2019). Deep learning in medical imaging and radiation therapy. *Medical Physics*, 46(1), e1–e36. https://doi.org/10.1002/mp.13264.

Shaikh, F. J., & Rao, D. S. (2021). Materials today: Proceedings predication of cancer disease using machine learning approach. *Materials Today: Proceedings*, https://doi.org/10.1016/j.matpr.2021.03.625.

Sunny, J., Rane, N., Kanade, R., & Devi, S. (2020). Breast cancer classification and prediction using machine learning. *International Journal of Engineering Research & Technology (IJERT)*, 9(2), 576–580. https://doi.org/10.17577/ijertv9is020280.

Zhu, W., Xie, L., Han, J., & Guo, X. (2020). The application of deep learning in cancer prognosis prediction. *Cancers*, 12(3), 1–19. https://doi.org/10.3390/cancers12030603.

Index

Note: **Bold** page numbers refer to tables and *italic* page numbers refer to figures.

Milton Keynes UK
Ingram Content Group UK Ltd.
UKHW051536141024
449569UK00001B/51